THE DIGITAL DION

Fig. 1. Hieronymus Bosch, *Ship of Fools* (1490–1500).

The Center for Transformative Media, Parsons School of Design, is a transdisciplinary media research initiative bridging design and the social sciences, and
dedicated to the exploration of the transformative potential of emerging technologies upon the foundational practices of everyday life across a range of settings.

First published in 2016 by CTM Documents Initiative
An imprint of punctum books, Earth, Milky Way.
www. punctumbooks.com

ISBN-13: 978-0692270790
ISBN-10: 0692270795
Library of Congress Cataloging Data is available from the Library of Congress

Cover image: Perry Hall
Book design: Vincent W.J. van Gerven Oei & Natalia Tuero

The Digital Dionysus

Nietzsche and the Network-Centric Condition

Edited by
Dan Mellamphy &
Nandita Biswas Mellamphy

In memory of Bibi Pettypiece

Contents

Nietzsche and Networks, Nietzschean Networks: *The Digital Dionysus*

Dan Mellamphy & Nandita Biswas Mellamphy

NWW.I–IV, 2009–2013

The inspiration for this volume of essays, drawn from the proceedings of the Nietzsche Workshop @ Western (held at Western University, London ON, and the Center for Transformative Media at The New School, New York NY),[1] comes from the hypothesis that Nietzsche's thinking is pertinent to a phenomenon which can be described as the planetary propensity toward the digitization and networking of information. Moreover, "Nietzsche-Thought" — to lift a phrase from philosopher François Laruelle[2] — provides unique insights about the complexities

---

1   The Nietzsche Workshop @ Western (NWW) was co-organized by the editors of this volume in 2009 (NWW.I), 2010 (NWW.II), 2011 (NWW.III) and 2013 (NWW.IV).

2   As was stated in Nandita Biswas Mellamphy, "Nietzsche's Political Materialism: Diagram for a Nietzschean Politics," in *Nietzsche as Political Philosopher,* ed. Barry Stocker & Manuel Knoll (Berlin: De Gruyter, 2014), 78: "From the outset, Laruelle makes it clear that what he means by Nietzsche's 'thinking' does not refer primarily to what Nietzsche said or wrote — or neglected to say or write — but rather to the way in which Nietzsche's thinking functions, i.e. operates. Needless to say, with this type of agenda, Laruelle's interpretation does not focus on the hermeneutic, exegetical or doctrinal dimensions of Nietzsche's many explicit political statements; indeed one of Laruelle's main contentions is that although these signifying elements in no way need

NIETZSCHE AND NETWORKS, NIETZSCHEAN NETWORKS

of our contemporary network-centric condition, especially in relation to the all-important notion of "information," which has been conceptualized primarily in terms that are *protocological* and *computational*, hence almost exclusively *Apollonian* (or as Gilles Deleuze and Félix Guattari would say, "striated"), rather than *Dionysian* (or as Deleuze and Guattari would say, "smooth") terms. As Manav Guha argues in his contribution to this volume, the current military understanding of net-centricity is "a project of extreme striation involving the harnessing of *Dionysian energies* of the yet-to-be-processed with the *Apollonian reigns* of the processor."[3]

Primary among the conceptual tools provided by Nietzsche's thinking is the pairing of Apollo and Dionysus, which Nietzsche initially presents as artistic and psychological tendencies in *The Birth of Tragedy,* but later reconceptualizes more fundamentally as ontological and (in)formational tendencies out of which empirical matters/materials arise and are individuated in terms of the will-to-power's "form-giving" functions: "Thus the essence of life, its will-to-power, […] [involves] the essential priority of the spontaneous, aggressive, expansive, form-giving forces that give new interpretations and directions."[4] For Nietzsche (who took this from the ancient Greeks), *life itself*—or again, *will-to-power*—expresses itself through the duality of Apollo, god of the *eye*, of *vision*, of the *visual arts* (including musical *notation* and *composition*), of *order, memory,* and *civic affairs,* and Dionysus, god of the *ear*, of *hearing*, of *sonic perception, musical performance, dissonant dynamics, dissolution into soundscapes*

be repressed or suppressed, they are nevertheless secondary features of the fundamental design or layout (*agencement*) of Nietzsche's thinking. The basic and most important characteristic—the one that makes Nietzsche's political thinking unique from Laruelle's point of view—is the operation of an elementary and fundamentally non-signifying force-mechanics that activates the virulence of Nietzsche's thought."

3   Manabrata Guha, "*Networked Nightmares:* On Our Dionysian Post-Military Condition" (chapter three of this volume), 66.

4   Friedrich Nietzsche, *The Genealogy of Morals,* trans. Walter Kaufman (New York: Random House, 1967), II §12.

(or *immersion into noise*[5]), *intoxication, self-abandon, oblivion, and revelry*. Ontologically, the duality of Apollo and Dionysus is reflected in the constancy of becoming, of the regeneration and degeneration of all forms, as Horst Hutter suggests in his contribution to this volume.[6] *Informatically* (and *physiologically*, as Nietzsche would have surely said, and as Scott Bakker reminds us in his contribution to this volume), Dionysus symbolizes the "forgetfulness and random noise," the *pre-* or *proto*-individual "background of all media"[7] out of which arises the Apollonian signal qua ordering "principle of individuation" (the *principium individuationis* of *the Birth of Tragedy* §1–2).[8]

According to Nietzsche's thinking, then, we can conceptualize the *Apollonian* as the tendency toward concretization via selection, individualization, and formalization (e.g., the complex computational processes required for physiological formations, including cognition, representation, signification); the *Dionysian*, by contrast, is that tendency which continuously mediates the former — threatening to dissolve, disrupt, and dissipate it (chaos in this sense is the Dionysian weapon *par excellence*). To date, we have tended to view networks and our current network-centric condition in almost *exclusively* Apollonian terms — that is, in terms of networks of discrete elements, informational protocols, and platforms. From the Apollonian perspective, the Dionysian is "a chiasmic turbulence that the computationally-centric [viz. Apollonian] concept of network[s] tries to keep at bay."[9] The result is that "so far, there is no digital Dionysus"[10] — hence a fundamental aspect of network-centricity remains almost entirely occluded (i.e., unthought).

---

5   See Joseph Nechvatal, *Immersion into Noise* (Ann Arbor: Open Humanities Press, 2011).

6   Horst Hutter, "The Internet as a Development from Descartes' *Res Cogitans*: How to Render It *Dionysian*" (chapter two of this volume).

7   Cf. Friedrich Kittler, *Gramophone, Film, Typewriter,* trans. Geoffrey Winthrop-Young (Stanford: Stanford University Press, 1999), 2.

8   Friedrich Nietzsche, *The Birth of Tragedy and Other Writings,* trans. Ronald Speirs (Cambridge: Cambridge University Press, 1999), §1–2.

9   Guha, *"Networked Nightmares."*

10 Hutter, "The Internet as a Development from Descartes' *Res Cogitans.*"

What would it mean to re-imagine the network-centric condition in terms that privilege the Dionysian background of all information rather than its Apollonian signals and figures? This is a very complex question, and the essays in this volume are, first and foremost, experimental responses to this very question from various perspectives — political, politico-theological, philosophical, aesthetic, media-archaeological, psychological, neuro- and/or techno-physiological, etc. One gleans from Babich's essay, for instance (chapter one of this volume), that to understand the network-centric condition in Dionysian terms would entail a de-privileging of visible and optical aspects of mediation, (at)tuning one's ear instead to the hidden, dissonant, puls(at)ional, or rhythmic affinities of information flow here understood in *Dionysian* terms — that is, as the winding and widening "wound" out of which discrete Apollonian forms or "idols" emerge.[11] In a well-known and oft-cited passage from *Twilight of the Idols,* Nietzsche writes:

A maxim — the origin of which I withhold from scholarly curiosity — has long been my motto: *"increscunt animi, virescit volnere virtus"* (the spirits increase, vigor grows through a wound). Another mode of convalescence (in certain situations even more to my liking) is sounding out idols. There are more idols than realities in the world: that is my "evil eye" upon this world; that is also my "evil ear." Finally to pose questions with a hammer, and sometimes to hear as a reply that famous hollow sound that can only come from bloated entrails — what a delight for one who has ears even behind his ears, for me, an old psychologist and pied piper before whom just that which would remain silent must finally speak out.[12]

---

11 Babich, *"Digital Alexandrians:* Greek as Musical Code for Nietzsche and Kittler" (chapter one of this volume).
12 Friedrich Nietzsche, *Twilight of the Idols,* trans. Richard Hollingdale (New York: Penguin Books, 1990), 31.

It is the wound that permits sounding-out idols. Rather than think the conceptual pairing of Apollo and Dionysus as a dialectical dualism, it is revealing to think of it instead as a two-headed "interface" — a concept mobilized in this volume by Nicola Masciandaro. In the interface of Dionysus and Apollo (especially when relating this conceptual pairing to the notions of network-centricity and information), the *ear* (Dionysus), not the *eye* (Apollo), is revealed to be the aperture of subversion, overcoming, and transformation. As Nietzsche stated, Ariadne has Dionysus's *ears*, and Nietzsche's teachings address the disciples of Dionysus: those who alone possess such a third ear can hear his words. It was Sarah Kofman who noted that "the aphorism becomes a precaution against feeble minds, against the *profanum vulgus*; it allows one to express revolutionary ideas in the knowledge that one will be understood only by those who possess the third ear."[13] The ear deciphers the aphorism, and in so doing activates what Masciandaro calls a "navigational protocol" — *Dionysian love, amor fati*: "a medium that does not mediate," a kind of "magic non-medium at play between the solid of being and the liquid of thought."[14] As Masciandaro suggests, with Nietzsche we return "to the scene of modern philosophical decision in order to reopen the wound it hastily bound — to let it, like the blood of Saint Januarius, heal in bleeding anew."[15] Dionysus, as such, cures by cutting,[16] a theme that is explored in

13 Sarah Kofman, *Nietzsche,* trans. Duncan Large (Stanford: Stanford University Press, 1994), 116. See also Dan Mellamphy, "*Fragmentality*: Thinking the Fragment," *Dalhousie French Studies* 45 (1998): 82–98.

14 Nicola Masciandaro, "Nietzsche's *Amor Fati*: Wishing and Willing in *a Cybernetic Circuit*" (chapter seven of this volume), 132.

15 Ibid., 135.

16 The *Dionysian ear* is thus the *third eye of Shiva*: not the eye that *sees*, but the eye that *seers/sears* — the eye that hears; as Kodwo Eshun says, "the *3rd Eye* is a secret faculty that scans the non-visible spectrum for radio, ultraviolet, daemonic, acoustic waveforms" (*More Brilliant Than the Sun: Adventures in Sonic Fiction* [London: Quartet Books, 1998], 71, our emphasis). Enter the pineal eye of Georges Bataille: "the eye, at the summit of the skull, opening on the incandescent sun in order to contemplate it in a sinister solitude, is not a product of the understanding, but is instead an immediate existence; it opens and blinds itself like a conflagration, or like a fever that eats the being,

another one of the contributions to this volume: one in which Shan Bell "philosophizes with a scalpel."[17] In yet another contribution, Sarah Choukah suggests that the curative and transformative effects of these cuts — of this "cutting" — can be the catalysis for veritable *transindividuation*, precisely in the senses outlined by the techno-philosopher Gilbert Simondon.[18]

The current and prevalent computational paradigm of information and communication technology (e.g., "Big Data") is vindicated only at the cost of downplaying the double-sided interfaciality of information — and in particular, of denying the Dionysian aspect of the cybernetic interface. One of the reasons may be that Apollonian tools and Apollonian perspectives — which are designed to parse-out and calculate discrete elements within a medium or media — cannot compute the Dionysian aspect of information, which is incommensurable and cannot be rendered into discrete computable elements. Dionysus, unlike Apollo, *mediates* without *being mediated* — and this is, indeed, the troubling (even "nightmarish," *pace* Guha) Nietzschean insight regarding the doubleness of the interface. *To mediate without being mediated* can here be equated with a capacity *to bind without being bound,* to elude capture while at the same time being able to set traps and go undetected. In this very important sense, Dionysus is not a god that relies on the *logos* (word, measure, logic, or logical intelligence) as does Apollo, but rather on *mētis* (ruse, cunning, craftiness, double-dealings, and technical trickery), which for the ancient Greeks, as Marcel Detienne and Pierre Vernant have shown, was often conceptualized in terms of *nets,* i.e. as itself being *net-like. Mētis* — metic duplicity, technical trickery — involves an "interlacing of opposite directions [...] and imprints," producing

or more exactly, the head" (*Visions of Excess: Selected Writings,* trans. Allan Stoekl [Minneapolis: University of Minnesota, 1985], 82).

17 Shannon Bell, "'Philosophizing With a Scalpel': *From Nietzsche to Nina Arsenault*" (chapter 15 of this volume).

18 Sarah Choukah, "*The Rope-Dancer's Fall:* 'Going Under' as Undergoing Nietzscheo-Simondonian Transindividuation" (chapter eleven of this volume).

"an enigma in the true sense of the word":[19] "living bond[s]"/
double-binds that "bind" and "secure" but *themselves elude capture.*[20] To affirm the Dionysian aspect of the interface (which
Masciandaro aptly calls "willing within a cybernetic circuit") is
to affirm the background of all media, the smooth space of the
Dionysian non-medium out of which arises the interlacing of
oppositions that is necessary for the Apollonian emergence of
media and computable information or "data." In this manner,
as Dylan Wittkower suggests, Dionysus can be viewed as the
unofficial and occluded — as well as intoxicated — god of nets
and network-centricity.[21]

This, quite obviously, is not how Dionysus is *normally* viewed,
and it is also not how Nietzsche's thinking is usually presented.
It seems that Nietzsche — while acknowledged as a key figure
in relation to "post-modernism," for instance — is seen to have
limited insight with respect to networks and network-centricity:
the "Nietzschean Argument,"[22] while calling attention to "the po-

---

19 "[I]t is what the Greeks sometimes call *ainigma* and sometimes *griphos,* for
an enigma is twisted together like a basket or a wheel. In one of his dialogues,
Plutarch writes of the Sphinx twisting together her enigmas or riddles (*ain-
igmata kai griphous plekousan*), devising the questions which Sophocles describes as *poikila*: shimmering, many-coloured, shifting. The composition of
some of the best known riddles reveals the tangle of forms and the shimmering of different colours which give them the disturbing mobility of speech
which seems constantly vibrating, never for a moment remaining the same
as it was. […] The answer which allows Polyeidos to escape from the aporia
is the infallible grip with which he catches and binds the shifting and mobile
words of the riddle" (Marcel Detienne and Jean-Pierre Vernant, *Cunning
Intelligence in Greek Culture and Society,* trans. Janet Lloyd [Chicago: University of Chicago Press, 1978], 303–4); for more on the latter, see Marshall
McLuhan and Vilém Flusser's *Communication and Aesthetic Theories Revis-
ited,* ed. Tom Kohut and Melentie Pandilovski (The Video-Pool Media-Arts
Centre, 2015), 260–80.
20 Detienne & Vernant, *Cunning Intelligence in Greek Culture and Society,* 41–
42.
21 See Dylan Wittkower's essay on a Dionysian notion of gamification that
remains true to the earth, *"Farmville, Eternal Recurrence,* and the *Will-to-
Power*-Ups" (chapter thirteen of this volume).
22 Alexander Galloway and Eugene Thacker, *The Exploit: A Theory of Networks*
(Minneapolis: University of Minnesota Press, 2007), 7.

litical physics of action and reaction that exists within network structures," nonetheless fails to "account for conflict within networks — or better, between networks" (the latter c/o Alex Galloway's and Eugene Thacker's publication *The Exploit*[23]). From this perspective, Nietzschean arguments are too *local* — "in effect moving from node to node" — and even *atomistic* (this *despite* Nietzsche's explicit statements against atomism) to be able to be revealing about how networks behave:

> Nietzsche's notes in *The Will to Power* reveal this atomistic bias. Nietzsche begins from the analysis of "quanta of power" in constant interaction, and these quanta of power are understood somehow to compose the "will to power." Network structures challenge us to think about what happens outside scale — that is, between the jump from "quanta of power" to "will to power."[24]

Here the focus on Nietzsche's "atomistic bias" interprets Nietzsche in Apollonian terms — that is, literally in terms of the primacy of the Apollonian tendency which by definition and function *does* proceed by way of discretization, atomization, and individualization. Taken as a whole, the impact of Nietzschean concepts has enabled the conceptualization of power in material and relational — mainly *subjective* and *intersubjective* — terms, but not in relevant *systemic, machinic,* or *network* terms. This viewpoint seems to be responding to (and mobilizing) a particular kind of prevalent interpretation of Nietzsche inspired by Michel Foucault and Gilles Deleuze, adopted by phenomenologists and post-structuralists (this popular version of Nietzsche itself being part of the response to early twentieth-century interpretations of the "fascist" and later "literary" as well as "psychological" portraits of Nietzsche). Here — or rather, *therein* — Nietzsche is the icon of difference and differentiality as well as multiplicity and heterogeneity: from the

23 Ibid.
24 Ibid.

"thermodynamic" version of Nietzsche — the thinker of ener-getic and kinetic force-relationality or power-associations (Spi-nozan *power* and *potentiality*) as espoused by Georges Bataille and Pierre Klossowski — to Michel Foucault's "genealogical" Nietzsche and Sarah Kofman's "metaphorical" Nietzsche — the thinker of corporeality and discursivity — and Gilles Deleuze's "mutating"/"metamorphosing" Nietzsche (initially as the exem-plary thinker of "tragic contingency" — in *Nietzsche et la phi-losophie* — then subsequently of "nomad thought," "virtuality," and "immanentism." In this respect, Jean Baudrillard is another notable interpreter of Nietzsche in the historical developments of post-structuralism).

By theoretically rooting itself in subjectivity and intersubjec-tivity, however, the "Nietzschean Argument" is also perceived to root itself in a dialectical politics of identity and difference, which, while being a revealing lens for subjective and intersub-jective insight, does not provide any systemic or machinic ("ma-chine-system") vantage-or-viewpoint that would be relevant for understanding network-centricity. As we are reminded in *The Exploit*, "decentralized networks are not simply the opposite of centralized networks,"[25] and Nietzschean rebellion qua agonism and pluralism — while decentralizing power — does not solve the problem of hierarchical power altogether (nor does it ex-plain more diffused modes of power such as distributed or net-work control). The post-structuralist model of endless deferral or difference is therefore trapped in a kind of performative and communicative game-space that simply enacts and oscillates-between various positions, or "nodes" as Galloway and Thacker call them (post-structuralist discourses tend to understand these as "subject positions" or "subjective identities" that are embodied *corporeally*).

Perhaps there is no greater lesson about networks than the lesson about control: networks, by their mere existence, are not liberating; they exercise novel forms of control that oper-

25 Ibid.

ate at a level that is anonymous and non-human, which is to say material. The non-human quality of networks is precisely what makes them so difficult to grasp. They are, we suggest, a medium of contemporary power, and yet no single subject or group absolutely controls a network. Human subjects constitute and construct networks, but always in a highly distributed and unequal fashion.[26]

From the viewpoint of network theory/theories, hermeneutic, phenomenological and post-structuralist frameworks have been somewhat constrained by their own rationales and dialectical models (e.g., favoring theoretical over empirical dimensions of thought) and have emphasized energetic and vitalistic interpretations that focus on differentiality and multiplicity in intersubjective terms. What post-structuralism has tended to leave undertheorized, as such, is the nature of the impersonal and perpetual mediation machine *itself*, the machinic aspects of network-centricity that are anonymous, non-organic, and non-human. Even though Nietzsche has been acknowledged to be the "bridge between the processual/machinic philosophies formulated in Greek thought (predominantly Ionian cosmology) and the post-structuralist/post-modernist enterprises emanating from France in the 1960s and beyond with such figures as Lyotard, Foucault, and Derrida,"[27] there is a strong tendency to resist interpreting Nietzsche outside the register of the "organic" bias in his philosophy of life. What we are trying to suggest here is that the post-structuralist-inspired "Nietzschean Argument," insofar as it shows a bias towards the *organic*, is "missing the boat," so to speak (giving a nod to the cybernetic etymon), with respect to an important insight about how "distributed" control works in networks. Far from being a "liberation" demanding either optimistic or pessimistic human-centered responses (or a combination of *both*), from the perspective of the *anonymous,*

26 Ibid., 5.
27 Mark Halsey, "*Ecology and Machinic Thought*: Nietzsche, Deleuze, Guattari," *Angelaki: Journal of Theoretical Humanities* 10.3 (Dec. 2005): 34.

non-human, machinic–cybernetic, and *distributed* tendencies of current and future planetary conditions, any emphasis on anthropocentrism can only be seen as another tactic in an overall strategy of pyramidal/hierarchical control. Rather, what is really *needed*, argue the political theorists of media, is to understand how networks "act politically, both as rogue swarms and as mainframe grids."[28]

So, are we forced to agree that the "Nietzschean Argument" cannot tell us anything meaningful about how networks *work*? If we had to stop at the post-structuralist vision of Nietzsche, then we might, indeed, be forced to concede. But we shall not stop here. As Scott Bakker stresses in his contribution to this volume, Nietzsche was actually and actively thinking *past* post-structuralism *a century before it*![29] Perhaps we get an intuition of Bakker's claim in Laruelle's distinct-and-compelling yet overlooked and generally-unknown take on Friedrich Nietzsche — his 1977 *Nietzsche contre Heidegger: thèses pour une politique nietzschéenne.*[30] While admittedly not disengaged — not *yet* disengaged — from post-structuralist theory, and while it doesn't offer a *machinic* Nietzsche *per se* (this is also lacking in Deleuze and Guattari as well as in Derrida's "Nietzsche and the Machine"[31]), Laruelle's *Nietzsche contre Heidegger* is nevertheless a rather remarkable rethinking of the material political effects of a "Nietzsche Machine," a way of Nietzschean thinking that Laruelle defines as a generic schema or "ensemble of rela-

28 Galloway and Thacker, *The Exploit*, 15. "Like it* or not, the new culture is networked and open-source, and one is in need of intelligent interventions to evaluate it," states Alexander Galloway on the very first page of *The Interface Effect* (Cambridge: Polity Press, 2012), a book and book title with many resonances in this volume (most explicitly in chapter seven and the present introduction).

   * "Like it," love it — in the spirit of Nietzsche's *amor fati* — or not.

29 R. Scott Bakker, "Outing the 'It' that Thinks: *On the Collapse of an Intellectual Ecosystem*" (chapter eight of this volume).

30 François Laruelle, *Nietzsche contre Heidegger: thèses pour une politique nietzschéene* (Paris: Editions Payot, 1977).

31 Jacques Derrida, "Nietzsche and the Machine," trans. Richard Beardsworth, *Journal of Nietzsche Studies* 7 (Spring 1994): 7–66.

tions [of power] without terms, crossed within a chiasmus or a problematic":[32]

> In the sense that one speaks of *logical* or *mathematical* machines, *reading* machines, *calculators*, or *infernal* machines, there is a "Nietzsche Machine" — but with a way of operating that is specific to it, since it is an intrinsically *political* machine rather than *logical* or *mathematical*. [...] [T]here is only *affinity*, no *identity*, between what Nietzsche calls "forces" — which are non-signifying elements [that] [...] become an autonomous process of rebellion. [...] [T]he rationale of the Nietzschean revolutionary power thus begins to appear: Rebellion and Mastery are in a relation of positive disjunction without mediating negativity. [...] They are not predominantly exclusive to one another; they are not closed entities of transcendent essence to one another in the onto-theological or gnostico-christian manner; their relation of co-belonging is *a relation of duplicity rather than of duality*.[33]

In Laruelle's quadripartite — rather than dialectical — schema, a schema he calls the "Nietzsche Machine," the Dionysian (that is to say, the *non-signifying* but *active* and *unmediated* forces, or what he calls "Rebellion") mediates the Apollonian (that is to say, the signifying forces of "Mastery"), but only as the other side of a duplicitous interface. "The Nietzschean Cut contains no term, no essence, but only relations of duplicity and of chiasmus."[34] Both poles of the interface are active in the "Nietzsche-Thought" (i.e., in Nietzschean thinking); the one does not

---

32 Laruelle, *Nietzsche contre Heidegger,* 11. Rather ironically, we would argue that (despite his critique of Deleuzian thought) Laruelle — in his post-1970s "non-philosophy" works — adopts the Deleuzian portrait of Nietzsche-as-theorist-of-"difference" and thereby makes Nietzsche part of his own critique of differential philosophy. In this sense, Laruelle's earlier engagements of Nietzsche as political materialist, in his pre-"non-philosophy," are much more subversive and compelling takes on Nietzsche(an) thought.

33 Ibid., 19 (All translations by the present editors). Also see Biswas Mellamphy, "Nietzsche's Political Materialism."

34 Ibid., 33.

annul or sublate the other, but instead *crosses-over* or better-yet *double-crosses* the other. This "duplicity" (as Laruelle calls it) accounts for the presence of both fascistic and subversive tendencies in a Nietzschean mode of thinking. It is from this duplicity that Laruelle develops a theory regarding the inherently political function of Nietzschean thinking: "The Nietzsche-Thought is a complex political process with two 'contradictory' poles that *are not mediated*: the subordinate relation of a secondary 'fascistic' pole (*Mastery*) to a principal revolutionary' pole (*Rebellion*). Nietzsche became fascist to better defeat fascism; he assumed the worst forms of Mastery to become the Rebel. [...] We are all fascist readers of Nietzsche, we are all revolutionary readers of Nietzsche."[35] Indeed, Laruelle goes as far as to claim that "[t]his internal duplicity of the two poles in relation to immediate contradiction and its plasticity makes Nietzsche superior to Marx for reflecting on the political problems of our times."[36]

This principle of methodological duplicity is intrinsic to the interface of Dionysus and Apollo and thus also intrinsic to the Nietzsche Machine (the function of which, as has already been suggested — following Laruelle and borrowing a phrase from Masciandaro — is to "cure" by "cutting"). Both the "fascistic" and the "revolutionary" poles (what Heike Schotten, in her contribution to this volume, describes in terms of "master"-and-"slave" or "strong"-and-"weak" types, which we have contextualized in terms of Apollonian and Dionysian tendencies[37]) are intrinsic not only to Nietzsche's texts, but to the Nietzschean conception of *will-to-power* in general. The built-in duplicitous interface of Dionysus and Apollo is a mechanism that collapses not just all *subjectivities* but all *ecosystems* of thought and experience. This intrinsic explosion or extrinsic implosion is often felt as something that is not only *morally uncomfortable,* as Schotten suggests, but also, following Bakker, as *revelatory and*

35 Ibid., 9.
36 Ibid., 28.
37 Heike Schotten, "Reading Nietzsche in the Wake of the 2008–9 War on Gaza" (chapter six of this volume).

numinous, and perhaps even as the (re)gaining of a vital *"sweet-ness,"* as Masciandaro says.

The Cloud, we remind ourselves, is *both* vaporous (Diony-sian) *and* vectoral (Apollonian).[38] Nietzsche might still qualify as the thinker of the yet-unthought contingencies of network-centricity — not just a thinker of ecosystems, but more pre-cisely, as Bakker asserts, "an annalist of collapsing ecosys-tems" (and in this case not only biological, but *informational* ecosystems). "He understood that the Enlightenment would not stop exploding our ingrown vanities, that sooner or later the *anthropos* would fall along with the anthropomorphic [...]. [T]his is the moment he had glimpsed, however obscurely: the moment when our methods crumble, and our discursive domain slips away — when science asserts its problematic cog-nitive rights."[39] Nietzsche is *the* thinker of the dethroning and decline (i.e., fall) of the *anthropos* and the collapsing of anthro-pocentric ecologies. Thinking about the network-centric con-dition through the Nietzschean Interface prompts a revalua-tion — and perhaps even eventually a transvaluation — of our current conception of information, as well as the in*formational* nature of our being, which Guha describes as an incomputable and impersonal "Becomingness that drives our Being."[40]

Laruelle's notion of "generic ecology," which is to be un-derstood neither as a *general* ecology nor as an ecological *phi-losophy* (since philosophy is but one "productive force" among others — such as science, art, and religion — from the Laruel-lian vantage-point) might be useful here. "Generic ecology" is concerned with what Laruelle described as the "generic de-growth" in which philosophy is not only reduced to being one "productive force" among others, but in which this movement of *degrowth* or *receding* becomes *constitutive* of philosophy it-

---

38 We take the notion of "the vectoral" from our colleague at The New School, McKenzie Wark; see his *Virtual Geography: Living with Global Media Events* (Bloomington: Indiana University Press, 1994), 3–26. E.g., Ch. 1.1 on the "vector."

39 Bakker, *"Outing the 'It' that Thinks,"* 157.

40 Guha, *"Networked Nightmares,"* 77.

self.[41] "Obsolescence," as Jen Boyle's contribution to this volume highlights, becomes a fundamental functional feature of life itself — not just the "vital site of events and processes of becoming (becoming history; becoming machine; becoming human) but suddenly, violently, grasped as an imagething of the dead object."[42] The customary vitalist interpretive focus on *life, death, growth,* and *organicism* gives way to a double-headed (Janus-faced[43]) understanding of the equally important role of *non-life, degrowth,* and the *inorganic* (or *non-organic,* inclusive of the *cyborganic,* and, as in Guha's contribution, the *inforganic*): a richer but also darker and — in the senses invoked by Thacker's contribution to this volume[44] — more *pessimistic* understanding of information and network ecology. This is admittedly a hard pill to swallow (or, for fans of *The Matrix,* a very well-"Red pill"

41 François Laruelle, "*The Degrowth of Philosophy*: Towards a Generic Ecology," lecture at Miguel Abreu Gallery, New York (Nov. 20, 2012).

42 Jen Boyle, "*The Will-to-Obsolescence:* Nietzsche, Code, and the Digital Present" (chapter twelve of this volume), 198.

43 Janus, the *god at the top of the heap* (Mount Olympus), is also *the god of the garbage heap* and of all custodians of the latter (janitors), as the editors of this volume explained in a paper — "What's the 'Matter' with Materialism?: *Walter Benjamin and the New Janitocracy*" — presented to the *Congress of the Social Sciences and Humanities* at the University of Toronto Munk Centre for International Studies in May 2002. The two faces or sides of the Janus-face look not only *backward* and *forward* — into the *background* as well as into what is *foregrounded* — but also, in addition, *upward* and *downward*: up to the loftiest of Olympian (viz. Apollonian) *heights* and down to the grimiest chthonic (viz. Dionysian) *depths*. According to Babich in her contribution to this volume, Nietzsche had "noted in passing — *in passage, in transit* — that behind the scenes, every porter wants to have an admirer" (chapter one, 47)…"wants to" precisely because in the typical Janus-faced interface this is not the case. Here again we have "Wishing and Willing in a Cybernetic Circuit" (chapter seven). "The natural connection between the cybernetic and Nietzsche's *amor fati* is evident in their intersection within the principle of interface as the site of steering or helmsmanship (*kubernēsis*)," states Masciandaro, "Nietzsche names this love [viz. this *amor fati*] under the double sign of *Januarius*: at once the two-faced god of beginnings/doorways/gates and the saint whose annually liquifying blood signals the miracle of spiritual renewal" (131–32) "For Nietzsche," says Babich, "we are here to learn to love one thing; that is *amor fati* […] life as it is" (chapter one, 34).

44 Eugene Thacker, "*All for Naught*" (chapter nine of this volume).

indeed, with darkened tinges/tinctures of Baudrillard/Lewis-Carroll); *as disciples of Dionysus would say*, however, the bitter pill goes down much better with wine — and here Gary Shapiro reminds us, in "A Philosophy of the Antichrist in the Time of the Anthropocenic Multitude,"[45] that the *Antichrist*'s true name is *Dionysus* (*wink, wink*).

The duplicitous interface of the Nietzsche Machine collapses the unitary and sovereign principle of *life-as-growth* or *life-as-mastery*. Instead of a transcendental theory of life that privileges the Apollonian aspect — a clear example of this being the liberal biopolitical view, as outlined in Julian Reid's contribution,[46] in which life and the legitimacy of liberal regimes remain firmly grounded in promises to secure futures through the continual mastery and technologization of life, which amounts to what Dominic Pettman, in his contribution, describes in terms of a "hierarchical parsing of species-based ontologies"[47] — the Nietz-

---

45 Gary Shapiro, "*A Philosophy of the Antichrist in the Time of the Anthropocenic Multitude*: Preliminary Lexicon for the Conceptual Network" (chapter four of this volume).

46 Julian Reid, "*Occupying God's Shadow*: Nietzsche's *Eirōneia*" (chapter five of this volume), 49.

47 Dominic Pettman, "*A Horse is Being Beaten*: On Nietzsche's Equinimity" (chapter ten of this volume). Hutter's *donkeys** (his statement that "we are all donkeys that celebrate for a while, welcoming new donkeys to the celebration before singing our songs of goodbye" in chapter two of this volume, 49) lead, via various *Holzwege*, to Nietzschean *mania* (or *frenzy*, as Nechvatal says in chapter fourteen) and through this† to Pettmanian *equinimity*: "a horse-like mind: wild, kicking, unbridled — yet because of this, more sensitive to alterity, and capable of responsible response. The common hierarchical parsing of species-based ontologies is thus dispelled for an intense form of intersubjective feedback: a negative and diminishing spiral which inverts the disciplined joy in things which Nietzsche sought in his less stricken days" (chapter ten, 181). Nietzsche and Nietzschean thought come across as a veritable Trojan Horse — in both the *classical* and *computational*, technically *Greek* and techno-*Geek* senses — in that it packs in itself what Guha describes as the "night*mare*" of Apollonian arrangements (Apollonian arrangements qua Pettman's "common hierarchical parsing"). One might recall here the passage on equinimity *avant la lettre* in Gilbert Durand's *Structures anthropologiques de l'imaginaire: Introduction à l'archétypologie générale*, the first edition of which was published by the Presses Universitaires de France in

sche Machine ruthlessly cuts-up/cross-cuts (mixes, modulates) any relation one might make between life, being, and thinking. "Tuning into" the Dionysian tonalities of information becomes a kind of *tragic fatum* for the subject (cf. Pettman's account of Nietzsche's *equinimity*) — a necessary attunement, admittedly — but one that is also felt as *amor fati*: a love not just of *life* (the sovereignty of life) but of the *unlife/non-life* of life (the non-sovereignty or contingency of life) or that "point of identity between law and sweetness lost in the splitting of life into *bios* and *zoē*."[48] Perhaps herein lies Nietzsche's most unique contribution to contemporary theorizations of network-centricity: the "Nietzsche Machine," like Heraclitean fire, cures by cutting and *creates* by *destroying*. "Dare one hope for a philosophy of futility? Phosphorescent, moss-ridden aphorisms inseparable from the thickness and ossification of our own bodies, inseparable from the stillness of breathing"?[49]

The Nietzsche Machine *connects* — connects *objects, subjects, what-have/haven't-you* — by *cutting*, making bodies part of the collapsing ecosystem(s) of thinking and being. The philosopher of futurity is, after all, a *vivisectionist*, as Nietzsche declared in *Beyond Good and Evil* §211–212, and would indeed "philoso-

---

1960 and second/updated edition in that most Orwellian — not to mention *Animal Farm*ville‡ — of years, 1984.

* Which recalls an image we discovered when putting together an essay for *Foucault Studies* in 2005: see the first page (a full-page photo of Foucault on a donkey) in *L'Actualité Poitou-Charentes: Revue Trimestrielle de l'Innovation Régionale* 51 (Jan–Feb–Mar 2001). PDF.Actualite-Poitou-Charentes.info/051/VINHUIT.pdf (accessed October 2005).

† "[A]s a friend of a friend said about [Robert Bresson]," Pettman noted in his lecture, "every film in his oeuvre essentially says, *Life sucks, then you die.* However, in the case of [Bresson's] Balthazar there is a caveat: *Life sucks, then you die. But you're a donkey*" (again: in chapter ten of this volume).

‡ A nod to Wittkower's essay (chapter thirteen). One of the sources in Wittkower's contribution, Ian Bogost, posted the following question on Twitter (which we are adding to this endnote at the very last minute, or "in the last instance," as Laruelle would say): "Are *My Little Ponies* transformers now? They turn from ponies into *Equestria Girls*? Or is that something else entirely?" — *"In my day, a pony was a plastic horse!, grandpa shouted at the empty room."* Twitter.Com/iBogost/status/660268080916926464, Twitter.Com/iBogost/status/660268849909010432 (Oct. 30, 2015).

48 Masciandaro, "Nietzsche's *Amor Fati*."
49 Thacker, "*All for Naught*," 163.

phize with a scalpel,"[50] to use (once again) Bell's titular phrase from her contribution to this anthology of essays. Bodies and bodily order(s) break apart into multiplicities, and even further into flux and incommensurability.[51] The Dionysian aspects of the process of becoming, the frenzied underside of beauty,[52] and the "cut"[53] — or what we might call the Dionysian "hack" — each entail various intensities of entanglement between drifting detritus, materials, and materialities (e.g., in the Krokerian sense of that "body drift" wherein Judith Butler becomes the alter-ego/embodiment of Friedrich Nietzsche and/or a "Nietzsche *in drag*" — here be *drag*ons — in the sense taken up by Bell in her reading of Nina Arsenault's body/bodies). But it's not just about recombinable bodies and body parts (or what poet Christopher Dewdney called "permugenesis" in a more geophilosophical/ geopoetic *"Erde treu"* context[54]). The *curative* capacity of the Dionysian hack comes from what can be called — following Gilbert Simondon and (in this anthology) Sarah Choukah — its "amplifying" effects, in which (as Choukah very nicely explains) "great magnitude can be triggered by relatively little quantities of energy."[55] What the curative aspect of transindividuation produces is not a single or singular distributed being — as in the

---

50 Nietzsche, *Beyond Good and Evil: Prelude to a Philosophy of the Future,* trans. Judith Norman (Cambridge: Cambridge University Press, 2002), §211–12.

51 Arthur Kroker's presentation at our third Nietzsche Workshop (Oct. 1, 2011) was published the following year, 2012, in a book with the very relevant/very topical title of *Body Drift: Butler, Hayles, Haraway* (Minneapolis: University of Minnesota Press , 2012).

52 Joseph Nechvatal, *"Aesthetic States of Frenzy:* Nietzsche's Aesthetic Palimpsest" (chapter fourteen of this volume).

53 Shannon Bell, *"Philosophizing with a Scalpel."*

54 See Christopher Dewdney, *Permugenesis* (Gibsons, BC: Nightwood Editions, 1987), *A Palaeozoïc Geology of London Ontario* (Toronto, ON: Coach House Books, 1974), and *Concordat Proviso Ascendant: A Natural History of Southwestern Ontario* (Berkeley, CA: The Figures, 1991). "Ich beschwöre euch, meine Brüder, bleibt der Erde treu und glaubt Denen nicht, welche euch von überirdischen Hoffnungen reden! Giftmischer sind es, ob sie es wissen oder nicht" (Friedrich Nietzsche, *Also sprach Zarathustra: Ein Buch für Alle und Keinen* [Chemnitz: Ernst Schmeitzner, 1883], I, §3).

55 Choukah, *"The Rope-Dancer's Fall,"* 186.

Apollonian version(s) of network theory — but rather a singular contagious becoming in which the material activities of ecosystemic collapse nonetheless undergo a process of amplification-without-figuration in which all bodies fold back onto and into their Dionysian background (e.g., random noise).

In terms of communicative mode(l)s, the contagious or virulent aspect of today's "viral media" can thus be understood as Dionysian because its mode of expression proceeds by way of the positive amplification of information (rather than by way of negation, negativity, or the negotiated parsing of information). In this sense, even the *Erinyes* (the *Furies*) of Greek antiquity would be accomplices of Dionysus. What Galloway calls "furious media" — after the *Furies*, that "bloody ravening pack" described by Aeschylus, amongst others — so as to distinguish this mode of mediation from two other, more well-known, communicative models (namely the *hermeneutic* and *iridescent* mode(l)s), can also be called a *Dionysian* mode.[56] If hermeneutics en-

---

56 "Given the convoluted twists and turns of Hermes' travels, the *text* is best understood as a *problem*. Likewise, given the aesthetic gravity of immediate presence in Iris's bow, the *image* is best understood as a *poem*. Thus, whereas hermeneutics engages the problem of texts, iridescence engages the poetry of images, be they visual or otherwise. Hermeneutics views media (of whatever kind — be it text, image, sound, etc.) as if they were textual problems needing to be solved. Yet iridescence views these same media as if they were poetic images waiting to be experienced [...]. The culminating moment of hermeneutics is always a type of mystical revelation — a lightning-strike. Yet the culminating moment of iridescence is an aurora, a blooming — the glow of a sacred presence," writes Galloway in "The Love of the Middle" (a version of which was presented at the 2013 *Apps And Affect* conference in London ON, as "*Three Middles*: Mediation in Networks"). See Alexander Galloway, Eugene Thacker, and McKenzie Wark, *Excommunication: Three Inquiries in Media and Mediation* (Chicago: University of Chicago Press, 2013), 46, 55. The key passage for us is the following one: "*After Hermes and Iris*, instead of a return to hermeneutics (the critical narrative) or a return to phenomenology (the iridescent arc), there is a third mode that combines and annihilates the other two. For after Hermes and Iris there is another divine form of pure mediation: the distributed network, which finds incarnation in the incontinent body of what the Greeks called first the Erinyes and later the Eumenides, and the Romans called the Furies. So instead of a *problem* or a *poem*, today we must confront a *system*. A third divinity must join the group:

gages problems of the text, and iridescence engages the poetry of images, then "furious media" engages affects as agents of ontological sabotage (cf. Guha's essay) and communicates through contagion, cutting through the distributed logic of the swarm. The Dionysian mode is thus a weaponized environment where transindividuation can have disruptive, even lethal effects; as Guha notes, "the Apollonian mask that covers the visage of the genius is stripped aside to reveal a truly Dionysian core, which is corrosive to the cohesiveness of the network."[57]

It has been our aim in this introduction to show that "Nietzsche-Thought" does indeed provide unique insights about the complexities of the contemporary network-centric condition — especially in drawing attention to the occluded Dionysian dimension of information, mediation, and technological transduction. We have tried to give an overall thematic portrait of how the various essays in this volume can be considered to engage Nietzsche-thinking, as well as engage in the activity of thinking about network-centricity along with Nietzsche. We would very much like to thank (and *do* so here, in this closing paragraph of our introduction) the students in the Department of Political Science, at the Centre for the Study of Theory and Criticism, and in various other centers and departments in the vicinity of Western University who participated in the first three Nietzsche Workshops @ Western (NWW.I 2009, NWW. II 2010, NWW.III 2011) as well as all of those who ventured to The New School in New York for the fourth one (NWW.IV, 2013). We would also like to thank the late great Bibi Pettypiece — to whom and in whose memory this anthology is dedicated — for her dynamic support of the workshop initiative, and our colleague Ed Keller, Series Editor of the CTM Imprint under which this volume has been published, whose fantastic presentation at the third Nietzsche Workshop (NWW.III) is one of the very-much-missed missing-pieces of this anthology. Thanks also go

not a man, not a woman, but a pack of animals" (56, our emphases). *Incipit Dionysus!*

57 Ibid., 75–76.

to Jeff Moen at the University of Minnesota Press for permission to reprint the lecture that Arthur Kroker presented on October 1, 2011 at NWW.III, subsequently published in *Body Drift,*[58] to Eileen A. Joy, Vincent W.J. van Gerven Oei, and Natalia Tuero at punctum books, and—last but not least—to the authors and presenters themselves: you have all made the Nietzsche Workshops truly wonderful events.

— DM+NBM, October 2015.

58   Kroker, *Body Drift,* 29–62.

01

Digital Alexandrians:
Greek as Musical Code for Nietzsche and Kittler

Babette Babich

NWW.IV, April 13, 2013

The will to power interprets.
— Friedrich Nietzsche[1]

The *Cyborg*-Nietzsche appeals to us — indeed the pastiche-in-general appeals to us — like the bookplate-image from Alfred Soder's *Nietzsche in the High Mountains,* discretely placed not on the front of the dust-jacket but the back of Steven E. Ascheim's *Nietzsche Legacy.*[2] Nietzsche-On-Demand can be found at the click of a button: the *Hitler*-Nietzsche? ... got that; the *Ayn-Rand*-Nietzsche? ... got that; the *Naturalist-* or *Brian-Leiter*-Nietzsche? ... also got that. The *Analytic*-Nietzsche we have from John Richardson to Aaron Ridley, the *"New"*-Nietzsche still with David Allison and the shining feathers of Alphonso Lingis. And with Friedrich Kittler — as Nandita Biswas Mellamphy has already acknowledged,[3] along with a host of

1   Friedrich Nietzsche, *Kritische Studienausgabe,* trans. and ed. Giorgio Colli and Mazzino Montinari (Berlin: De Gruyter, 1980), 12: 2 [148], 139.
2   Steven Ascheim, *The Nietzsche Legacy in Germany 1890–1990* (Berkeley: University of California Press, 1992).
3   Nandita Biswas Mellamphy, "Nietzsche & the Engine of Politics," in *Nietzsche and Political Thought,* ed. Keith Ansell Pearson (London: Continuum/

typewriter-and-keyboard networking enthusiasts, including a certain Arthur Kroker — we already have a *Media*-Nietzsche, tracked from several angles, several perspectives. As Nietzsche himself has told us, "There are myriad eyes. Even the sphinx had eyes. And consequently there are myriad *truths,* and consequently there *is* no truth."[4] Thus we suppose a multiplicity of trans- and over-humans (are we not all already post-human?) if only to overcome the last humans, as we imagine the trans-human phantasm in our own image.[5]

Well and good. Yet Jean Baudrillard — who wrote not only on women and self-marketing in the interim,[6] in addition to the politically articulated cultural logic of marketing and branding (a good complement to the Frankfurt School)[7] — might be the ticket for an illumination of the best sense in which none of us can have "oil and mercy enough"[8] for either women or men, trans or cis, in this age of simulation, simulacra, seduction, and virtuality. Indeed — and I will come back to this later — Kittler reads his Nietzsche by sidestepping Nietzsche, riffing off his typing habits and his typists. And we follow suit: these days we decide what (and who) to read on the basis of citation frequency: there are those clicks again. Today's cybertheorists, however, avoid philosophers — maybe with exception of Bruno Latour

Bloomsbury Books, 2013), 140–60.

4 Nietzsche, *Kritische Studienausgabe,* 11: 34 [230], 498.

5 I discuss this phantom in my essay on "Friedrich Nietzsche and the Post-/Trans-/human in Film and Television," in *The Palgrave Handbook of Post-Humanism in Film and Television,* ed. Michael Hauskeller et al. (London: Palgrave Macmillan, 2015).

6 Jean Baudrillard, *De la séduction* (Paris: Editions Galilée, 1979). Unfortunately this is more entrenched than sheer Gallic insight can afford; this is mainstream capital advantage, closer to the critical reflections in Pierre Bourdieu's *Distinction* (Cambridge: Harvard University Press, 1984), but without the breadth or critical range. See Daniel Hamermesh, *Beauty Pays: Why Attractive People are More Successful* (Princeton: Princeton University Press, 2013).

7 Jean Baudrillard, *The System of Objects,* trans. James Benedict (London: Verso, 1996 [1968]).

8 Nietzsche, *The Gay Science,* trans. Josefine Nauckhoff (Cambridge: Cambridge University Press, 2001), §68.

(but even he prefers to address himself to a shifting panoply of speculatively minded, object-oriented ontologists).

In this way, the focus on the subject has come full circle. Now we tell ourselves the secret lives of "things," "object thought," as if we hadn't been doing that all along. We've never been modern, as Latour rightly insists, nor indeed objective, where to be object-oriented leaves us still not thinking, *still* where Heidegger found us some time ago. Not even Kittler was as much of a thing/object fetishist as his followers today, grateful for his now lasting silence, would have had him be.

And yet the new world order of total mobilization has now become totally integrated, connected, beyond *branché*. Every dream the forgotten Lyotard ever had for Internet and wireless connectivity has been achieved.[9] Shall we not have some version of Nietzsche along for the ride?

Connected by some thinkers to the humanist enthusiasm for techno-transhumanism, we could ask why Nietzsche asks us to revalue values — after all, aren't we already doing that? Didn't the free thinkers of Nietzsche's day do that? Weren't they enlightened enough? Did they not in fact already go beyond what had been regarded as good and beyond what had been regarded as evil? Why, using the mouthpiece of his *Thus Spoke Zarathustra,* does Nietzsche urge us to "overcome" humanity unless to remind us to get over ourselves and our petty wanting, our longing, for immortality? But we do not want to overcome humanity because we do not want to go to ground. Can we not devise ways to live forever? Sure we can, so Ray Kurzweil hopes, but that too — here Nietzsche mocks us from the end of his nineteenth century — is still youth.[10]

---

9 I discuss Lyotard in a hermeneutically turned reflection in *"Thus Spoke Zarathustra,* or Nietzsche and Hermeneutics: Gadamer, Lyotard, and Vattimo," in *Consequences of Hermeneutics: 50 Years After Gadamer's* Truth and Method, ed. Jeff Malpas and Santiago Zabala (Evanston: Northwestern University Press, 2010), 218–43.

10 I have a reflection on this in a German essay written on the new desire(s) for body modification, with brain transplants being the ultimate example of such: see my "Körperoptimierung im digitalen Zeitalter, verwandelte Zau-

We prefer Nietzsche the humanist because we do not want to follow his questions to what he called their "ultimate consequences," as Nietzsche radicalizes the critical turn in philosophy. As Kant himself inaugurated this turn and then left us, as it were, as a tightrope-walker — or as Nietzsche wrote, a "rope-dancer" — without a net. Kant was a humanist, but he had no trouble setting aside or denying the logic of his own consequentiality to make room, as he put it, for faith. Nietzsche — *post* Schopenhauer, *post* Feuerbach — is likewise no kind of humanist, no more than Heidegger ever was.

Obvious in the case of the author of two volumes entitled, wearily enough to make the point from the get go, *Human, All Too Human* — and who then tops them off with a second volume of mixed maxims and republished the whole again together with a postscript, a *memento mori*: *The Wanderer and his Shadow*. We are pilgrims on this earth, all so many wanderers, and for Nietzsche — fan of antiquity as he was — this only entailed that we are here to learn to love one thing. That is the meaning of *amor fati*, that is life as it is.

But most of us want life *otherwise*. Trans-futurists as we might call ourselves, we are ahead of ourselves, which is the fundamental point of futurism. If we have not been modern since Rome (or, better said, since Nietzsche's Alexandrian). Much rather, we've been trans-futurists ever since Lucian fibbed the first science-fiction fantasy story into existence as a genre in his dialogue a "True Story" (the Greek title, *Alēthē Diēgēmata*, doesn't quite convey that for us).

Lucian's master in satire was Menippus. And like true scholars everywhere, classicists to date prefer Menippus (he was so much better than Lucian). This is an incontrovertible preference because we have no exact text of Menippus to contradict our admiration: what we know of Menippus is channeled through Lucian, who commends Menippus for introducing the art of "truthful lying." Lucian, himself perfected the art of truthful

berlehrlinge, und Übermenschsein," in *Körperphantasien*, ed. Andreas Beinsteiner and Tanja Kohn (Innsbruck: Universtitätsverlag Innsbruck, 2016).

lying by using the philosophical conundrum, Cretan as we are told, of proclaiming himself to be lying whilst lying and thereby warning the listener not to be fooled. Heirs to David Hume's skepticism as we are today, we may read this in the spirit of Epicharmus's encomium: "always remember not to believe."[11]

Nietzsche also alludes to the Lucianic constellation of vanity, contrasting the perspective of the self-absorbed individual down to the smallest gnat by contrast with the vast view from above, from the heights of the sky in *On Truth and Lie in an Extra-moral Sense.*

Like Hume, Nietzsche was fond of Lucian's mockery of the lifestyle adopted by humans, beings who were no more than, as Sophocles called them, creatures of a day. If the point of philosophy is to teach us the art of living — and if life includes limitation and failure, stumbling and sickness, aging and decay, in addition to the yoke of the erotic, of procreation, of growth — life should bring us at the very least to the thought (as Nietzsche endeavored to underscore) of death.

But we are not inclined to think of death, as Heidegger spent a lifetime trying to suggest. And we are even less inclined to think of Nietzsche and death. For this reason, paradoxically or absurdly enough — especially for the parodistic sensibilities of those fond (as Nietzsche was) of Menippo-Lucianic satire — all of us are hell-bent in our ambition to live in the future, cannot wait to get there. It is all we talk about: digital humanities, digital social science, trans-humanism, what to do when we can (finally) do whole-body or brain transplants or when we can clone ourselves to make spare parts for future transplants (we seem to have given up on turning off the aging gene) or build giant space arks to sail the solar seas or make nanobot bees to replace the ones we are killing now or grow meat in a lab or a fetus in a

11   David Hume used the quote from Epicharmus as an epigraph and read Lucian on his deathbed. I discuss this — with additional references to Hume's reading of Lucian in the literature — in "Becoming and Purification: Empedocles, Zarathustra's *Übermensch,* and Lucian's Tyrant," in *Nietzsche and the Becoming of Life,* ed. Vanessa Lemm (New York: Fordham University Press, 2014), 245–61; 359–68.

vat. Because we are sure that technology is moving so fast that we want to be the first in this future too, just as Nietzsche wrote in his aphorism, "The Thought of Death." I am all for this too; I still want that jet-pack. And why not *want* the latest, coming, newest thing? It is not only that we are not interested in scholarship even as scholars; younger researchers want the cutting edge rather than old books, hence everyone pretends to have read all those old books (not that they have) and skips the effort of repeating all the old questions everyone pretends to have asked (or answered).

Reflecting at the beginning of the fourth book (in its initial publication this would have been the *last* book) of *The Gay Science,* in the aphorism on "The Thought of Death," Nietzsche notes "[h]ow even now everyone's shadow stands behind him, as his dark fellow traveller!"[12] For Nietzsche the metaphor is utterly Greek: the world of shades, and the Nietzsche who had earlier appended an extra book entitled *The Wanderer and His Shadow* to his *Human, All Too Human* here alludes again to death in the same Lucian-suffused spirit.

Lucian himself wrote conversations of a zombie sort, set among the bones and the shades of the Greek afterworld: dialogues of the dead, posthumous musings. Note (as I have in so many of my own writings of late) that Lucian was an essential correspondent interest for Nietzsche inasmuch as Nietzsche was himself a specialist in the work of Diogenes Laertius, Lucian's contemporary — the same Diogenes, as Jonathan Barnes reminds us, no scholar of antiquity can afford to overlook (Barnes calls him the porter — the Cerberus, if one likes — of classical philology).[13]

The classical allusions continue as Nietzsche in this same aphorism writes:

12 Nietzsche, *The Gay Science,* §278.
13 Jonathan Barnes, "Nietzsche and Diogenes Laertius," *Nietzsche-Studien* 15 (1986): 16–40. Helmut Heit and Anthony Jensen have reprinted Barnes's essay in their recent collection *Nietzsche's Value as a Scholar of Antiquity* (London: Bloomsbury, 2014).

It's always like the last moment before the departure of an emigrant ship : people have more to say to each other than ever; the hour is late; the ocean and its desolate silence await impatiently behind all the noise — so covetous, so certain of its prey. And everyone, everyone takes the past to be little or nothing while the near future is everything; hence this haste, this clamour, this outshouting and out-hustling one another. Everyone wants to be the first in this future — and yet death and deathly silence are the only things certain and common to all in this future![14]

The aphorism is extraordinary. It begins with a labyrinthine reference to life "in the midst of this jumble of lanes, needs, and voices" and speaks of what Nietzsche calls his one "melancholy happiness."[15] But the Menippo-Lucianic metaphor of the shadow inveighs Nietzsche's happiness; once again we hear "[h]ow even now everyone's shadow stands behind him, as his dark fellow traveller!"[16] The ship metaphor is not limited to Lucian and may be found throughout the whole of antiquity (including Plato and beyond), but it is true that Lucian has his Hermes journey with Charon in various settings, collecting mortal souls (mostly unwilling) for a final transport in said ship…

The image of the ship about to depart is a cliche, and toward the end of his own life Kittler too draws upon the metaphor. It may be found at the outset of Epictetus's *Enchiridion* — in §7 — and it is more generally or even helpfully available in Marcus Aurelius's *Mediations* 3.3. Don't go too far and be ready to drop everything when the captain calls, is still good advice for cruise-going travelers today, but it is the metaphor that matters, especially as the metaphor has a Norse resonance beyond its Greek origins. In Nordic myth, a final ship built of dead men's nails, Naglfahr, sails at the end of times.

---

14 Nietzsche, *The Gay Science,* §278.
15 Ibid.
16 Ibid.

All ghost stories, hardly worthy of the dreams of our philosophy, we might say. As Nietzsche himself reflects, we are not
interested in thinking of our "dark fellow travelers" — much
less of Charon, Hermes, and so on. (Indeed, we are allergic to
hermeneutics likely for this reason.) Rather, what we want (and
what we mean to get at long last) is a *new* future. Hence we do
not want to follow Nietzsche where this fourth book of *The Gay
Science* proceeds to go, that is — as Nietzsche's demon spells it
out — down to the last spider of what he calls *das größte Schw-
ergewicht,* that which is eternally the same ("and there will be
nothing new in it"[17]).

To Nietzsche's thought-question, be it of real or imagined
purchase on our lives, we have all of us — already and in advance — answered a decisive "no." Dedicated as we are to that
hoped-for-future (not the shadow, not "death and deathly silence"), we are not the anti-Alexanders whom Nietzsche hoped
to find, but perfectly *Egyptian* Alexandrians — perfectedly *modern*. And our new, digital age allows us to break free of the old
bonds of scholarship, cutting more Gordian knots than ever. If I
now try to trace what Nietzsche meant, it still remains for us to
ask why this matters (i.e., what are Nietzsche's nets to be, here
and now?).

The question Nietzsche often asks in his works and of his
texts — *what is a word?* or better yet: *what is a code?* — is key
here, interwoven with the same essential deciphering, in addition to the archaeologies of texts and textures (the inhaled dust
of pages interleaved with pages). Along with the intercalations
of the writerly/readerly text, along with the physiognomy and
profundities of flesh and surfaces, along with the geologies — the
descrying of deep time — that Nietzsche traces as part of the
desecration of the divine sensorium (the stochastic time of cosmology playing all possibilities to eternity, *da capo*), along with
all of these there are his peregrinations, timetables, and plans.
The same Nietzsche who had a fixed position from which he
retired (his university job which also included teaching at the

17 Nietzsche, *The Gay Science,* §341.

local high school) was an itinerant, traveling scholar. In a sense, Nietzsche's image stands over all conferences, for travelers underway to knowledge and searching out places to write, or at least places to write about, good places to think, as both Graham Parkes and David Krell have tracked these, as indeed have Gary Shapiro and Paolo D'Iorio and Thomas Brobjer too, and Robin Small and Heribert Treiber, just to name a very few of the names of those scholars who follow Nietzsche's traces.

I began by noting that Nietzsche seems to be all things to everyone, and I mentioned that among so many others, we may also blame Kittler for this. Unlike most of Nietzsche's readers, however — especially today, especially those trained in schools that also boast a lot of analytic philosophy — Kittler knew rather a lot about music, mathematics, historical and contemporary psychology, and cybernetics, not merely for teasing but for *using, deploying, parsing, coding, hardware hacking*. And Kittler started, as Nietzsche started, with the text (of course: not as Nietzsche did, but still).[18]

Kittler's "ship," as we say, has come in for him — not merely in the sense of the Stoïc metaphor that has us waiting for the captain to call, ready to drop everything for that certain eventuality (what Heidegger called the possibility of the ultimate impossibility of all our own possibilities), but also in the better sense of promised fame or recognition. If we read Kittler now (as just a few years ago scholars simply smirked and said "no thanks, I'll pass," calling him a Romantic, capital-R, or a Flake, capital-F), what we do not do is pursue the lessons that Kittler had to offer (and now that he has died we shall also have Kittler

18 I think one might be careful about taking this too far. Kittler has a lovely scholarly reference to Nietzsche's "Geschichte der griechischen Literatur" but no evidence that he read Nietzsche on meter or quantitative rhythm; and there Kittler does not differ from the majority of Nietzsche scholars (see my chapters on Nietzsche and the Greeks in *The Hallelujah Effect: Philosophical Reflections on Music, Performance Practice and Technology* (Surrey: Ashgate, 2013).

scholars vying for title to his legacy).[19] Like Nietzsche and Heidegger, Kittler's lessons involved breaking down the standard
story of all the truths we know and the things we assume about
those truths without further reflection. The philologist needs to
learn to read, and Nietzsche argues that the philologist above
all needs to learn to read with his (or her) ears. He meant that
(reading with one's ears) as literally as one can imagine. There
is for Nietzsche music not in addition to or as a supplemental
coding (the "notes"), but in the words themselves.

Kittler reminds us that music goes in different directions
and toward different ends. The point echoes in media studies
of radio, and (as Adorno and Anders and Arnheim had already
pointed out) already in the 1930s radio is never merely radio,
but served any number of other functions and was heard in any
number of other ways to all kinds of ends.[20] Thus the DJ-artist/
philosopher Steve Goodman starts his study of *Sonic Warfare*
with an epigraph drawn from a film that seems tailor-made for
Kittler's purposes (almost repeating Kittler's metaphors), "We'll
come in low out of the rising sun and about a mile out, we'll
put on the music. — General Kilgore, *Apocalypse Now*."[21] Kittler
too (and this is no small part of the reason his fans love him)
cites Pink Floyd lyrics to support his claim that "[i]nterception,
chopping, feedback, and amplification of war reports: *Sym-
pathy for the Devil* means nothing else."[22] The Rolling Stones'

---

19 See, just for a start, the several contributions to the 2011 issue of *Thesis Elev-
    en*.
20 See my discussion of Günther Anders on radio and Theodor Adorno (in
    connection with the Princeton Radio Project) in "Adorno's Radio Phenom-
    enology: Technical Reproduction, Physiognomy, and Music," *Philosophy &
    Social Criticism* 40.10 (Oct. 2014): 957–96.
21 Steve Goodman, *Sonic Warfare: Sound, Affect, and the Ecology of Fear* (Cam-
    bridge, MA: MIT Press, 2010), xi.
22 Friedrich Kittler, *Gramophone, Film, Typewriter,* trans. Michael Wutz and
    Geoffrey Winthrop-Young (Stanford: Stanford University Press, 1999), 120.
    See further, in this context, Geoffrey Winthrop-Young, *Kittler and the Media*
    (London: Polity, 2011), 129*ff.* Winthrop-Young elaborates some of Kittler's
    reflections on Nietzsche in his book, but the more philological level is not
    his concern in that context.

apocryphal reports of the mash-up/shoot-em-up composition of their *Beggar's Banquet*[23] together with the Beatles' compositional conventionalities is chilling, and given Goodman's *Sonic Warfare* analytics, all too persuasive. Musicians compose by cutting and pasting, but that is still all too analogue. Today one can code — reading in letters for notes — random preparations. Just as Kilroy scrawled, John Cage himself *had already been there*.

And yet we cannot hear it. Kittler's suggestion is not acoustic but rather that Nietzsche is "really" "a film-theory before its time," writing as he does as a half-blind philosopher — "–14 diopters" (so writes the myopic Kittler) — condenses a wonderfully complex observation down to the same story everyone tells: "describing both *The Birth of Tragedy* in ancient Greece and its German rebirth in the mass spectacles of Wagner."[24] Going on to offer marvelous free-associative accounts of light and dark, media conflation — and despite his own sensitivity to music — Kittler's analysis occludes Nietzsche's project, which was about learning to "hear" the music of the text rather than a reverse nostalgia for a cinematic spectacle not yet available.

Where Kittler misses Nietzsche's insights, he is nonetheless sensitive to the achievements of the master of Bayreuth: "reducing his audience to an invisible mass sociology and the bodies of actors (such as the Rhine maidens) to visual hallucinations or afterimages against the background of darkness."[25] Word-painting Kubrick's *2001,* Kittler's media phenomenology of light and above all darkness (today's theorist will insist that this is somehow an "after phenomenology")[26] holds to the idea that "all movie-theaters, at the beginning of their screenings, reproduce Wagner's cosmic sunrise emerging from the primordial dark."[27]

---

23 Kittler, *Gramophone, Film, Typewriter,* 120. Kittler cites as his source here the Rolling Stones' *Beggars Banquet: Songbook* (New York, 1969).

24 Ibid., 120.

25 Ibid., 121.

26 See here the contributions to *Digital Light,* ed. Sean Cubitt, Daniel Palmer and Nathaniel Tkacz (London: Open Humanities Press, 2015).

27 Kittler, *Gramophone, Film, Typewriter,* 122.

Where Kittler may fall short when it comes to Nietzsche is not in any failing to tell us much about Nietzsche the man (if we needed to know more than the romantic reports of illness and afflictions already retold by Stefan Zweig and soberly reported by David Allison and everyone else) but in his argument that the author of *Twilight,* philosophizing with his "hammer," merely or simply channels in so doing his own visual pathology. This is a Cartesian conventionality taken to its furthest logical extension: the philosopher is a seeing machine. In support of his case, Kittler invokes the Berlin newspapers, as Nietzsche cites this report about himself (ego-surfing would be one of the oldest academic absorptions — as Marcus Aurelius already reproaches himself).[28]

"Nietzsche himself successively described his condition as quarter-blindness, half-blindness, three-quarter blindness (it was for others to suggest mental derangement, the next step in this mathematical sequence)."[29] Fixing on the optical, Kittler obscures Nietzsche's acoustic tuning. If Nietzsche posed his "questions with a hammer,"[30] he used the hammer as a tuning-fork — sounding out "that famous hollow sound which speaks of inflated bowels" — and coded as he wrote "for one who has ears behind his ears, for an old psychologist and pied piper like me."[31]

---

28 Kittler's analysis repeats the summary judgment of the 1882 *Berliner Tage-blatt*: "The well-known philosopher and writer [*sic*] Friedrich Nietzsche, whose failing eyesight made it necessary for him to renounce his professorship in Basel three years ago, currently lives in Genoa and — excepting the progression of his affliction to the point of complete blindness — feels better than ever. With the help of a typewriter he has resumed his writing activities, and we can hence expect a book along the lines of his last ones. It is widely known that his new work stands in marked contrast to his first, significant writings." See Kittler, *Gramophone, Film, Typewriter,* 203. Kittler's subsequent footnote points us to Nietzsche's letter of March 17, 1882 (292, n. 88).

29 Ibid., 200.

30 Nietzsche, *Twilight of the Idols,* trans. R.J. Hollingdale (New York: Penguin Books, 1981), 21.

31 Ibid.,

As a media theorist, Kittler focuses on optical media, beginning his study with a marvelously politically risqué reflection on the optical fiber networks we take for granted — why would we not? Today they are standard everywhere:

As is well known, nuclear blasts send an electromagnetic pulse (EMP) through the usual copper cables, which would infect all connected computers. The Pentagon is engaged in farsighted planning: only the substitution of optical fibers for metal cables can accommodate the enormous rates and volumes of bits required, spent, and celebrated by electronic warfare.[32]

This is powerful stuff, and to be sure Nietzsche's own "tuning-fork" [*Stimmgabel*] was designed to bring what wished to remain unsaid, unspoken, unheard-of, to come-to-word: "precisely that which would like to remain silent must become resonant," he explained.[33]

Unlike Kittler, I am not concerned to argue here that Nietzsche was a film-theorist *avant la lettre*. For me it is enough to do the archaeology of thinking through his work to note that his dynamite exploded ancient philology therapeutically (and just where things then were not right as rain, as the experts then insisted — from Wilamowitz to Jaeger and so on, to the scholars still sitting in the same chairs today).[34]

Kittler's attention to the old tropes of Wagnerian filmic darkness and homosexual academia is attuned to both more conventionally risqué music as well as Kittler's own memories.[35]

32 Kittler, *Gramophone, Film, Typewriter,* 1.
33 Nietzsche, *Twilight of the Idols,* 22.
34 See here, again, the contributions to — and note the title of — *Nietzsche's Value as a Scholar of Antiquity,* ed. Anthony Jensen and Helmut Heit (including my own essay "Nietzsche's Philology and the Science of Antiquity," 233–62).
35 Both Rüdiger Schmidt and Joachim Köhler seem to have transcribed Kittler's reflections into monographs of their own design (and on the personal and the intimate there is of course no limit, especially if one reaches back to Nietzsche's youth and ideally too even before he begins writing; Hermann Josef Schmid offers us several volumes on this theme).

But after so much submersion into the detritus of Nietzsche-the-cripple and Nietzsche-the-addict (both of which Kittler invokes) we have long lost the connection between music and word: Nietzsche's own and original code-breaking. Beautiful as Kittler's associations with Ariadne and Salomé are (though Kittler seems to be speaking more of the opera than of Lou Andreas herself) and worthy of further reflection as Kittler's account of the (otherwise unnamed) women who take dictation and transcribe manuscripts (their names are literally legion), Kittler still and yet effaces important aspects of Nietzsche's reflections as he highlights that "The poet of dithyrambs is once again only a secretary who puts the words of one woman, von Salomé, into the mouth of another woman, Ariadne."[36] Stealing just a bit more from Derrida — via Lacan, of course via Lacan — than from Heidegger, we have for Kittler an earworm. Better said: we have some kind of queer ear-violation going on, far more blatant — whatever else may be said — than Derrida's *Otobiographies*.

We are still reaping the consequences of ignoring not only Nietzsche's typewriters and the market sources for the same (on which theme Kittler is impeccable), as we might also ignore the existence of ferry schedules from one side of Lake Orta to the other. Just which Sacro Monte did Nietzsche climb, if we speak with Kittler here, together "with his Russian love"?[37] And although we are still not quite clear about the Nietzsche–Salomé connection (if Lou was not the impeccably objective source one might have wished, who, we should reflect, ever is?), one thing is certain: Kittler wondrously undertakes to reconstitute in his works the feminine bodies of Nietzsche's *Schreibkraft*: his writing-corps (important as this body of assistants was for Nietzsche, as Kittler shows, and evidenced by the fact that Nietzsche himself carefully lists their names in his letters — letters duly

36 Kittler, *Gramophone, Film, Typewriter,* 213.
37 Ibid., 209. See, for further context and further references on Lou, Pascale Hummel's edited collection *Lou Andreas Salomé, muse et apôtre* (Paris: Philologicum, 2011).

commented upon by a series of dedicated scholars in the editions we now have of the volumes of the *Friedrich Nietzsche Briefwechsel–Kritische Gesamtausgabe,* edited by Norbert Miller and Renate Muller-Buck).

For his own part, we began by noting that Nietzsche did not quite or really follow a wild odyssey, pulled by this allure or by that wild sea as Luce Irigaray can seem to imply, nor indeed was he drawn by the appeals of any maenad frenzy, but only a very domesticated course directed him. Nietzsche followed extant circuits of trains and postal coaches. Thus, cripple as we may choose to call him (Kittler does), Nietzsche had more help than only that afforded by his occasional writerly assistants, both paid and unpaid (and the unpaid always do more work). Nietzsche sought out a portable typewriter, Kittler tells us, partly because he expected that it might travel with him along with his traveling trunks (here I might add that it was only Descartes who sought to take a woman — a virtual one, and for the ordinary reasons of convenient relief — in his shipboard luggage; although that ended badly for both the doll and his reputation; and Kierkegaard suggested the same option to his Regina, rather sadistically counting on its negative effect for his own purposes; *that,* on the other hand, ended just as K. had wished it). In Nietzsche's case, the circuit ran from Basel to Tribschen and back again, and from Beyreuth to Venice and so on, as he also traveled from Sils to Venice — and indeed it is probably worth it for anyone reading this to try to get to Venice as soon as possible. Just because. Here it will not be my point to rehearse the different trajectories of Nietzsche's travels, and although I am surprised that this has not as yet systematically been done, my point is much rather that it *can* be done. Hence we may retrace the networks alone, as they offered possible circuits, of which possibilities Nietzsche followed only certain ones.

In other words, roads and trains take you there: taking Nietzsche to Rome, but first to Messina, via rail and via boat, rather than straight to Lou's arms (there's a whole other story here), but also and eventually to Nice, with excursions to Eze, and again and again to Italy where, just as the train travels, he found himself in Turin — at the end of what would be his conscious self-recognizance — and he could be rescued, retrieved by those who brought him back again (via Switzerland and a stop in a clinic, then the longish trip home by train via Naumburg to Weimar, where, after several awful years, he finally died).

The Nietzsche who wrote while walking, who told us to trust nothing that did not make us want to move, want to dance, himself walked only for constitutionals — immensely long as they were by New York standards; Nietzsche took his walks sometimes in the morning but mostly in the afternoon, after his midday meal and between headaches. It was not Nietzsche but Hölderlin who crossed half a country and then some at the news of the death of Suzette, his love, illicit and borrowed as she was (married, indeed, to Hölderlin's employer). Hölderlin was not a stand-up fellow when it came to love and morals — he left the woman pregnant, and abandoned her and their child — but he was able to walk. Nietzsche arguably had his own set of character problems, but he was not by any stretch a walker on the level of Hölderlin; and the reason (at least in part) was that unlike Hölderlin — who was a creative genius who was himself his own instrument — Nietzsche (*contra* Kittler) did not see himself as a writer. "I am no writer," he wrote. We will dispute him, but what he meant has everything to do with his nets. Nietzsche drew what he wrote out of himself alone, but he was as he thought of himself: scientifically minded — a scholar — he needed his books.

Books were the recording technology of his day, and they were for him (as for all of us) memory chambers, memory palaces. When Nietzsche travelled, he took his books (some he owned; we know some of these; some he borrowed; we do not, because we cannot, know all of these — and this means that no bibliographic listing of Nietzsche's library can ever be complete and any such list is and must be misleading for just this reason), he folded his tents — his nets, that is to say his books (owned and/or loaned), his notebooks, packets of active correspondence, old letters too. Some of these books he would ship out ahead; some he packed into trunks that other people were employed to carry for him.

Nietzsche was a nineteenth-century traveler, and travelers at the time had both porters even when they had limited funds. Let us forget neither the ports (travel stops/travel itineraries) nor the porters — the whole network — and neither let us forget that Nietzsche had sufficient occasion to observe the comings and goings of porters, and that he noted in passing — *in passage, in transit* — behind the scenes, every porter, wants to have an admirer.[38]

---

38 In German: "und wie jeder Lastträger seinen Bewunderer haben will" (Frie-drich Nietzsche, "Ueber Wahrheit und Lüge im aussermoralischen Sinne," *Kritische Studienausgabe* 1, 875.

02

The Internet as a Development from Descartes' *Res Cogitans:*[1] How to Render It *Dionysian*

Horst Hutter

NWW.III, October 11, 2011

The vision of the human condition that emerges from both ancient Greek tragedy and pre-Christian philosophy involves the
fundamental duality of Apollo and Dionysus, among other divinities, naturally. Accordingly, life is defined and ordered by
the influence of both of these divinities. As such it involves definite form, growth and change through time, as well as finitude
and the dissolution of every form into chaos and death. Apollo
and Dionysus both always win and ultimately always also lose.
Nothing lasts, except the constant regeneration of new forms
of growth and movements toward the future that transit brief
presents, before becoming memories of the past. From this perspective we are indeed all goats that sing and dance for a while
before vanishing into the nihilating nothing.[2] Or, in another
image, we are all donkeys that celebrate for a while, welcoming new donkeys to the celebration before singing our songs of

---

1   The link between Descartes' *res cogitans* and the Internet has been suggested
    to me by my son, the filmmaker Harald Hutter (he is philosophically edu-
    cated and does most of his work on the Internet).

2   The root of the word "tragedy" is both the Greek word *tragos* (goat) and *ōida*
    (song). The doings and sufferings of characters in plays, especially power-
    hungry rulers, are thus described as the manifestations of singing goats.

goodbye.[3] Yet the fact that every singing donkey or goat stands under the influence of two divinities has also given birth to much hope and longing for eternity and the promise of escaping from the depredations of time. Some of these structures of hope have been based on vehement attempts to defeat Dionysus altogether and enthrone a permanent Apollo.

A common understanding that has emerged from some ancient mythologies consists in the designation of a human totality as a temporary union of an "immortal" mind/soul that inhabits a mortal "body." The considerable variety of religious myths that existed in antiquity have attempted to deal with the tragic insight into the temporary union of soul and body, either by rejecting temporality altogether, or by accepting it as a form of testing and examination of souls. We thus find Gnostic and Manichean ways of dealing with the suffering that emerges from temporality by rejecting bodies, and especially the erotic procedures for creating new bodies altogether, or, at best, accepting these as trials of suffering that prepare us for eternity. Both views involve a repression of Eros down to the most elementary level.

In general, the monotheistic myths that emerged in late antiquity have been most successful in structuring the consciousness of the masses of humans up to our present. These myths have been successful in interpreting the living and always temporary unions of Apollonian forms and Dionysian dissolutions of these forms as temporary trials and preparations for eternal life in union with the one true divinity. This interpretation of living bodies has led to a valorization of supposedly immortal souls and contempt for mortal bodies. The adoption of a proper mix between these two attitudes would then lead to a corresponding mix of punishment and rewards in and for eternal life. Thereby the great numbers of sufferers were granted also the vision of being able to see their oppressors tortured, punished, and them-

3 Friedrich Nietzsche, *Also Sprach Zarathustra* IV, 1–3, "Das Eselsfest," *Kritische Studienausgabe,* ed. Giorgio Colli and Mazzino Montinari (Berlin: De Gruyter, 1980), 4, 390–94.

selves rewarded for obedience to the various moral and legal codes.[4] Finite life thus had acquired enormous meaning. These myths also enabled the creation of much-needed help communities that were based on the modes of conduct shaped by these very myths. Yet the fact that these visions were phrased in terms of always ambiguous myths also led to constant questioning and divergent interpretations. These in turn called for constant verifications and explanations in terms of rational arguments.

Religious myths powerfully shape human conduct, but always leave room for multiple interpretations. Meanings are never self-evident, but require explanations in terms of literal, allegorical, tropological, and anagogical levels of meaning. The understanding of any *mythos* thus always depends on the labors of humans skilled in the refinements of the *logos*. Religious myths thereby provide powerful and indispensable supports for moral codes and the shaping of habits of conduct, which, in turn, create and sustain politically organized faith communities.[5]

In the following I shall evoke briefly some developments in the succession of *logoi* of the Christian mythologies and show how a relatively late development of these *logoi* was defined as the most influential division between *res cogitans* and *res extensa* within the Cartesian mind/body duality. Before doing so, we need to recall a most important difference between the ancient mythology that informed tragedy and the Christian mythology which Descartes may have aimed to save from internal, nihilistic disintegration.[6]

4   Cf. the quotes in the *Genealogy of Morals* from fathers of the church on the delightful spectacles that await the saved souls in heaven: Nietzsche, *Kritische Studienausgabe*, 5, 283–85.

5   Every human political order is based on mythologies that require rational explanations, which aim to be correct but never succeed in being completely correct. For Nietzsche's profound understanding of mythology and his attempt to design the myths for a new religiosity, see Ernst Bertram, *Nietzsche: Attempt at a Mythology,* trans. Robert Norton (Chicago: University of Illinois Press, 2009).

6   Cartesian mind–body dualism has been enormously influential in shaping the whole evolution of technological society since its first formulation. For

Both the ancient tragic mythology and the Christian mythology begin from an acceptance of human mortality. Both of them postulate each individual human being to be a temporary conjunction of a soul or mind and a body. Both of them take cognizance of human suffering. However, in ancient tragedy and in philosophical understandings derived from it, the forces of the dual divinities Apollo and Dionysus govern each individual. But these divinities govern both each soul and each body, and neither of them promises or is able to deliver immortal life. Neither of them abolishes human finitude and suffering. Hence the division between soul/mind, on the one hand, and body, on the other, is not congruent with the duality between Apollo and Dionysus. Both divinities encourage obedience to moral codes and point toward forms of action that enable humans to reduce but never to abolish suffering. Suffice it to mention here the famous command from Apollo at Delphi, *mēden agan,* that is to say, always to respect one's limits. Similarly, we may think of the psychic health benefits deriving from orgiastic dancing devoted to Dionysus and his rites. At this point we can become aware of the profound differences between the ancient polytheistic myths and the various monotheistic myths, both Christian and Islamic, and to a certain extent, also Judaic.[7]

We may begin this discussion of the differences between pre-Christian and Christian forms of religiosity by pointing to the profound difference between the concepts of sin and of human error. In tragic mythology, humans can commit grievous errors, but such errors are not inborn, even if the tendency to commit certain errors may be passed along several generations. But there is no original sin in all humans, which is inherited through the act of conception. The tragic vision certainly knows and discusses the transmission of desires for revenge, even down through some six generations. But these are seen as politi-

that development see Friedrich Georg Juenger, *Die Perfektion der Technik* (Frankfurt: Vittorio Klostermann, 1939).

7   The temple of Apollo at Delphi, with its famous inscriptions, and the annual orgiastic festivals devoted to Dionysus, show a form of soul craft oriented to this world and not some beyond.

cally and socially conditioned tendencies to do wrong. And as such they may be corrected. Humans are always limited in their understandings of the realities of their situations. They may be governed by strong passions, but such traits are the results of faulty educations. The Greek word for error, *hamartia,* comes from the domain of archery and simply means that anyone can miss the target. It is, of course, also the word used in the Christian myths to designate "sin." The pagan meaning, by contrast, is very close to the Zen notion of missing the mark in archery. It has nothing to do with an inborn bad sinfulness. It can be corrected through training efforts. Original sin, by contrast, can only be remedied through special divine intervention.[8]

However, the profoundest difference between tragedy and Christianity concerns the different visions of the "body," the "flesh." Christianity postulates that humans have an immortal soul that is entombed in a corrupt and corrupting body. The purpose of life is to save the soul, to avoid eternal damnation, and to achieve salvation, so as to dwell with the divine after death. And this is best when done as quickly as possible. Only the immortal soul has value, the body is despicable. And the most contemptible aspect of the body, the greatest source of sin, is sexual desire. This must be controlled and suppressed as efficiently as possible. Hence Nietzsche's statement seems justified, that Christianity gave Eros poison to drink. He did not die from it, but became a vice.[9] It seems significant that New Testament Greek does not have any form of the word *erōs,* in any one of its grammatical variations. It is, as if the word had disappeared from the Greek language when the New Testament was written, which is not the case. The positive aspect of Christian contempt for the body and the emphasis on working and striving for the salvation of the soul lies in the fact that it seems to give infinite meaning to any finite human life. Life is no longer finite, and

8   For a post-Christian attempt to sketch a new vision of the human condition close to Buddhism, see Eugen Herrigel, *Zen in the Art of Archery,* trans. R.F.C. Hull (New York: Vintage Books, 1953).

9   Nietzsche, *Kritische Studienausgabe,* 5, 102; *Beyond Good and Evil,* trans. Judith Norman (Cambridge: Cambridge University Press, 2002), §168.

death has lost its sting, as the saying goes. But even this positive aspect has not sufficed to provide the saving means for preventing the nihilistic disintegration of Christian cultures over the last century or so.

The phrasing of the original Christian messages in the Gospels in the form of *mythoi* required constant efforts of rational explanation across the centuries. The possible varieties of meanings have been enormous and are best grasped in terms of some Hegelian dialectical analysis. The positivity of the message had to be constantly defended against doctrines that might undermine the faith. The two main articles of faith that required defense have been the existence and nature of the divinity, and, very importantly, the connection between the concept of an immortal soul or mind, and its relation to the mortal body, which seemed to furnish so many obstacles to efforts to lead the life of faith. Seemingly one of the most significant of such efforts of saving the Christian faith have been the writings of Descartes, which aimed to prove the existence of God as well as the existence of the immortal soul. Beginning from a position of universal doubt, the *dubito ergo sum,* his discourses on first philosophy have been enormously influential. They have shaped the whole history of all the sciences, as well as the history of philosophy and theology since their publication. The distinction he made between *res cogitans* and *res extensa* has established a very profound mind/body dualism that has furnished one of the leading foundations of Christian culture since. Indeed, I am arguing that the evolution of the digital world and the Internet is a technological development of the concept of the *res cogitans*.[10] The Internet is the result of Descartes' concept of a collective immortal soul, with all of its problems, chief among which is the absence from the Internet of anything bacchantic and Diony-

10 Descartes' *Meditations on First Philosophy* is one of the most influential attempts to construct a *logos* in defense of the Christian *mythos*. To be sure, it did not succeed — but still was able to shape the whole history of Western philosophy since. See René Descartes, *The Philosophy of René Descartes,* trans. John Cottingham (Cambridge: Cambridge University Press, 1996), 2, 1–62.

sian. As such, it is a major threat to the further evolution of the human species, and the saving of the earth, if nothing Dionysian can be recuperated. So far there is no digital Dionysus, and there cannot be, given the forceful separation of soul/mind from body that the Internet has established. As such it is, however, a most powerful tool for the Apollonian ordering of the totality of the social and political realities of the human species.

The Internet is the profoundest way so far of realizing the Christian project of separating mind and soul from body. As such it is the most efficient way of crystalizing the Cartesian project of separating the *res cogitans* from all physical reality, the earth and all of its forms of life. It creates a whole world where the body is a nuisance. This world is populated by virtual "persons" that have a life of their own in a reality activated solely by mind. The coming of the smartphone has extended the reach of this mental world, as it is no longer necessary to sit in front of a computer so as to be a citizen of this realm. It is possible to live in the "mind" all the time, and the next stage might well be the control of dreaming by this domain. Indeed, such might already be the case, as the dimensions of current psychic disorders have not been fully explored.[11]

However, the Internet is suffused with melancholia, as it seems to be populated by anxious Apollos that yearn for their Dionysian companions. Apollos also need their bodies, even if they are mortal and attached to the fated Dionysian chaos of death and disintegration. A telling indication of the longings in this entirely mental world for the body and the "flesh" is the fact that, according to some sources, as much as 70% of this world of the mind is occupied by pornography. So far this seems to be a major presence of Dionysus. However, here as well as elsewhere, the medium is by no means the message. Whatever meager forms of the Dionysian the anxious Apollos are allowed to enjoy is wholly controlled by the imperatives of the capitalist market, governed by hungry wolves who feed on immortal souls. It may

11 A remarkable case of such psychic derangement is the case of an academic who wished to drop his body and live in the World Wide Web.

well be that, if no new access to Dionysus is found, the bodies of these anxious Apollos will simply wither away into this world-wide web of souls, together with a despoiled earth.

We can no longer engage in contempt for the earth, the "body of the human species." We need to find access again to a Dionysian dimension — a post-Christian one, to be sure — and unify it with the *res cogitans* that has become almost global. We have to learn how to dance again, so as to permit the Apollos in the Internet to manage their anxieties and rages in a creative fashion. In the following I shall explore some possibilities to render the digital world Dionysian for the control of the largely negative emotions of anxiety and rage. For this we need to become self-shaping human beings who establish a regime of the soul that is better at managing the inner conflictual multiplicities. Perhaps indeed we need to move closer to the promised condition of the over-human and again proceed upwards in our metaxy, our in-between animality and over-humanity, reawaken the animal in ourselves and learn to respect the animal kingdom.

The digital world, as it exists at present, without a sufficiently significant Dionysian dimension, powerfully reinforces established political orders. These established orders, especially those based on monotheistic mythologies, by privileging the so-called "soul" and disdaining the so-called "body," impose a consensual hallucination, a "veil of Apollo" on the herd minds that populate them. This veil resists being understood by anyone as a fiction. Modern societies thus tend to be spectacles of unleashed collective self-evasions in which almost all are untrue to themselves. Almost everyone is the "other" and few are themselves, except in moments of spontaneous awakening to the terrors of their situation.

In such a situation, dance becomes a prime form of contemplation, which, by focusing the ego on the body, permits access to the ground of all human doing and being. This ground is not subject to human willing, to the "little reason" of the ego, and it is not definable in any arbitrarily relativist rhetoric. This ground becomes "visible" and is experienced, even if only temporarily, once the veil of Apollo has been lifted from the Dionysian deep eternity of life, with its inevitable possibility of death in any now. In dance we awaken the insights of the animal in us and acquire a sound mindedness that permits us to dispense with the forced self-repression of decadent and almost always anxious puritans. To be sure, dance in this way provides benefits similar to those to be gained from body-centered ascetic practices of Eastern forms of religiosities. These awaken in us a process knowledge that gives us insights into our own deep, deep eternity of time, into the great reason that always anyhow guides both the great reason of our body and the little reason of our intellect.

But one needs to recall that the ancient tragic vision of human life foresaw the judicious management of conflicted emotionalities by ascetic practices centered on the body and by the tragic theater. Thereby Apollonian forces of order came to be integrated with Dionysian forces of chaos and disintegration. Periodic rituals of communal dancing, imitating movements of either war or peace, or both, would then serve to manage and control the tyrannical surges of the human soul. Erotic and aggressive movements, initially always involuntary, and coming from deep within, could be brought under conscious control by introducing movements of dancing that could be learned and consciously practiced. Thereby the many involuntary aspects of human existence could be rendered partially voluntary. Living could become conscious, even without being oriented to immortal life. The ancient tragic worldview, as well as ancient philosophical practices, could thus render finitude acceptable and leave all hopes for immortality on the level of mere hopes, as something that all of us would know about soon enough. But these hopes would be seen simply as children of Pandora and certainly did not require any proofs through faith, which is so aptly described by the founder of Christianity as "the substance of things hoped for and the evidence of things unseen."[12] The gains for political orders would be as real in the tragic vision as those coming from religiosities based on a psychological ordering of the soul by a faith promising eternal life.

12   Heb. 11:1.

Here it becomes necessary to discuss a fundamental factor of the human condition. Human individuals are in reality dividual, that is to say, each one of us has both an inborn primary nature and an acquired second nature. The pressures coming from the social environments into which we are born and in which we grow up condition this second nature into us. These two factors are necessarily always in conflict with one another, a conflict required by the need for domestic peace of every political order. Inborn nature is governed by conflicts between powerful passional forces. These conflicts, say between tyrannical erotic drives and strong thymotic compulsions, need to be regulated and governed, so that humans living together do not descend into a war of every one against everyone else. The function of inbred moral codes is to enable each dividual to repress and/or modify inborn impulses so as to achieve self-control and thereby peace with one's neighbors. The established political orders, deriving from monotheistic myths, for example, aim to contain the tyrant Eros within the institution of "holy matrimony." As is amply known, however, this institution is in obvious disintegration. Moreover, this aspect of the nihilistic disintegrating of monotheistic cults now temporarily coincides with the *res cogitans,* the digital ordering of the collective, human mind/soul. This conjunction now calls for a new political psychology, one that finds new ways for ordering the conflictual multiplicity of the human soul. The difficulty then is how to condition in a new second nature, which is necessarily in conflict with the old conditioning. A new form of the Dionysian has to be bred into and merged with the old monotheistic Apollonianism. An enormous task of re-education hence awaits us, a task which may take a lot of time. The Internet may be a powerful tool helping us in this task. It is to be hoped that the suffering that always accompanies such endeavors will not be too severe, and will not involve a massive destruction of the earth, the "body of the human species." A chief task here then is how to use the Internet so as to establish a new Dionysus. But before reflecting on the Dionysian possibilities of the *res cogitans,* it seems necessary to explore a bit further the dimensions of dance.

A human life that fully embodies the tragic vision requires an interaction between both divinities. The world of work, the management of everyday life, would need the sovereignty of Apollo. Dionysus here has to submit to Apollo. This needs the successful containment of the conflictual and chaotic forces of the human soul, both erotic and thymotic. There are many humans who know what is good for them, but who are unable to act on this insight. The attainment of insight and the ability to act on it require a steady practice.

A major obstacle to a reconditioning of psychic forces into a post-Christian second nature, based on a Dionysian vision, is lack of honesty. Humans tend to hide their compulsions, especially erotic ones, into conventionalities based on the impersonal "one": one does not do this, one does that. It may well be that only deep suffering could dispel the veil of Apollo and force an awakening to the needed tasks. Only once a minimal amount of honesty with oneself has been achieved can the spiritual exercises of reconditioning begin. These exercises have to be body-centered and aim to manage the surface forces of the soul. Music with its rhythms and melodies has to control and guide the movements of the human totality. The inherent "musicality" and rhythmicity of the unconscious forces, as described long ago by Pythagoras, are thereby awakened and guided in an orderly manner. This helps the intellect, the little reason, to assume its proper role as a secondary and serving aspect of the totality. An already available form of such sacred movements and chanting is the widespread culture of gospel music services. This is especially significant as this sacred practice has arisen within existing forms of religiosities.

It seems obvious from the above that the most successful form of Dionysian dance is the dance practiced in groups. Many so-called primitive cultures also know periodic rituals in which the regular social order is suspended in favor of wild forms of dance and musicality. Such periodic festival interruptions in honor of Dionysus, with dancing Maenads, were a standard feature of ancient tragic cultures.

Modern raves and musical festivals, aptly referred to as temporary autonomous zones, would seem to be attempts to invite Dionysus back into modern life.[13] Such events permit suspensions of forces of consciousness into periods of autonomy for the wild aspects of the human soul. Rock and pop concerts seem to be similar autonomous zones. The fact that these are mass events would seem to indicate widespread awareness of the deficiencies of traditional forms of sacred rituals. They give reasons to hope that the Dionysian may yet return to help the formation of rituals that may help in the needed salvational labors. A further aspect of hope is the fact that these temporary autonomous zones have arisen at the same time as the *res cogitans* with its anxious Apollos.

The chief aspect of the Internet that seems to furnish its considerable melancholia is the fact that the anxious Apollos inhabiting it are solitary and isolated. Any reconditioning via dance would hence have to begin with solitary forms. These could constitute the beginning of a return of Dionysus. It may pointed out here that the *res cogitans* contains many forms of groupings, with such aspects as Facebook, Twitter, and Tumblr. This cannot be denied. Perhaps it might be possible for Facebook friendship groupings to meet for regular Dionysian encounters. Thereby the isolation of anxious Apollos may be overcome and the *res cogitans* enter into the service of both Apollo and Dionysus. All is not lost, and the Internet may yet establish a better connection between all species, become the noösphere and thus save the earth and the biosphere.[14]

13 Hakim Bey, *The Temporary Autonomous Zone: Ontological Anarchism, Poetic Terrorism* (Brooklyn: Autonomedia, 1991).
14 For the concept of the noösphere, see the Internet sources on Pierre Teilhard de Chardin and Vladimir Vernadsky.

03

Networked Nightmares:
On Our Dionysian Post-Military Condition

Manabrata Guha

NWW.II, May 6, 2010

> *In many ways, "chasmic turbulence" is the imprimatur of the*
> *21st century. Is it surprising, therefore, that we talk of the Mul-*
> *titude rather than the Singular?, of the Distributed in place of*
> *the Pyramidal? How does this play out in the strategic-military*
> *context? Can we even talk about strategy and strategic organi-*
> *zations like the military under these conditions? — Shouldn't*
> *we be talking about a post-military condition?*
> — Unnamed Commenter at a Senior Military Commanders'
> Conference in New Delhi, India, 2014.

1. Hardware

While the world made fun of Donald Rumsfeld for his observations regarding the "unknown unknowns" gaffe, hidden in
the rhetoric *a quiet revolution in military affairs* was underway.[1]
More precisely, it was a subtle but significant revolution in military *concepts*. Mass and firepower — the traditional metrics of
military capability — were not (as is most often argued) under-

---

1   Secretary Rumsfeld and General Myers, "DoD News-briefing," United States
    Department of Defense (Feb. 12, 2002), http://www.defense.gov.

mined; rather, they were being augmented (and recontextual-ized) with a terminological turn that reflects, if nothing else, the significance of the impact of the Age of Information on military affairs. At the very least, the conduct of war was being recon-sidered in a network-centric sense.[2] But this focus of attention on networks (and netwars) came at a cost. It entailed recogniz-ing the imperative of the "Distributed" at the cost of the "Py-ramidal," where the design of the latter underwrites the formal strategic-military structure of a nation-state. At first, this drew a lot of protest and resistance in strategic-military circles, par-ticularly in the United States. But later, through various stages that saw, among other things, the constitution, operation, and disbanding of one of the most curious "offices" created by the us Department of Defense — the Office of Force Transforma-tion[3] — the rabid furor over the network-centric concept has, for the most part, ebbed. Some consider it to have failed in its promise to "transform" war and combat and, to that extent, ef-forts to theorize "network-centric warfare" have slipped under the radar of both military thinkers and of their civilian counter-parts.[4] Others claim to notice — a view naturally championed by the Pentagon — how some of the operative principles (albeit in heavily modified forms) have infiltrated the subsequent de-velopment of doctrine and other operational practices. Most importantly, however, it is in the speculative and arcane space

2   Vice-Admiral Arthur K. Cebrowski, U.S. Navy, and John J. Garstka, "Net-work-Centric Warfare: Its Origin and Future," *Naval Institute Proceedings* 124-1-1-139 (Jan. 1998).

3   *Office of Force Transformation,* U.S. Department of Defense, "Five Goals," http://OFT.OSD.mil/top_five_goals.cfm. For an interesting perspective of the OFT in light of the rumors about its closure, see Christopher P. Cavas, "Pentagon May Close Transformation Office [that] Helped Establish Inno-vative Outlook to DoD Challenges," *Defence News* (Aug. 28, 2006), http://OFT.OSD.mil/. See also Geoff Kein, "Office of Force Transformation Taking New Shape Inside DoD," *Defense Daily* (Sep. 5, 2006), http://OFT.OSD.mil/library/library_files/article_519_DEFENSE%20DAILY%20September%205%202006.doc.

4   Sean Lawson, "Is Network-Centric Warfare (Finally) Dead? Only *Partly*" (Aug. 14, 2010), http://www.SeanLawson.net/?p=772.

where concept–technology pairings are experimented with that the network-centric concept — applied to the problematic of war and combat — has had, and continues to have, its greatest impact.

Essentially, the network-centric concept is a simple one and its lineage can be outlined with reference to the work done by Paul Baran in the 1960s.[5] Baran was tasked to investigate the optimal design of a strategic-military command, control, and communication (C3) system that would survive a potential Soviet nuclear attack over the polar route against the North American continent.[6] But stripped of its military vestiges, the key point at stake in the concept is the perception of the high levels of efficiency — which is often, but erroneously, presented as efficacy — that accrues when objects/things are networked, i.e., connected, in a way that facilitates the exchange of information and data between them.

When applied to the strategic-military domain, this marked a break from the dominant way of envisioning the nature and function of objects in a space of conflict. Traditionally, in the strategic-military context, singular objects have drawn the greatest attention. In other words, the focus of interest was (and, to a large extent, remains) the platform. "Platform" here means the weaponized objects that co-constitute the battlespace, like tanks, guns, planes, ships, weapon-suites, individual soldiers,

---

5   This lineage can be drawn further to the work of Dr. J.C.R. Licklider who headed, among other things in a very distinguished career, the Information Processing Techniques Office. Here, Licklider was instrumental in conceiving, funding, and managing the research that led to modern personal computers and the Internet which, arguably, may be considered to be one of the earliest and most influential accounts of the network-centric concept. See Katie Haffner and Matthew Lyon, *Where Wizards Stay up Late: The Origins of the Internet* (New York: Simon & Schuster, Touchstone Editions, 1998). See also Paul Baran, *On Distributed Communications,* Vol. 1: *Introduction to Distributed Communications Networks* (Santa Monica: RAND Corporation, 1964).

6   Paul Baran, "On Distributed Communications Networks," RAND Corporation paper P-2626 (Santa Monica: RAND, 1962), http://www.RAND.org/pubs/papers/P2626.html.

diverse kinds of weaponry, etc. This focus on platforms does not contradict the various combinatory groupings into which they can be organized. Thus, for example, in the context of the operational art of war, concepts like "combined arms warfare,"[7] "jointery,"[8] "integrated operations,"[9] etc., are instances where the focus on platforms has not diminished despite such platforms being organized in ways that optimize the lethal effects of their combined, joint, integrated capabilities. In a more abstract sense, platforms could also include the economic, scientific, and technological infrastructure particular to the strategic-military context. When considered as platforms, such infrastructure may also be said to contribute in critical and foundational ways to the comprehensive military and warfighting capabilities of nation-states. As such, platforms are what allow for comparative and competitive assessments to be made that purport to measure the warfighting potential and capabilities of military establishments globally.[10] Naturally, from within such a platform-centric perspective, the battlespace is conceptualized accordingly. Among other things, it is considered to be populated by objects that are assigned a value in terms of capability and firepower. And, in base terms, particularly when considered in terms of "the last man standing" or "the last bullet available," notions of victory and defeat were and continue to be dependent to a large extent on such platforms.[11]

7   See, for example, Jonathan M. House, *Toward Combined Arms Warfare: A Survey of 20th-Century Tactics, Doctrine and Organization* (Hawaii: University Press of the Pacific, 2002).

8   See, for example, Trevor Taylor, "Jointery & the Emerging Defence Review," *Future Defence Review,* Working Paper 4, RUSI (Nov. 2004).

9   See, for example, "Capstone Concept for Joint Operations: Joint Force 2020," http://DTIC.mil/cgi-bin/GetTRDoc?Location=U2&doc=GetTRDoc. pdf&AD=ADA568490.

10 The International Institute for Strategic Studies (IISS) publishes a credible and well-respected analysis called *The Military Balance.* http://www.IISS. org/en/publications/military-s-balance.

11 A landmark publication in this context is Stephen Biddle's *Military Power: Explaining Victory and Defeat in Modern Battle* (Princeton: Princeton University Press, 2006).

The network-centric point of view, on the other hand, while not dismissing the object or the platform, draws attention to the cumulative and coordinated effects that diverse sets of such platforms can generate when linked to each other in innovative ways. The baseline argument is that the cumulative and coordinated effects of a set of "networked" objects or platforms are greater than just the sum of the effects that each object or platform is independently capable of creating or generating. And, the necessary prerequisite for this is the network (of relations) that is shared by, or that may be constituted between, objects or platforms.[12] The corresponding image of the battlespace, therefore, is one where networked entities struggle with their adversarial counterparts to design and deliver a variety of effects in a bid to gain what in the past US military doctrine has openly referred to as Full-Spectrum Dominance.[13] As a consequence, in the emergent network-centric concept of war, the battlespace and networked battle entities are considered to be ensembles of Information and Communication networks *with lethal capabilities*. For our purposes, we cannot help but observe and appreciate the dependency that this understanding of network-centricity has on hardware (comprising clients, servers, routers, etc. and their associated protocols). As it stands today, therefore, the networked military machine can be said to be constituted by military hardware that is being augmented with increasingly sophisticated and "smart" networking technologies which, in turn, are tied together by a strict set of operational protocols.

The lure of the network-centric paradigm, however, is clear enough. The "holy grail" that this theory of warfare posits is a "transparent battlespace." "Transparency" in this context means a state or condition — regardless of its existent condition — which is amenable to cognition, analysis, and engineered transforma-

12 See, for example, David S. Alberts, John J. Gartska, and Frederick P. Stein's *Network-Centric Warfare: Developing and Leveraging Information Superiority* (Washington: US DoD, CCRP, 2003).

13 For an optimistic overview of the concept, see *Dominant Battlespace Knowledge,* ed. Stuart Johnson and Martin Libicki (Washington: National Defense University Press, 1996).

tion with a singular aim: to derive the maximally possible and sustainable advantage in and on the battlespace. As such, the notion of a "transparent battlespace" is a direct response to the famous Clausewitzian problem concerning the "fog and friction of war." Put another way, it could be said that what the theory of network-centric warfare argues for is a radical solution to the problem of (battlespace) uncertainty by transforming the "unknown unknowns" into "known knowns." And how is this transparency (and transformation) to be achieved? The growing ubiquitousness of a plethora of sensors and other data collection systems, combined with sophisticated computing systems, driven by complex algorithms that analyse huge volumes of data and underwritten by a growingly pervasive surveillance system appear to be the way by which the ideal of battle-space transparency is to be achieved. As such, in Deleuzo-Guattarian terms, it is a project of extreme striation involving the harnessing of Dionysian energies of the yet-to-be-processed with the Apollonian reigns of the processor.[14]

The theory of network-centric warfare, as it is currently being operationalized, is still in the gradual process of updating previously analogue platforms and systems into digital ones. Notice, however, that this project of updating and upgrading does not diminish the primacy of the platform. It is the platform which is being upgraded and digitized. And, while platforms will, over time, be constituents of a network, the fact should not be missed that they are, in the final analysis, legacy systems, that is to say, systems that were designed as stand-alone units and with a functional envelope that — at least in design — did not include operating as an integral part of a weaponized network. That said, the emergent profiles of tactical and, in some cases, strategic surveillance (and strike) systems do reveal their constituents being designed to operate as a part of a network by default — be that in terms of data collection or data analysis or

14 Gilles Deleuze and Félix Guattari, "1440: The Smooth & the Striated," in *A Thousand Plateaus: Capitalism and Schizophrenia,* trans. Brian Massumi (Minneapolis: University of Minnesota Press, 1987), 474–500.

other more kinetically-oriented forms. In short, to appropriate Floridi's phrase, a limited form of reontologization is under-way — from the Analogue to the Digital — in global strategic-military affairs.[15]

2. Wetwares

However attractive this vision may be to the theorists of net-work-centric warfare, there is — as has previously been hint-ed — a significant limitation at play. To appreciate the nature of this limitation, it is helpful to consider an even more extreme version of the network-centric paradigm which has been hint-ed at in some of the more speculative literature on the subject. Such a version suggests envisioning Nature-as-such — from the macro to the nano scale — as a complex web of relations.[16] This version, which at first glance resembles a set-up taken from ei-ther a "new age" text or a dystopian sci-fi novel, is not (at least conceptually) as outrageous as it may appear to be. One way to understand this version would be to think in terms of a word that crops up quite frequently in Chinese military-theoretic literature: "informationalization."[17] And, while it is not clear if Chinese military theorists are familiar with the works of Simon-don when they use the term "informationalization," Simondon's concept of "reticularity" is one that applies quite well in this context.[18]

---

15 Luciano Floridi, "A Look into the Future Impact of ICTs in our Life," *The Information Society: An International Journal* 23.1 (2007), Section II.

16 I would tend to agree with the conservatism shown by Floridi when he es-chews the "Matrix" model for what he refers to as "the evolutionary, hybrid sense represented by an environment such as New Port City, the fictional, post-cybernetic metropolis of *Ghost in the Shell*" (*The Ethics of Information* [Oxford: Oxford University Press, 2013], 10.)

17 A useful compendium of instances of the word "informalization" is available in Timothy L. Thomas, *Decoding the Virtual Dragon: Critical Evolutions in the Science and Philosophy of China's Information Operations and Military Strategy* (Fort Leavenworth: Foreign Military Studies Office, 2007).

18 See, for example, Gilbert Simondon on "Technical Mentality," trans. Arne DeBoever, in *Gilbert Simondon: Being and Technology*, ed. Arne DeBoever

The dictionary defines reticularity as being "a pattern or arrangement of interlacing lines resembling a net." But in the Simondonian context, this "arrangement of interlacing lines" applies not only to technological objects (Simondon refers to "technical objects"), but to all things and objects, including the human. This "arrangement of interlacing lines" further plays out as the network of relations *between* objects and things *and within* objects and things themselves. The network-centric concept, when considered in this sense, plays out in two ways: In the "intra" sense, the notion of network-centricity allows for the structural consideration of any object — in- or non-human — as a reticular system, that is to say, as a network-centric system. In other words, it could be said that this network-centric system is the sum-total of the network of relations that the various constituents of the system share with each other, in terms of functionality, capability, and proximity, among other things. Not only does the network represent the sum-total of the functions and capabilities of the constituents of a given object or thing, it is also that what lends consistency — an internal consistency — to the said thing or object. In the "inter" sense (and continuing with a strain of Simondon's work) the notion of reticularity extends between objects and things. Considered in this way, the understanding of "the network condition" (and "the networked condition") approaches something akin to the Deleuzo-Guattarian concept of "the plane of consistency."[19] This suggests that while our commonplace view of things and objects presumes their singularity (i.e., their individualness) and, more often than not, gives it primary importance, such a view — in the Simondonian sense — is misplaced. In other words, this perspective holds that every object (or thing) shares, in a distinctly origi-

et al. (Edinburgh: Edinburgh University Press, 2012), 1–19. Also see Muriel Combes, *Gilbert Simondon and the Philosophy of the Transindividual,* trans. Thomas LaMarre (Cambridge, MA: MIT Press, 2013), and the 2010 update to E.N. Mellamphy's 1980 translation of Simondon's treatise *On the Mode of Existence of Technical Objects.*

19 Deleuze and Guattari, *What is Philosophy?,* trans. Hugh Tomlinson and Graham Burchell (New York: Columbia University Press, 1994), 35.

nary sense, some degree of relationality with an indefinite (i.e., emergent) number of other objects and things and across multiple registers (milieus). When seen from this point of view, the call of modern Chinese military theorists to "informationalize" the battlespace and the forces that operate within such battlespaces takes on a distinctly different meaning than the lattice of pipes — wired or wireless — through which "information" flows. What I am attempting here is to draw attention to how this kind of a pervasive connectivity (or networking), which I am associating Chinese military theorists' term "informationalization," is cast more in informational terms than in computational (and hardware-centric) terms.[20] In effect, the kind of net-centricity that is being invoked here is natively "smart" and structurally transient. It is opportunistic (to explore the potential for connectivity) but it is not predatory. It is fluid and tactical. It is recurrently regenerative — thus resilient — and eminently adaptable. And, it is always in-*formation*. It could be said that the network is both in-*formation* and Information. It is that which transacts and that which is transacted or, as Marshall McLuhan said, "the medium is the message."[21] As such, this understanding of a network, networking, and information contradicts and is, indeed, in excess of an understanding that is underwritten by clients, servers, and protocols.

There is no denying the fact that this extreme understanding of net-centricity is highly abstract. But one can readily appreciate the attraction that it would have for strategists, futurists, and theorists of war and combat. The very prospect of being able to envision the battlespace and combat units in informational terms, which allows for the application of the net-centric point of view without the limits and strictures (collectively, and in the broadest of senses, protocols) of the hardware that gives the more commonplace notion of net-centricity its distinct materi-

20 My preference would be to use the word "connectivity" instead of "network"/"networking," as the former invokes a kind of comprehensive engagement as opposed to the latter.

21 Marshall McLuhan made this insightful observation in *Understanding Media: The Extensions of Man* (New York: McGraw Hill 1964).

ality, is liberating. The distinction is a subtle but important one. As Floridi puts it, the focus of interest in this instance is on *information* rather than on *computation*, though the latter is a key constitutive element of the former — at least in the Digital Age.[22] The literature on network-centric warfare and evidence from the battlespace suggests that this radical version of network-centric warfare, while not easily discernible, certainly underwrites some of the thinking that is taking place on such matters. Thus we find that while we may be at the nascent stages of such a process, strategists and theorists who are involved in long-range "blue sky" and speculative projects concerning military affairs are already considering the prospect of war, and of waging war, in informational (battle) spaces which, in turn, has led them to explore what is sometimes described as the cognitive dimension of war and combat.[23] Nevertheless, on close analysis, we find that at the conceptual register the bottleneck that bedevils such efforts is precisely what we have alluded to earlier, namely the problematic of thinking outside the imagination of networks conceived in computational rather than informational terms.

This problem is perhaps best encapsulated by means of two examples. The first is the redesigning of the global military communications network that underwrites the US strategic-military establishment. In the late 1980s, the legacy system, better known as the World-Wide Military Command-and-Control System (WWMCCS), was gradually transformed into the Global Information Grid (GIG).[24] But the inclusion of the word "information" in the GIG is misleading; like its predecessor, the WWMCCS, the GIG is a hardware and firmware solution. In other words, the GIG is a constellation of objects/things and the wired and wireless linkages between them — scattered across four domains

---

22 Floridi, "A Look into the Future Impact of ICTs in our Life."

23 An early text that invokes such a way of thinking about war and its conduct is Alvin and Heidi Toffler's *War and Anti-War in the 21st Century: Survival at the Dawn of the 21st Century* (New York: Little, Brown & Company, 1993).

24 See Thomas B. Allen's *War Games* (New York: McGraw Hill, 1987), 219. On the GIG, see the *Global Information Grid Project* residing within the US National Security Agency, http://www.NSA.gov/ia/industry/gig.cfm.

(land, air, sea, space) — which facilitates the movement and flow of information and communications. Underwriting this constellation of objects/things are what Galloway refers to as the "protocols" that allow for the negotiation and communication between them.[25] At first glance, the difference between these two systems may appear obvious. For example, in structural terms, whereas the WWMCCS was much closer in terms of structural design to the more traditional C2 systems of the past and thus was more hierarchically oriented, the GIG — both by deliberate design but also by the imperative of the technologies used — is a more flattened structure. Notice, however, the functional similarity of the WWMCCS and the GIG. Both systems have essentially the same task: to facilitate the flow of information and communication. Considered in this way, the net-centricity implicit in this model then remains hardware- and protocol-centric. The "content" (sometimes data, sometimes information) that is transacted through the network is, to all intents and purposes, irrelevant to it. When considered in this light, this model remains mired, to steal a phrase from William Lind, in the third generation.[26] It may be considered "third-generation" because it can be argued that the only thing that has effectively changed is the way battlespace information flows. And, even this change is marginal in the sense that the traversing of information still takes place subjected to the "protocols" of the strategic-military command and control system. When seen from this point of view, the effort to recast military force in network-centric terms is better described as an exercise in digitization rather than, to again use the word popularized by the Chinese military theorists, "informationalization."

25 Aleaxander Galloway undertakes an extensive and interesting look at the notion of protocols in his *Protocol: How Control Exists after Decentralization* (Cambridge, MA: MIT Press, 2004).
26 William S. Lind, *The Four Generations of Modern War* (Finland: Castalia House, 2014).

Our second example is the ongoing Soldier-as-a-System or SaaS project.[27] The Soldier-as-a-System project is underwritten by a singular concern: How to increase the operational and combat efficiency of the individual combat soldier? The efforts thus far have succeeded in triggering the technologization of the (human) soldier by progressively encasing him or her in layers of wearable computing, sensing, and data-transmission devices. The sensors, in such a scheme of things, have a dual function: while the sensor suite is designed to enhance battle-space awareness, it is also tasked with monitoring the health and vitality of its wearer. Further improvements are being made to this basic design that will allow for the augmentation of specific capabilities of the soldier, such as endurance, cognitive awareness, weapons-integration, and health-management systems, among others. But this represents only one aspect of the SaaS project. The other critical aspect involves it being a part of a network of other objects/things such as static or mobile combat and communication devices. The claim is that, when considered cumulatively, such enhancements and augmentations allow for an increase in the combat capability of the soldier, integrate the soldier with other battlespace units, and coordinate and calibrate the design and delivery of the desired effects. Keeping in mind the current state of technological development, by all accounts the results appear to be positive. If we push this development process into a speculative future, based on current developments, we would not be amiss to suggest that a weaponized cyborg is within the horizon of achievability. Yet the conceptual bottleneck remains, for there is no denying the computational bedrock on which the notion of the weaponized cyborg is dependent. The cyborg, despite being organized around the human soldier, is a sophisticated human-computational system, and is as a consequence both augmented and limited by the protocological imperative that underwrites computing and communication systems. In

27   See, for example, Maren Leed and Ariel Robinson's *Realizing the Vision: The Soldier/Squad System* (New York: CSIS/Rowman & Littlefield, 2014), http://www.CSIS.org/files/publication/140402_Leed_RealizingVision_Web.pdf.

this context it is also necessary to recognize, as Floridi points out, that there exists a difference between the processor and the processed.[28] This difference, though considerably narrower than what we experience in our practice of everyday computing life, remains in the case of a weaponized cyborg, although it is layered beneath "skins" of wearable computational devices.

How then is this computationally inspired understanding of networks and the corresponding vision of network-centric warfare limited or limiting? In the first instance, let us begin by recognizing that the materialist understanding of networks, i.e., the understanding of networks in specifically computational terms, restricts us to thinking about ways by which information is transacted. It draws our attention toward the lattice of pipes, wires, and other communication protocols that overlay what Floridi refers to as a "dead world" or an (apparently) inanimate world.[29] This overlay is the emergent battlespace and it is here that the efforts to institute and maintain transparent battlespaces are made. When considered in this way, the promise to deliver a transparent battlespace makes sense. Theoretically, it is possible to think in terms of pure transparency in the battlespace because in its ideal state and considered in computational terms it is a closed system. As Martin Libicki remarked in the context of battlespace sensors, "a fine-enough mesh [...] will catch anything."[30] However, as Clausewitz and numerous others have described, the battlespace is anything but a closed system.[31] It is a space in-*formation* and is consequently turbulent. To date, the

---

28 Floridi, "A Look into the Future Impact of ICTs in our Life," 6.

29 Ibid., 7.

30 Martin Libicki, *The Mesh and the Net: Speculations on Armed Conflict in a Time of Free Silicon* (Washington: National Defense University, 1994), 30–31, http://www.DTIC.Mil/cgi-bin/GetTRDoc?AD=ADA278484.

31 Carl von Clausewitz, *On War,* ed. and trans. Michael Howard and Peter Paret (Princeton: Princeton University Press, 1984), 580. Specifically, Clausewitz asserted that "[w]ar is the realm of uncertainty; three quarters of the factors on which action in war is based are wrapped in a fog of greater or lesser uncertainty." This allusion to "a fog of greater or lesser uncertainty" clearly suggests that Clausewitz was acutely aware of the "openness" of war and of the battlespace.

battlespace has been negotiated by means of applying amassed firepower or maneuver. Where digital military systems are being contemplated, the attention has shifted to agility in and on the battlespace.[32] But the intractable problem concerning the fog and friction of war that denies the fulfilment of the promise of a transparent battlespace remains.

Clausewitz, as is well known, has a Kantian solution to the problem of the fog of war. Beginning by asserting that the military genius is a special entity, Clausewitz suggests that it is only the military genius who, possessing the acute faculty of synthesizing (involving the use of pure reason, of practical reason, and resulting in acts of judgement) multiple flows of information, is best placed to choose a course of action. Let us pause here for a moment and pay close attention to what Clausewitz is telling us. He begins by saying that it is the genius who makes rules (which we could read as protocols), thus suggesting that the genius is not in any way bound to any protocological restrictions and is free to transgress any and all codes or modes of operation. This cognitive and operational flexibility runs directly against the assertion that Clausewitz also made regarding the importance of doctrine and training in the context of war, where doctrine and training play the same role that protocols play in the context of computers and other digital systems. To be sure, Clausewitz assures us that an army populated by geniuses would be a very poor one. But his point about the radical alterity of the military genius when compared to other soldiers cannot be missed. In the context of network-centric warfare, the Clausewitzian military genius is a dangerous and destructive character, for his defining propensity is to transgress protocol, thereby calling into being a chiasmic turbulence that the computationally centered concept of network(s) tries to keep at bay.[33]

---

32 See, for example, David Alberts's *The Agility Advantage: A Survival Guide for Complex Enterprises and Endeavors* (Washington: Command & Control Research Program, 2011).

33 For an extended discussion on the Clausewitzian notion of the "genius," see my monograph, *Reimagining War in the 21st Century: From Clausewitz to Network-Centric Warfare* (London: Routledge, 2011), 41, 72, 78–85, 88, 169.

3. Nightmares

To those theorists and strategists who continue to champion the computationally underwritten vision of net-centricity there are at least three nightmarish conditions with which to contend. Each of these conditions cascade on top of the other to reduce the structured and protocologically arranged net-centric battlespace into a mess and to introduce us to what I will refer to as the post-military condition. Of these, the first is the presence of, to appropriate the title of one of Walter Benjamin's most curiously titled pieces, "the destructive character."[34] The Clausewitzian genius is a close approximation of such a destructive character, but this image can be stretched a little further. The military genius undertakes not to leave a path of deliberate destruction in his or her wake. Yet, the genius must destroy, for it is the only way by which new, innovative, and asymmetric paths are forged. In the process, the genius tears off the veils of protocols and other rules that obscure the seething uncertainty that underwrites the battlespace. Eliminating the protocological imperatives that bind the battlespace and its constituents allows the genius to re-fashion hitherto striated space into smooth space, and it is here that the networked military, i.e., a computationally-centric networked military, loses traction. Bereft of protocological guidelines, the war machine experiences slippages as the volume of information overwhelms its processing capabilities. In its place, the genius revels in this maelstrom of information. The genius is able to seamlessly make and sever connections between disparate sources and kinds of information, thus forming and deforming connections and patterns, which elide the more rigid and protocologically organized network(s). Thus, actions of the genius may appear contradictory, and the Apollonian mask that covers the visage of the genius is stripped away to reveal a truly Dionysian core, which is corrosive to the cohesiveness of the

---

34 Walter Benjamin, "The Destructive Character," in *Reflections: Essays, Aphorisms, Autobiographical Writings,* trans. Edmund Jephcott (New York: Schocken Books, 1986), 301–3.

network. As a consequence, the military genius is able to wreck the strategic (pre-)disposition of the network. Operationally speaking, the military genius reflects a tactical fluidity that outwits the computational agility that such weaponized networks are being designed to exhibit. In essence, the threat that the military genius poses to the protocologically organized networks is that of disintegration. It is a threat that is directed at the heart of the network-centric warfare project, which aims, in the final analysis, to contend with the uncertainty principle.

In the context of war and combat, the weaponized cyborg is the most refined version of the human–machine conjoining project thus far. While appearing fantastic, such an entity is, as I have shown, a mundane aggregation of layers of computational capabilities around a human core. As such, the motive force that drives the cyborg is its computational capabilities, which are both local and distributed. The "unique selling proposition" that the cyborg offers in the battlespace is the availability and application of "computing power" to the prosecution of combat, with the caveat that the battle takes place in what Floridi refers to as "dead places." This qualification is necessary and an important one. While cyborgs, given their individual and collective computing capabilities, may be able to act on and respond to rapidly changing events, they cannot contend with transformations in their conditions of possibility. In other words, cyborgs can only operate against non-animated backgrounds (alternatively, in "dead spaces"), which the protocologically-organized networks provide. This is why cyborgs can seamlessly operate in computationally underwritten conditions of which they are themselves, in part, a product. Floridi refers to such cybernetic organisms as information organisms or *inforgs*.[35] Floridi's understanding of inforgs, while a functionally oriented one, is nevertheless interesting. What is at stake in Floridi's understanding is the evolutionary adaptation of human agents to a digital environment.

---

35 Floridi, "A Look into the Future Impact of ICTs in our Life," 9. Note that Floridi is not the only theorist who speaks of "inforgs." See also his *Philosophy of Information* (Oxford: Oxford University Press, 2011), 311–36.

Floridi claims that the "threshold between here (analogue, carbon-based, offline) and there (digital, silicon-based, online) is fast becoming blurred."[36] As a consequence, Floridi claims that "we are all becoming connected informational organisms (*inforgs*). This is happening not through some fanciful transformation in our body, but, more seriously and realistically, through the re-ontologization of our environment and ourselves."[37] The point, while an interesting one, does not push the conceptual envelope. Perhaps the matter can be presented in another way.

Without undermining the obvious benefits that the Digital Age has brought in its wake, it could be said that perhaps the most significant benefit that it has brought has been to introduce us to the ubiquity of information. We have learned to recognize the presence of information in virtually every aspect of life and existence. While it is another matter that much of this information bypasses us, either because we are yet to recognize it, appreciate its significance, or not possess the instrumentation by which these flows of information may be tapped into, we are now more than ever aware of ourselves being submerged in a sea of information. But our awareness does not exhaust itself here. Instead, it leads us to further recognize the informational and *in-formational nature* of our being. In other words, we have begun to recognize, albeit faintly, the Becomingness that drives our Being. These recognitions identify us as pure informational organisms and are in excess of Floridi's more conservative speculations concerning "connected informational organisms." The distinction is both a subtle and a far-reaching one. The connectivity that Floridi's inforgs boast of is computationally dependent. Thus, there is always some degree of mediation and routing to such computational dependency, which, as Galloway has pointed out, is protocol-dependent. The inforgs that I am positing are transient aggregations of information independent of any protocological imperatives. These aggregations are as much information as they are *in-formation*. And, as such, they

36 Floridi, "A Look into the Future Impact of ICTs in our Life," 4.
37 Ibid., 9–10.

share the same ontological space with their peers as they do with that which constitutes them. For the theorist of net-centric warfare, such inforgs are a critical problem, because the threats that such entities present are ontological in nature rather than posing merely "dumb" kinetic threats. This ontological threat is twofold in nature. While on the one hand inforgs violate with gay abandon the protocological underpinnings of the net-centric concept, on the other hand such entities are well placed to play the role of "ontological saboteurs" by virtue of sharing the same ontological space as the constituents of the computationally-underwritten version of networks. As such, they are able to undermine the ontological consistency that underwrites the net-centric concept.

The third nightmarish condition that presents itself to the theorists and strategists of net-centric models of warfare involves the recognition of the volume of information, the rate at which it is generated and what it represents. The sheer volume of information and the diversity of its sources are overwhelming. It is for this reason that protocols have been created that allow for the sifting of large volumes of data and information to enable their structuring and organization. But what is particularly nightmarish about this condition? Given that faster and more powerful generations of sensors and computing systems are in the pipeline, the equation between processing power and the volume of information being generated will eventually tip over in favor of the former. However, this is an optimistic assessment and one that, in part, assumes the finitude of information and of its combinatory capabilities. Nietzsche, perhaps best of all, captured the intensity of this state of affairs in an elegant manner. In Nietzschean terms, the conditions instituted and marked by the veritable flood of information may be described as being

> a monster of energy, without beginning, without end; a firm, iron magnitude of force that does not grow bigger or smaller, that does not expend itself but only transforms itself; as a whole, of unalterable size, a household without expenses or losses, but likewise without increase or income; enclosed

by "nothingness" as by a boundary; not something blurry or wasted, not something endlessly extended, but set in a definite space as a definite force, and not a space that might be "empty" here or there, but rather as force throughout, as a play of forces and waves of forces, at the same time one and many, increasing here and at the same time decreasing there; a sea of forces flowing and rushing together, eternally changing, eternally flooding back, with tremendous years of recurrence, with an ebb and a flood of its forms; out of the simplest forms striving toward the most complex, out of the stillest, most rigid, coldest forms striving toward the hottest, most turbulent, most self-contradictory, and then again returning home to the simple out of this abundance, out of the play of contradictions back to the joy of concord, still affirming itself in this uniformity of its courses and its years, blessing itself as that which must return eternally, as a becoming that knows no satiety, no disgust, no weariness: this [...] Dionysian world of the eternally self-creating, the eternally self-destroying, this mystery world of the twofold voluptuous delight [...] "beyond good and evil," without goal, unless the joy of the circle is itself a goal; without will, unless a ring feels good will toward itself — do you want[...] [a] solution for all of its riddles? [...] — This world is *the will to power,* and nothing besides! And you yourselves are also this will to power — and nothing besides![38]

Under such conditions, the structural integrity of the net-centric concept falters. Given that the intent behind positing the concept of the transparent battlespace is to contain and pacify precisely "the monster of energy," the intensity and radical indeterminacy of the condition described by Nietzsche undermines such efforts. And, in a peculiarly circular way, the net-centric paradigm ends up confronting precisely that very condition

---

38 Friedrich Nietzsche, *The Will to Power,* trans. Walter Kaufman (New York: Vintage Press, 1973), 550, §1067.

that Clausewitz cautioned against, albeit for a different set of reasons — the radical uncertainty that marks the space of battle.

4. Addendum

What, then, of the military condition? To all intents and purposes, the current strategic-military system is an outdated and outmoded one. This is not because such systems do not and are not employing cutting-edge technology. Rather, it is because the organizing principle of the military *per se* is now defunct. More than anything else, it is ill-designed to address the chiasmic turbulence that we are in the process of triggering as we rediscover ourselves as *inforgs* and, as such, as integral constituents of the aforementioned turbulence. Further, as inforgs, we are also discovering our propensity to think and act tactically, which requires us to eschew more strategically oriented modes of organization and operabilities. And given that we, as inforgs, always already inhabit an informationally driven ecology, we exist in a condition that requires us to craft newer modes of martial operabilities. For, as inforgs, we live in a Post-Military Condition.

04

A Philosophy of the Antichrist
in the Time of the Anthropocenic Multitude:
Preliminary Lexicon for the Conceptual Network

Gary Shapiro

NWW.IV, April 13, 2013

ANTICHRIST. Nietzsche's not just being scary and shocking. He speaks of a "philosophy of the Antichrist" in one of the more explicitly political sections of *Beyond Good and Evil*,[1] in fact in a long concluding aphorism in §8, "Peoples and Fatherlands." He reviews the mixed accomplishments of figures who helped to teach the nineteenth-century concept of "the higher human (*Mensch*)," including such diverse men as Napoleon, Wagner, Stendhal, and Heine. While all invented various forms of cultural hybridity (*cf.* **übernational**), escaping the limits of nationalism, still all reverted to religion, and none "would have been capable of a philosophy of the Antichrist." In the late preface to *The Birth of Tragedy* Nietzsche ventures to reveal the **Antichrist**'s true name: Dionysus. The book *The Antichrist*, completed by Nietzsche and published later in distorted form by his sister Elisabeth, was first described as the initial one of four in *The Transvaluation of Values*, and later as the work's whole. In choosing the name and figure of **Antichrist** is Nietzsche sim-

---

1   Friedrich Nietzsche, *Beyond Good and Evil*, §256, in *Basic Writings of Nietzsche*, trans. Walter Kaufmann (New York: Random House, 1992), 387.

ply aiming at ultimate blasphemy, a poke in the eye for Christianity? Some scholars take this view and would translate the book as *The Anti-christian* (Daniel Conway acknowledges his terminological change by writing *The Antichrist[ian]*). While either works as a translation of the German term, leaving aside Nietzsche's usage, the lexicon reads Nietzsche's invocation of the **Antichrist** in terms of his rejection and parody of a specific set of Christian theological–political concepts involving specific ideas of time and history which he saw as the source of his *bête noire,* the Hegelian idea of **Weltgeschichte**. Thinkers like Carl Schmitt, Giorgio Agamben, and Ernst Kantorowicz have shown that much Christian political thought, beginning with early church fathers like Tertullian, legitimated worldly power, as that which deferred the coming of **Antichrist**. The texts providing a (rather questionable) basis for this view were those letters attributed to Paul that attempt to discourage the view that the end of the world was imminent. Instead, "Paul" said there was a delaying, restraining power (a *katechon*) holding back the appearance of **Antichrist**. Eventually this was understood to be the Roman empire (even prior to its Christianization) and the idea was then applied to its successor states. Agamben has this complex of ideas in mind when he says that much Western political theology is *katechontic*. The **Antichrist**, then, is that which appears with the collapse or dissolution of the state. As early as *Human, All Too Human,*[2] Nietzsche suggested that the form of the European nation-state was fragile in a world of increasingly **nomadisch** peoples who were not as firmly attached to territory and tradition as their forebears. One sign of this fragility was the state's readiness to discover security threats which it countered by declaring a state of exception or **Notzustand**. Like Schmitt, Nietzsche sees that such sovereignty operates on a theologic; its legitimacy requires thinking of the political state of exception as parallel to the miracle by which God asserts his sovereignty over the world and nature. Part of the long and difficult process of

2   Nietzsche, *Human, All Too Human,* trans. R.J. Hollingdale (New York: Cambridge University Press, 1986), §472–75.

understanding God's death is seeing that the state with its claims to sovereignty is one of several "shadows of God" that persist after his disappearance.[3] Nietzsche announces a philosophy of the **Antichrist** which will not only split the world's history in two but also marks a break with the time of *Weltgeschichte,* the Christian–Hegelian construction of political time that owes so much to Christianity's accommodation to the *Welt,* more specifically to the state, said by Hegel to be "God's march through the world."

An important step in the development of katechontic thought was taken by Hippolytus of Rome (ca. 200 CE) in commentaries on apocalyptic texts from Old and New Testaments. He interpreted them to mean that the end times were at least several hundred years away. Without this extension of time, which was gradually increased, the meta-narratives of Christian history that eventually morphed into the stories of *Weltgeschichte* or *Weltprozess* would not have been possible. Nietzsche's critique of Hartmann's conception of the *Weltprozess* includes a sneer at the author for assimilating his own narrative mélange of Schopenhauer and Hegel to the Christian idea of the last days and the coming of **Antichrist**.[4] Nietzsche was conversant with this tradition. A former student of theology from a ministerial family, his closest adult friend and housemate for several years was Franz Overbeck, an anti-theological theologian. According to Agamben and Andreas Sommer, Overbeck anticipated Nietzsche's genealogy in his critique of Christian canon formation, and was engaged with him in a common project of deconstructing liberal Protestantism's evasion of its radical disconnection from messianic consciousness. A "philosophy of the Antichrist" then is one that sets aside the narratives of Christianity and *Weltgeschichte* concerning the *Welt* (first rejected and then conditionally accepted in Christianity) and instead celebrates the

3   Nietzsche, *The Gay Science,* trans. Josefine Nauckoff (New York: Cambridge University Press), §108.
4   Nietzsche, *Untimely Meditations,* trans. R.J. Hollingdale (New York: Cambridge University Press, 1983), II §9.

Erde, the site of human energy, activity, productivity, and movement.

ERDE. Earth, the sphere of actual, living, human habitation, as distinguished from the "world beyond," and somewhat more subtly from the *Welt*. When Zarathustra begins his discourses by calling for loyalty (*Treue*) to the earth and later seeks disciples (*Jünger*) in this enterprise, the political aspect of the term becomes evident. This is even more explicit in *Zarathustra*'s chapter "On Great Events" (*cf. grosse Ereignis*), in which the noisy, exaggerated howlings of politicians and what we would call "public intellectuals" are juxtaposed with true great events that approach quietly "on dove's feet" and somehow mesh with the self-renewing earth. The usage seems implicit in later writings. *Beyond Good and Evil* speaks, for instance, of the battle for hegemony (*Herrschaft*) over the earth in the next century.[5]

GARTEN. Garden. If humans are loyal to the *Erde* it could become a garden.[6] From the standpoint of active and exuberant power, the garden is a site of growth, cultivation, and artful perspective. When conditions are not yet ripe for this, the garden can be a more enclosed and relatively private site of thought, rest, and friendship, on the model of Epicurus's garden. The symbol can be expanded to embrace contemporary ecological concerns.

GROSSE EREIGNIS. Great event. According to Alain Badiou, *Also Sprach Zarathustra*'s chapter containing this term is the most important in the book. He assimilates Nietzsche's thought to his own concept of a holistic change that elicits fidelity to a new form of universality. Indeed, Nietzsche begins his 1876 *Untimely Meditations* §4 with an account of such a great event that he thinks is happening then; he explicitly states that such

5   Nietzsche, *Beyond Good and Evil*, §208.
6   Cf. Nietzsche, *Thus Spoke Zarathustra*, trans. Graham Parkes (New York: Oxford University Press, 2005), III §13.2

events are rare, transformative in unanticipatable ways, evoking and inspiring fidelity to their principle. Badiou downplays or ignores the emphasis that Nietzsche gives to *Erde* in naming the site of such great events in this and related texts. The last such great event, Nietzsche says, was Alexander's linking of East and West. The nascent great event is Wagner's decoupling of West from East. However absurd the thesis and comparison, it shows Nietzsche thinking geophilosophically and sketching, however abstractly, an alternative to Hegel's *Weltgeschichte* whose transitions involve inclusions and transformative absorptions (*Aufhebungen*). At the same time it suggests questions about the Christian pattern of Hegelian teleology, whose Trinitarian structure is its signature. Unspoken here is that the first event enabled the Christianization of Europe, and that Wagner makes its de-Christianization possible. Wagner could then be thought of as a "positive" *Antichrist*. It's well known that Nietzsche soon saw Wagner as more of an actor than a cultural hero (perhaps he'd already entertained such doubts). *Beyond Good and Evil* §256, frequently remembered for its closing ironic rhymes on Wagner's path toward Rome, also declares that none of the great nineteenth-century figures who enacted various versions of cultural hybridity was capable of a philosophy of the **Antichrist**. Although Nietzsche's later speculations and often bizarre notebook entries can seem as strange as the comparison of Alexander and Wagner, he consistently says or implies on a "formal" level that the great event is one of the earth, as in the summation in *Ecce Homo*: "[T]here will be wars unlike any yet on the *Erde*. Only from myself on will there be great politics on the *Erde*."[7]

MENGE. Probably most accurately translated as "multitude"; while "crowd" or "throng" are not necessarily misleading, they do not capture as well Nietzsche's distinction between relatively homogeneous masses (*Massen*) and the diversity of the **Menge**. This is especially important in reading *Beyond Good and Evil,* the book that begins to speak of "a philosophy of the **Antichrist**."

7   Nietzsche, *Ecce Homo,* "Destiny," §1, in *Basic Writings of Nietzsche,* 387.

Beyond Good and Evil §256 maintains that "this is the century of the *Menge*," with Nietzsche emphasizing the term. For a clear sense of the masses/multitude distinction, see *The Gay Science* §149 ("The failure of reformations"), where Nietzsche says that a religious reformation cannot succeed, no matter how brilliant and charismatic its leaders (as in ancient Greece), if the population is composed of "a *Menge* of diverse individuals," but stands a chance where there are *Massen*. Luther's Reformation is a sign of the backward status of Germany and the European north. In the context of *Beyond Good and Evil* (§213, §256, §269) the *Menge* are not a cross-section of the population but "the educated, the enthusiasts" (§269), those who flock to the theater or to admire those they take to be "great men." Two sources of Nietzsche's usage are especially notable: 1) Luther's Bible typically uses *Menge* to describe those non-disciples who listen to Jesus, at least occasionally, with interest and enthusiasm; 2) Goethe's *Faust* opens with a "Prelude in the Theater" in which director, writer, and a clown discuss the attributes of the *Menge* before whom the play will be performed. The Biblical emphasis looms in the background of Nietzsche's warning to philosophers of the future to avoid the fickle, thoughtless taste of the *Menge*; the second underlines his diagnosis of the century as one of theater or spectacle. Failure to see the masses/multitude distinction is ironic, given that the *Genealogy of Morals,* explicitly labeled by Nietzsche as a guide to understanding *Beyond Good and Evil,* stresses the importance of noting nuances in the various Greek and Roman terms for diverse social groupings.[8] Unfortunately, both the recent Cambridge and Stanford translations of *Beyond Good and Evil* render *Menge* as "masses."

MENSCH. Human; often translated tendentiously as "man." The *Mensch* is in danger of becoming totally tamed and regularized, losing all sense of adventure and novelty, the *letzte Mensch*. Nietzsche thought this tendency was driven by increasing bureaucratization and organization of life around fetishistic no-

---

8   Nietzsche, *Genealogy of Morals,* I §10, in *Basic Writings of Nietzsche,* 387.

tions of individual and group security and by systems of thought (e.g., Hegel, D.F. Strauss, Hartmann) which anticipated what we now call "end of history" theories. The possibilities of the *Mensch* and its relation to animal and earth are still to be discovered. The most promising future is one where the *Mensch* is loyal to the earth and creates a glorious *Menschen-Erde*. Yet until now, the production of "an animal with the prerogative to promise"[9] has been focused on training humans to accept and live within an economy of *Schuld*; accordingly, Nietzsche suggests that *Mensch* derives from the Sanskrit *manas,* suggesting something like "the measurer," meaning the one able to measure what is due to and from itself.

MENSCHEN-ERDE. The human earth. While there is obvious emphasis on the experiential or phenomenological aspect of the human earth, the term can also be taken as a literal equivalent of the recent geological category of the anthropocene, the era when human habitation begins to change the earth and its atmosphere, especially since the end of the last Ice Age, ca. 10,000 BCE. (This date coincides roughly with the first proto-urban settlements and with the "moral" phase of *Hauptgeschichte* Nietzsche outlines in *Beyond Good and Evil* §32 and fills in further in *Genealogy of Morals* II §16–17). The experiential and the geological/archaeological senses can be seen as relatively passive and active sides of the same thing, human embodiment in the environment. On the one hand, Zarathustra declares in "On Great Events" that *Menschen* are a skin-disease on the *Erde*; they have desecrated and overlaid its beauty. On the other, he tells us elsewhere that the *Mensch* and the *Menschen-Erde* are unexhausted and undiscovered. The human earth, having come to seem like a dismal cave, could be transformed into a *Garten*, as he and his animals agree in his convalescence. "What direction will humans give to the earth?" is Nietzsche's overriding question. So far as the **Antichrist** figures as a symbol of hegemony over the earth, this question is central to a philosophy of the **Antichrist**.

9   Ibid., II §1.

NOMADISCH. Nomadic. When Nietzsche speaks of the increasing nomadic character of the modern European,[10] we must guard against reading this anachronistically as referring to the lifestyle of more or less solitary individual travelers, emigrants, and the like. As Deleuze reminds us, nomads are first of all peoples, although they typically lack a state organization; second, nomads do *not* travel — they roam within a certain territory (even if it has vague or porous boundaries), sometimes in response to seasonal changes. In Emerson's essay "History," Nietzsche read an account of human group formations that includes both state and nomad types on an equal basis. Nomads may lack a *Welt* in Hegel's view, but they inhabit the *Erde.* A similar perspective, argued in more scholarly fashion, is found in Friedrich Ratzel's *Anthropo-Geographie,* which Nietzsche was reading and marking in the 1880s.

NOTZUSTAND. or *Ausnahmezustand.* Usually translated as "state of emergency" or "state of exception." Philosophers and political theorists should be familiar with the discussions of the concept in Schmitt and Agamben. In the state of exception the sovereign suspends some portion of "normal" law for the sake of the existence of the state (*Staat*) itself. Nietzsche was familiar with and alluded to Bismarck's use of the state of exception in the 1870s as part of his cultural war (*Kulturkampf*) in which, on this analysis, he attempted to solidify state power by raising fears of Catholic subversion. Other well-known deployments of the state of exception include Lincoln's suspension of *habeas corpus* in the US Civil War and Nazi Germany's use of the state of exception clause of the Weimar Constitution to suspend (rather than nullify) that constitution itself. The Weimar provision itself was based on law from the Bismarckian *Reich.* In *Human, All Too Human* §475, Nietzsche says that the transnational (**übernational**) tendencies of trade, migration, and other movements and interactions of peoples are eroding the national identity

10 E.g., Nietzsche, *Human, All Too Human* §472–75; *Beyond Good and Evil,* §242.

desired by the state. In response, the state attempts to evoke nationalism through imaginary security threats. But, he says, "this artificial nationalism is as dangerous as artificial Catholicism once was, for it is in essence a *Notzustand* and beleaguerment forcibly inflicted by the few upon the many, requiring artifice, deceit, and force to maintain its authority." Translations tend to miss the specific *legal* network of concepts at stake, with phrases like "state of siege" or "state of distress." Schmitt defines the sovereign as the one who decides upon the exception (cf. George W. Bush on the US president as "decider"), emphasizing the parallel between the sovereign's suspension of state law and God's of natural law through miracle. For Nietzsche the state is one of the "shadows of God,"[11] and in *Untimely Meditations* §3.4 he compares the absolute claims of the contemporary state to those of the medieval church. The katechontic tradition would legitimize protecting state sovereignty by deploying the state of exception.

ROME. In the Biblical Revelation, as originally understood, Rome is demonized. Taking the side of ancient Rome and the possibilities of its renewal in the Renaissance, Nietzsche identifies with the **Antichrist**.[12]

SCHULD. Writing in the late nineteenth century, a time conscious of newly accelerated global financial crisis, Nietzsche sketched a political economy based on debt rather than exchange, in the classical liberal model. The civilized *Mensch* is born in debt, accumulates more, and passes this on to the future. In the *Genealogy of Morals* Nietzsche articulates a genealogical analysis of how the archaic sense of *Schuld* as debt of goods, services, or money also acquired the psychic and religious meaning of guilt. The earliest human social forms, Nietzsche argues, consist of networks of debtors and creditors. These are not only the first economic relations — so that debt, for example, is prior to

11 Nietzsche, *The Gay Science,* §108.
12 Nietzsche, *The Antichrist,* §58, in *Twilight of the Idols and The Anti-Christ,* trans. R.J. Hollingdale (New York: Penguin Books, 1971), 179–80.

barter or to money — but are coeval with the emergence of the human (*Mensch*) as the animal capable of making promises and of measuring everything. The *Genealogy of Morals* traces the development of the debt regime, from tribal and familial contexts to the state's emergence; he shows how *Schuld* first acquires a religious coloring with debts to national gods and leads finally to the madness of monotheism in which the debt/guilt becomes overwhelming and unpayable (except through God's own sacrifice, for which believers now assume another unrepayable debt).

Philosophy itself is complicit in this madness, Nietzsche's Zarathustra argues, in a chapter fittingly entitled "On Redemption (*Erlösung*)," Zarathustra compresses the history of the Western philosophical tradition, from its first surviving sentence credited to Anaximander to its latest manifestation in Schopenhauer's pessimism, when he declares what madness preached:

> Everything passes away, therefore everything deserves to pass away! And this is itself justice, that law of time that time must devour its children [...]. This, this is what is eternal in the punishment "existence": that existence itself must eternally be deed and guilt again. Unless the will should at last redeem itself and willing should become not-willing."[13]

Nietzsche had several allies in his project of redemption, a redemption that would affirm the innocence of becoming (its freedom from debt and guilt, *das Unschuld des Werdens*); perhaps we should call this unmortgaged becoming. One was the North American sage who inspired him in his youth, Ralph Waldo Emerson. Emerson began his deceptively brief and simple "Gifts," his meta-economic theory, with another apparent allusion to Anaximander and his tradition, which could stand as an emblem of world economic crisis: "It is said that the world is in a state of bankruptcy; that the world owes the world more

13   Nietzsche, *Thus Spoke Zarathustra*, 122.

than the world can pay, and ought to go into chancery and be sold."[14]

So whether in the philosophical tradition that extends from Anaximander to Schopenhauer, in global economic relations, or in the theological complex of *Schuld* and *Erlösung,* the future is either completely and irretrievably mortgaged, an open-ended, indefinite amortization like the debt to the company store, or ought to be rejected as providing the illusion of satisfied desire.

ÜBERNATIONAL. Transnational, no longer bound by the ideology and practices of the nation-state. *Beyond Good and Evil* §242 speaks of the "increasing similarity among Europeans," as they detach themselves from their original conditions of site and climate, and the "slow approach of an essentially **übernational** and *nomadisch* type of person." The term "transnational" has become current in the academic field of American Studies, although introduced in Randolph Bourne's 1916 essay "Transnational America." Bourne's brief reviews and essays on Nietzsche are probably the most perceptive US responses to his work before 1920.

VATERLAND. Fatherland. Those who cling to archaic conceptions of sacred territory when the *Menschen-Erde* are said to be guilty of *Schollenkleberei,* being obsessed with and stuck in the mud or muck.[15]

VOLK. People or folk. Nietzsche is clear in his criticism of the fetishistic essentialism of the term as employed to legitimate the nation-state in the century of the *Menge.*

WELT. World. While Nietzsche's usage is not consistent, he often speaks critically of the *Welt,* especially in dealing with the term's appearance in contexts such as Hegelian *Weltgeschichte*

14 Ralph W. Emerson, "Gifts," in *The Complete Works, Vol. III, Essays: Second Series* (Boston and New York: Houghton Mifflin and Company, 1904), ch. 5.
15 Nietzsche, *Beyond Good and Evil,* §241.

and Eduard von Hartmann's *Weltprozess.* As early as his critique of the latter he complains about being compelled in reading Hartmann to constantly hear "the hyperbole of hyperboles, the word world, world, world!"[16] Instead, he suggests, we should be hearing about the human (*Mensch*). In the case of both the more traditional Hegelians and Hartmann, the word designates a totality or unity that transcends not only individuals, but groups and associations. For Hegel, the *Welt* is essentially impossible and inconceivable except as a structure of the state. Hegel goes so far as to maintain that there is no world for peoples who do not have a state.[17] Nomadic or non-state peoples are for Hegel "mere nations (*Nationen*)," that is, groups affiliated only by reproductive or family lineages. In contrast, Nietzsche never despises the *Erde,* and the term becomes increasingly prominent from *Thus Spoke Zarathustra* on, sometimes qualified as the *Menschen-Erde.* What distinguishes *Erde* from *Welt* in this conceptual network is that *Erde* is a full site of human life, not requiring to be understood either in terms of an absolute teleology or as requiring the political form of the state.

WELTGESCHICHTE. World history, a term especially identified with Hegel, although English translations typically omit the "world" in his *Philosophy of World History,* perhaps because they would rather not confront its restrictive sense of *Welt.* Nietzsche often speaks with contempt of *Weltgeschichte.* Beyond his rejection of Hegel's idealistic, absolutistic, teleological, and politico-theological history, Nietzsche suggests that geography, in a broad sense, cannot be subordinated to history in Hegelian fashion. The *Menschen-Erde* takes precedence over the state.

WELTPROZESS. World-process, a central concept of Eduard von Hartmann's philosophy of history in *Philosophy of the Unconscious,* one of the most widely read books of systematic phi-

16 Nietzsche, *Untimely Meditations,* II §9.
17 G.W.F. Hegel, *The Encyclopaedia Logic,* trans. William Wallace (New York: Oxford University Press, 1971), 279, §549.

losophy of the late nineteenth century. The conclusion of Nietzsche's *Untimely Meditations* §2 mischievously reads Hartmann as if the author of the "great book" had set out to write a parody of Hegelian thinking of the end of history, grotesquely mixing the spirit of that idea with Schopenhauer's conception that wisdom consists in willing nothingness. Hartmann thought it inevitable that after humanity's youth (Greco-Roman belief that this present world is sufficient for happiness), medieval adolescence (striving for salvation in the beyond), maturity or modern enlightenment (aiming at using knowledge of humans and nature to produce a better future world), and old age (where even the last of these is revealed as illusory), the only alternative is Schopenhauerian recognition of the futility of the search for happiness, and so acceptance or pursuit of the end of humanity. With respect to Nietzsche's later gestures toward a philosophy of the **Antichrist**, it is notable that he regards Hartmann's **Weltprozess** as a belated version of the Christian narrative with its end-of-the-world scenario, as in *Revelation*.

05

Occupying God's Shadow:
Nietzsche's *Eirōneia*

Julian Reid
NWW.II, May 6, 2010

It is a truism, after Schmitt, to say that all modern political concepts are secularized theological ones. Politically speaking we
have yet to emancipate ourselves from the tyranny of theological reason. Never less so than in this current era in which we
remain subjected to what Schmitt called "liberal metaphysics."[1]
And so it is the case that the struggle with neoliberalism must
be a struggle against the continuities of its theology. Contrary
to Nietzsche, God is far from dead: we haven't quite finished
the job of killing him — nor perhaps could we, were we up to
the task. In actual fact, to be true to Nietzsche, his proclama-
tion that "God is dead" was followed directly by a claim as to
the "shadow" that God continues to cast over us in spite of his
"death" and a warning that, in spite of his death, "we still have
to vanquish his shadow."[2] That "God is dead" merely means that
he continues to live in a different way, *as a shadow of himself.*
The problem Nietzsche posed for us has subsequently been un-

1   Carl Schmitt, *Political Theology: Four Chapters on the Concept of Sovereignty,*
    trans. George Schwab (Chicago: University of Chicago Press, 2005), 62.
2   Friedrich Nietzsche, *The Gay Science,* trans. Walter Kaufman (New York:
    Vintage, 1974), 167.

derstood as that of how to vanquish that shadow; how to secure the demise of God such that we might escape the many ways in which that shadow continues to be thrown over us, preventing us from realizing our emancipation from religion. How, in other words, to sever the relation of religion to the modern, ridding us of the scourge of religion that continues to afflict our thinking and practices.

But there is an irony in this formulation of the problem of God's shadow that has been hitherto missed. One cannot vanquish a shadow. Reduced to being a shadow of himself, God is suddenly at his strongest, and least susceptible to death or even injury. Of course one can attempt to fight a shadow, and to do so is itself a well-established art in both Western and Eastern traditions of the martial arts, but not one of which the meaningful aim can be to vanquish the opponent, but through the practice of which one aims to strengthen oneself by the engagement with an opponent who is unsurpassable: oneself. In the case of our combat with God's shadow, too, it is a question of a struggle with ourselves, and ourselves at that precise point when we are, as we moderns more or less are, mere shadows of ourselves. God's shadow is our own, and the challenge, to vanquish it, cannot be fulfilled because we, as mere shadows of ourselves, are too weak for it. The struggle over the death of God is that of two shadows cast over each other, too weak to see the nexus that regardless of their twoness actually binds them together.

Let's put aside the question of whether Nietzsche understood this, or whether his choice of metaphor was simply poor. The formulation of the problem of God's shadow is paradoxical — but that it is so, is a false problem; the paradox, indeed, is necessary. For it is an error to approach the relation of religion to the modern, as so many of Nietzsche's followers have done, as if it were a contingent one. By that I do not mean to deny the importance of confronting and struggling against the many ways in which religion limits our political horizons and life potential. There are many ways clearly in which it does. But that very task of confrontation and struggle against religion can only proceed within idioms of struggle and confrontation themselves made possible by religion. Let us take for example the problem of the continued power and influence of eschatological thinking in modern political discourse. So much of modern political discourse remains eschatological in terms of the ways it revolves around promises of a better and transformed life in the future. The nature of that promise finds its origins in Judeo-Christian civilization.[3] My collaborators Michael Dillon and Brad Evans have both demonstrated how the advent of liberal modernity and the birth of biopolitics did not do away with the eschaton but immanentized it within life itself.[4] The transcendental principle for liberal biopolitics is life, and the legitimacy of liberal regimes remains firmly grounded in their promises to secure life's futures. Indeed it is precisely that promise which continues to legitimize and incite the endless technologization of life, which has led us to the perverse paradox of a liberal modernity defined by a mastery of biological life as well as radical fear as to the catastrophic implications of such mastery, given the capacities of the species, so endowed now with the powers to destroy the very world on which it depends for its existence.

But the problematization of the nexus that continues to bind the religious with the modern, and the call to have done with it and move beyond it is no less eschatological. Another irony missed by those doing the calling.[5] How to secure the political from the religious? How to deploy the political such that it might move us into the beyond of both the biopolitical and the eschatological? How to remove the scourge of eschatology that infects our political thinking and practices? How to purify the political of its religious afflictions? These are the paradoxical and perhaps ultimately self-defeating stakes of the political critique of eschatological biopolitics.

3   Jacob Taubes, *Occidental Eschatology* (Stanford: Stanford University Press, 2009).
4   Brad Evans, *Liberal Terror* (Oxford: Polity Press, 2012); Michael Dillon, "Specters of Biopolitics: Finitude, *Eschaton* and *Katechon*," *South Atlantic Quarterly* 110.3 (2011): 780–92.
5   Ibid.

At the beginning of his essay on "Faith and Knowledge," Jacques Derrida asked whether "a discourse on religion can be dissociated from a discourse on salvation?"[6] Likewise, we might ask what would a politics be without a discourse on security? Securing the human from its modern subjection to the eschatological plans which liberalism has for it is a task that itself can only be achieved by a wielding of tools and weapons from the eschatological traditions of thinking bequeathed us by our Judeo-Christian heritage. That is the argument, at least, I want to propose and advance here. We won't be able to combat liberal biopolitics and its eschatology without deploying a counter-eschatology. And thus the struggle against liberalism requires a subject able to free itself from simplistically anti-religious reflexes and learn how to differentiate between the form of religiosity it chooses to go to war with and that which it requires in order to do so.[7]

An important starting point in the process of losing such reflexes is the recognition that there is no such thing as religion in the singular. Just as there is no such thing as Christianity or Judaism in the singular. Nietzsche himself understood this, his opposition to Christianity being more precisely to Protestantism: "[T]he mix of abnegation of the human will, its total inefficacy in the work of salvation, together with the authoritarian state and ruthless exploitation of the world."[8] Likewise eschatology is a multiplicity, open to and made itself by history, while all the time being itself the essence of history.[9] And thus the problem — if we accept there is one — of God's shadow today, cannot simply be said to be the continued shaping of political ideas and practices by religion, but the specificity of the particular regime

6   Jacques Derrida, "Faith and Knowledge: The Two Sources of 'Religion' at the Limits of Reason Alone," in *Acts of Religion*, trans. Gil Andjar (London: Routledge, 2010), 42.

7   Peter Sloterdijk, *Bubbles: Spheres 1*, trans. Wieland Hoban (New York: Semiotexte, 2011), 560.

8   Gillian Rose, *Mourning Becomes the Law: Philosophy and Representation* (Cambridge: Cambridge University Press, 1996), 142.

9   Taubes, *Occidental Eschatology*.

of religiosity that makes liberal biopolitics possible. This is precisely why, when we examine the works of the most acute critics of liberal modernity and its biopolitics we find that their own thinking concerning how to combat it is shaped by a refusal of any simplistically anti-religious reflex. One could choose from a wide range of thinkers as examples. But Michel Foucault and Peter Sloterdijk are, I think, not only two examples of this fact, but exemplary in the ways by which they have attempted to make use of religion, and the eschatological tradition of thought especially, in the struggle with liberal biopolitics. Both, of course, also take their cue from Nietzsche, and in ways that recognize the complexities of Nietzsche's own understanding of not only the difficulties, but the mistake of belief in the vanquishing, as such, of God's shadow.

There is not enough space go into great detail as to the different ways in which thinkers such as Foucault and Sloterdijk have gone about the task of using religion. I will simply give a brief sketch of how I think Foucault did this. On March 28, 1984, less than three months before his death, Foucault gave his very last lecture at the Collège de France. What was it that Foucault chose to talk about on that occasion? The lecture was on the subject of Christianity, and described the fundamental conflict within Christianity that led to the establishment of the Christian Church.[10] A conflict which, as Foucault told his audience, was fought and decided between two very different kinds of Christian subjects; the fearful, mistrustful subject of the Church versus the fearless and confident subject of the early pre-Church Christian era. Foucault's question, or that which he posed for his audience, was that not only of how to explain the victory of the former over the latter, but how to do so with a view to being able to understand the nature of the power of and struggle against liberalism better. We know from many of his precious lectures — most especially the *Security, Territory, Population* se-

10 Michel Foucault, *The Courage of Truth: Lectures at the Collège de France 1983–1984,* trans. Graham Burchell (New York: Palgrave Macmillan, 2011), 325–42.

ries he gave in 1978 — that liberalism, on his account, was born
from the "archaïc model of the Christian pastorate."[11] The pastorate sketched out and was the prelude to liberalism, he argued,
through its constitution "of a specific subject [...] who is subjected in continuous networks of obedience and who is subjecti-
fied through the compulsory extraction of truth [...] a certain
secret inner truth," which "becomes the element through which
the pastor's power is exercised, by which obedience is practiced"
and by which a "relationship of complete obedience is assured."[12]
That the truth of the pastoral subject was "internal, secret and
hidden"[13] was of essential importance for Foucault's explanation
of the specificity of the pastorate as a form of power, the par-
ticularity of the pastoral subject, and its continuities with the
biopolitical subject of liberal modernity.

Condemned never to be able to know its truth as such — that
is, form a "relationship with a recognized truth" — the pastoral
subject was likewise condemned to live out a life of permanent
obedience, humility, and servitude to a form of spiritual direction which was "absolutely permanent [...] directed with regard
to everything and for the whole of one's life," such that the entirety of his or her life became the object of continuous examination
amid pastoral practices of involuntary extraction.[14] The claim as
to the specificity of this form of subject called into being by the
pastorate and its continuity with the biopolitical subject of liberal
modernity was maintained by Foucault throughout his studies
of liberalism right up until his death. It was central, certainly, to
his explanation of the principle of self-limitation with which he
went on to define liberalism in *The Birth of Biopolitics* lectures in
1978–79. No doubt liberal discourses of economy were central
also to how it arrived at that principle. "Economics steals away
from the juridical form of the sovereign precisely that which is

11 Foucault, *Security, Territory, Population: Lectures at the Collège de France
    1977–1978,* trans. Graham Burchell (New York: Palgrave Macmillan, 2007),
    110.
12 Ibid., 183–85.
13 Ibid., 184.
14 Ibid., 182.

emerging as the essential element of a society's life, namely economic processes."[15] But beneath its advocacy of the principle of self-limitation Foucault shows us how liberalism rested not simply on a fundamental assumption as to the economic nature of the life of society, but fundamental assumptions as to the hidden nature of the truth of that life, the limits of what can be known of it, and the consequent preoccupation with the permanent surveying and extracting of its forever mutative truths as well as growth from it. The fundamental truth of life understood as economy is, as he explores, "the unknowability of the totality of the process. [...] [T]he economic world is naturally opaque and naturally non-totalizable. It is originally and definitively constituted from a multiplicity of points-of-view" and "[l]iberalism acquired its modern shape precisely with the formulation of this essential incompatibility between the non-totalizable multiplicity of society's life and the totalizing unity of the juridical sovereign."[16] Eschewing accounts of the supposed atheism of liberal political economy, Foucault shows how its assumptions as to the elusive nature of the economic life of the liberal subject, and the inability of the subject to ever know and tell the truth of that life as such, originated in the pastorate and its discourses on the elusive nature of the life of the pastoral subject.

"Truth" was also the concern of Foucault's very last lecture at the Collège de France, covering as it did the use of the term "parrhesia" or "truth telling" in early Christian texts. To his final audience Foucault described "the opposition between two major frameworks, two major cores of Christian experience." On the one hand, the experience specific to the very earliest forms of Christianity, of the "parrhesiac," a being possessed with an openness of heart, immediate presence, and direct communication of the soul with God, giving him the confidence, ability to speak the truth, to know the truth, and courage to act, be

15 Foucault, *The Birth of Biopolitics: Lectures at the Collège de France 1978–79*, trans. Graham Burchell (New York: Palgrave Macmillan, 2010), 282.
16 Ibid.

careless with his life, risk his life, to the point of martyrdom.[17]
Parrhesia as such was the courage to assert the truth that one is
confident of knowing and to which one wishes to bear witness
regardless of every danger. And on the other hand, the experience of the fear of the parrhesiac in the subsequent and institutionalized forms of Christianity which diagnosed parrhesia as
a kind of disease, an excess and danger to be prevented. And
which sought and succeeded in regrounding Christianity in a
completely other principle: that of trembling obedience, fear of
God, recognition of the necessity to submit to His will and the
will of those who represent him. This obedient subject did not,
and could not, have confidence in himself. He had to operate
on a principle of mistrust of oneself. He must not, it was understood within this other framework of Christian experience
that Foucault described, believe, imagine, or be so arrogant as to
think that he can secure his own truth and find a way of opening
to God by himself. He must be the object of his own mistrust,
an attentive, scrupulous, and suspicious vigilance. And only by
renunciation of self and the putting of this general principle of
obedience into practice would he be able to secure salvation.
So you have, as Foucault demonstrated in that last lecture, two
very different ways of conceiving how to fulfill the eschatological promise in Christianity. On the one hand through obedience, renunciation of self, care for life, and blind submission of
the will, and on the other through confidence, truth telling, risk
of life, and courage.

The task which I believe Foucault's studies of the degraded
subject constituted by the liberal project sets for us is to recover
that lost aspect to subjectivity, fundamental to early Christian
experience, which entails not the incapacity to know the truth
on account of its elusive nature, but the confidence of knowing and being able to tell truth. A subject very like that of the
early Christian "indifferent to the opinion of others and to the
structures of power."[18] A subject, also, for whom the term "hu-

17 Foucault, *The Courage of Truth,* 332.
18 Ibid., 318.

manity" refers to everything soft and pathetic among the living, and which regards itself and affirmed itself as a kind of beast. And yet a subject open in heart, which tells the truth it knows, on account of a confidence and trust in itself which gives it the courage to do so "regardless of every danger."[19] As Foucault shows us, it was only with the subsequent "stress on obedience in Christian life, in Christian practice and institutions, in relation to oneself as well as in relation to truth" that this confidence became obscured[20] and that Christians were taught, in place of confidence, to fear God, recognizing the necessity of submitting to his will and those who represent him. Likewise it was only then that the confidence that gave the early Christian subject his courage to tell truth in disregard of danger becomes diagnosed as "a sort of arrogance and presumption" requiring disciplinary and governmental attention.

There is, of course, another source in Foucault's studies of religious truth-telling practices that are of immense interest also: his journal writings from Iran in 1978 just prior to the Iranian Revolution. A revolution that he called "the first great insurrection against global systems, the form of revolt that is the most modern and the most insane." There he speculated on how Islam was working to transform the discontent, hatred, misery, and despair of Iranians into what he described as "a force," a way of being together, a way of speaking the truth and listening to truth, something that allows one to be listened to by others, and to yearn for something with them at the same time as they yearn for it. Islam was for Foucault the *spirit* which bound the Iranian people together, constituting a shared regime of truth more powerful than the simple biological fact of their being members of the same species, giving them the courage with which to risk their own lives in order to achieve the revolutionary change which they sought and dreamt about. He speculated on the major differences between the Islamic Modernity being sought through revolutionary means in Iran and the liberal

19 Ibid., 331.
20 Ibid., 333.

modernity that Iranian Muslims saw as archaïc and were rising up to overthrow in 1978. While liberal modernity produces a subject preoccupied by a fear of its vulnerability, the death and damage that can be done to its biological life, for the Muslim, Foucault argued, death is what attaches him or her to life. And while for the liberal subject the fear of death and damage initiates an ethic of constant care for life to ensure its wellbeing for the finite time of which it is capable, death gives him or her the courage to fight and ultimately act without care for his or her life. Not out of obedience to a law or authority but in renewal of a fidelity, to the eventality of a truth greater than life itself. A truth which cannot be coded by law, nor which simply belongs to a prophet, or other representatives, but to the people that truth inhabits, giving them the confidence and courage to risk their life in preservation of it.

Foucault's studies of twentieth-century political Islam and early Christianity were written at different times, to entirely different audiences, and never conjoined thematically. But it is obvious that there is a massive resonance between the very earliest historical forms of Christianity he analyzed and the political Islam of his and our present. Likewise that he saw in the later more institutionalized forms of Christianity the seeds of liberal modernity, biopolitics, and liberal subjectivity. And it seems to me that what Foucault is describing when he describes the experience of subjectivity in early Christianity and contemporary political Islam is a form of experience that can only posit itself in hostility to liberal modernity and its biopolitical subject; a form of experience which liberalism itself can only comprehend as threatening and fearful to its biopolitical project. So, if we want to found a politics beyond liberalism it is necessary that we learn something from these examples, themselves to be found within religious discourses and practices. Political subjects do not merely live in order to fit in with and adapt to existing times, or desire the sustainability of the conditions for their living the lives they do.[21] In contrast, they resist those conditions, and

21 Julian Reid, "The Disastrous and Politically Debased Subject of Resilience," *Development Dialogue* (April 2012).

where successful, overcome them, transforming time into that which it was not. A new time in succession of an old and destroyed time. The task is to affirm the eschatological confidence of the subject which entails not its experience of vulnerability to injury and fear of death, but the hubristic trust in itself and others with whom it decides what it wants, asserts what it possesses, and celebrates what it is able to do, in accordance with truths which transcend its existence as a merely living entity.[22]

---

22 For further discussion see Julian Reid, "The Vulnerable Subject of Liberal War," *South Atlantic Quarterly* 110.3 (2011): 770–79.

06

Reading Nietzsche in the Wake of the 2008–9 *War on Gaza*

C. Heike Schotten

NWW.I, May 12, 2009

In late January 2009, I sat down to re-read Nietzsche's *Genealogy of Morals*. I remember this otherwise uneventful event so distinctly because at that moment the first of Israel's series of twenty-first-century wars on Gaza was brutally and unremittingly underway. During that three-week-long military attack, Israel killed over 1,400 Palestinians, most of whom were civilians and approximately 400 of whom were children. Israel, in fact, deliberately *targeted* civilians — including children and humanitarian aid workers — assaulting Palestinians simultaneously by air, land, and sea, and deploying white phosphorus against them, a chemical intended to operate as a smokescreen for troop movements but when used as a weapon burns people's flesh down to the bone.[1] The brutality of Israel's war was all the

1   These facts have been amply documented by, among others, Amnesty International, "Israel/Gaza: *Operation Cast Lead*: 22 Days of Death and Destruction" (London: Amnesty International Publications, 2009); Amnesty International, "Failing Gaza: No Rebuilding, No Recovery, No More Excuses — A Report One Year After *Operation Cast Lead*" (London: Amnesty International Publications, 2009); John Dugard et al., "Report of the Independent Fact-Finding Committee on Gaza: No Safe Place" (Cairo: League of Arab States, Apr. 30, 2009); Richard Goldstone et al., "Human Rights in Palestine and Other Occupied Arab Territories: Report of the United Nations Fact-

more agonizing due to the fact that the people of Gaza were not allowed to leave there, Gaza itself being among the most dense-ly populated areas on the earth. This unrelenting, intentional, and indiscriminate massacre, conducted by one of the largest military powers in the world against a largely unarmed, civil-ian, refugee, and subject population, resulted in mass murder, rampant homelessness, devastation of Gaza's infrastructure, and destruction of the major institutions and workings of Palestin-ian daily life, including schools, universities, mosques, hospi-tals, and roads.[2] Opening the *Genealogy* had been the first break I had taken from non-stop news coverage of these bloody and horrific events — a diversion I felt compelled to undertake due to the demands of my professional life. The confluence of these two events, however — the situation of reading Nietzsche in the wake of the war on Gaza — confronted me, as if for the first time, with many of the difficulties with which I have struggled as a student of Nietzsche. In that moment I was transported back to the first time I had read the *Genealogy,* when I found myself stunned to encounter his bald advocacy of hierarchical domina-tion and merciless critique of those who object to it. Nietzsche's naming of the exponents of slave morality as the "oppressed" (*Gedrückten; Unterdrückten*[3]) — specifically in the context of his playful allegory of the lambs and birds of prey — itself told with the rhetorical intention of mocking all those who would

Finding Mission on the Gaza Conflict" (Geneva: UN Human Rights Council, Sep. 29, 2009); The Public Committee Against Torture in Israel, "No Second Thoughts: The Changes in the Israeli Defense Forces' Combat Doctrine in Light of *Operation Cast Lead*" (Jerusalem: The Public Committee Against Torture in Israel, Nov. 2009).

2   The devastation wrought by this war has not even remotely begun to be mitigated; see, for example, Amnesty International, "Israel/Gaza"; Amnesty International, "Failing Gaza."

3   Friedrich Nietzsche, *On the Genealogy of Morals*, trans. Walter Kaufmann (New York: Vintage, 1989), I §10, §13. German taken from Colli and Montin-ari. Also: *Twilight of the Idols*, in *The Portable Nietzsche,* trans. and ed. Walter Kaufmann (New York: Penguin, 1968); *Beyond Good and Evil*, trans. Walter Kaufmann (New York: Vintage, 1989); and *The Gay Science*, trans. Walter Kaufmann (New York: Vintage, 1974).

object to such "victimization" (as the eagles say, "we don't dislike them at all, these good little lambs; we even love them: nothing is more tasty than a tender lamb"⁴) — suggested to me that slaves and (other) oppressed people were simply the prey of other, naturally predatory, animals. Thus not only was victimization of the oppressed wholly unremarkable, but it was not even best understood as victimization; instead, their predation was better assimilated to one of the many, amoral workings of nature. This seemed to imply that oppression is inevitable and thus render anti-oppression politics (of which I was then an avid adherent) a resentful incarnation of slave morality, a moralization of otherwise natural (and thus unobjectionable) conditions, a political principle borne of envy, impotence, and revenge that sought to restrain and punish oppressors who could not do otherwise than oppress. Nauseated, I asked myself, could Nietzsche's critique of slave morality in the *Genealogy of Morals* be understood as justifying the brutality I was witnessing in Gaza?

Although today I am much less scandalized — even, indeed, rather persuaded — by Nietzsche's amoral reading of domination, I remain disturbed by the possibility that he may, indeed, provide justification for events like Israel's wars on Gaza: a possibility that is confronted only abstractly, if at all, in the secondary literature on Nietzsche, and never from any particular (explicitly avowed) political loyalty or concrete political event. While the classic studies of Nietzsche's political thinking include elaborate discussions and analyses of master and slave morality, they rarely, if ever, raise the important political implications of Nietzsche's contempt for slave morality or locate the consequences of this analysis in specific political events, movements, or policies.⁵ The major exception to this tendency is when Nietzsche's implication in the twentieth-century's fascist regimes and

---

4   Nietzsche, *On the Genealogy of Morals*, I §13.

5   See William Connolly, *Identity/Difference: Democratic Negotiations of Political Paradox* (Ithaca: Cornell University Press, 1991); Bruce Detwiler, *Nietzsche and the Politics of Aristocratic Radicalism* (Chicago: University of Chicago Press, 1990); Tracy Strong, *Friedrich Nietzsche and the Politics of Transfiguration* (Chicago: University of Illinois Press, 2000); Leslie Paul

imperial wars is under consideration.[6] Thus his critique has been considered either abstracted from specific political events or within a framework wherein Jewish people are the presumptive victims. One goal of this paper, then, is to disrupt both of these tendencies in the secondary literature on Nietzsche's philosophy.

To be clear, I have no interest in pacifying Nietzsche or appropriating him for my own twenty-first-century political sensibilities. Nor do I offer these reflections in a banal and self-congratulatory exercise in public hand-wringing. Furthermore, I am not asking if Nietzsche's philosophy is somehow compatible with morality, nor am I searching for some (version of) moral condemnation that Nietzsche might somewhere subtly authorize.[7] Rather, my inquiry concerns configurations of power: for Nietzsche, are they always just what they are, end of story? Does Nietzsche's critique of slave morality entail that we must affirm any and all expenditures of strength as such? While such questions may seem naïve or easily refutable, they are invited conclusions from his writing in general and from his discussion of slave morality in the *Genealogy* in particular. Dismissing them neither answers them nor resolves the dilemma raised by Nietzsche's awe-filled rhetoric of strength-worship, nor does it do the important work of taking seriously the "might makes right" assertion that, however many times it is "refuted," proves intractably to haunt not simply Nietzsche's philosophy, but also political theory, political science (witness "realism"), and politics in the "real world."[8] This paper is thus an attempt to determine, with

Thiele, *Friedrich Nietzsche and the Politics of the Soul: A Study of Heroic Individualism* (Princeton: Princeton University Press, 1990).

6   See essays in *Nietzsche: Godfather of Fascism? — On the Uses and Abuses of a Philosophy,* ed. Jacob Golomb and Robert Wistrich (Princeton: Princeton University Press, 2002).

7   See Philippa Foot, "Nietzsche's Immoralism," and Martha Nussbaum, "Pity and Mercy: Nietzsche's Stoicism," in *Nietzsche, Genealogy, Morality: Essays on Nietzsche's Genealogy of Morals,* ed. Richard Schacht (Berkeley: University of California Press, 1994).

8   As Nietzsche says, "It is certainly not the least charm of a theory that it is refutable; it is precisely thereby that it attracts subtler minds. It seems that

both a philosophical and political acuteness, what we can learn from Nietzsche (and, ultimately, what we cannot) about the war on Gaza, political warfare in general, and the viability of anti-oppression politics.

1. Strength and Superiority

Much turns on what Nietzsche means by "strength." Now, if "morality" constitutes the illegitimate subjectifying lie dreamed up by the weak to limit the strong and valorize the weak for being weak, then the *Genealogy* is incompatible with any condemnation of any expenditure of strength, no matter on what basis, and we have already reached the end of the argument. This is expressed most clearly in Nietzsche's famous analysis of his own allegory of the lambs and the birds of prey:

> To demand of strength that it should *not* express itself as strength, that it should *not* be a desire to overcome, a desire to throw down, a desire to become master, a thirst for enemies and resistances and triumphs, is just as absurd as to demand of weakness that it should express itself as strength.[9]

To refer to Israel's military assault on Gaza collectively as "war crimes," then, perpetuates the error that there is a "neutral substratum behind the strong man, which was *free* to express strength or not to do so" and indulges the "submerged, darkly glowering emotions of vengefulness and hatred" that seek to deploy this error in order "to make the bird of prey *accountable* for being a bird of prey."[10] Indeed, as Nietzsche observes elsewhere in the *Genealogy,* international tribunals in place of war are one of the symptoms of modernity's overall decline.[11]

the hundred-times-refuted theory of a 'free will' owes its persistence to this charm alone; again and again someone comes along who feels he is strong enough to refute it" (*Beyond Good and Evil,* §18).

9 Nietzsche, *On the Genealogy of Morals*, I §13.
10 Ibid.
11 Ibid., III §25.

Nietzsche is not the first to advance such a critique; it has haunted political theory since Plato. In the *Gorgias,* for example, Callicles accuses Socrates of slavishness and argues that laws were invented by weak people who knew they would lose out if the strong were left to their own devices. Unwilling to simply accept and receive their due — little to nothing — the weak devised laws, customs, and social mores in order to police and limit the few, superior, powerful ones who would otherwise get the "more" from life Callicles argues they deserve.[12] In typical fashion, Socrates inquires as to what exactly Callicles means by this word "superior." Does he mean stronger? For, Socrates observes, a handful of Callicles' slaves are stronger than he. Is Callicles honestly suggesting that because his slaves are stronger than him, they are therefore superior to him? Immediately relenting in the face of this objection, Callicles concedes that "strength" and "superiority" must be distinct.[13]

Nietzsche raises a similar such objection in the *Genealogy,* albeit not in his own voice. An unspecified interlocutor, named only as a "free spirit" by Nietzsche, offers the following rebuttal to Nietzsche's complaints about the triumph of the slave revolt in morality:

But why are you talking about "nobler" ideals? Let us stick to the facts: "the people" have won — or "the slaves" or "the mob" or "the herd" or whatever you like to call them. If this has happened through the Jews, very well!: in that case, no people ever had a more world-historic mission. One may conceive of this victory as at the same time a blood-poisoning (it has mixed the races together); I shan't contradict; but this intoxication has undoubtedly been *successful.*[14]

In other words, our "free spirit" asks, on what grounds can Nietzsche object to the triumph of the slave revolt in morality when it

12 Plato, *Gorgias,* trans. Donald Zeyl (Indianapolis: Hackett, 1986), 483c–484a.
13 Ibid., 498a–d.
14 Nietzsche, *On the Genealogy of Morals,* I §9.

has, in the most obvious and undeniable of ways, triumphed?[15] Is this not a sign of its overwhelming strength, and, thus, to be celebrated?

That the individual raising this objection is someone either contemptuously or at least skeptically referred to by Nietzsche as a "free spirit" suggests that he does not regard this objection highly. Just as the likely physical triumph of Callicles' slaves does not convince him of their actual superiority, so too does the victoriousness of the Jewish slave revolt not convince Nietzsche of its superiority. For while the Jewish slave revolt has been victorious — one that has "hitherto triumphed again and again over all other ideals, over all *nobler* ideals"[16] — Nietzsche still insists it is slavish or base, "an act of the *most spiritual revenge.*"[17] Nietzsche offers a similar disparagement of the triumph of the weak in *Twilight of the Idols,* criticizing Darwin for overlooking one of the most fundamental facts of modern life: it is precisely not the strong who triumph, but rather "the weak," who "prevail over the strong again and again, for they are the great majority — and they are also more *intelligent.* Darwin forgot the spirit (that is English!); *the weak have more spirit* [*Geist*]."[18]

Despite Nietzsche's complaints, then, what must be acknowledged is that the weak clearly are strong in some sense, if they triumph again and again. Indeed, according to Nietzsche himself, the Jews have set the stage of world history through the triumph of their slave revolt and the weak will continue to prevail on the basis of their "spirit" or "intelligence." But on what basis, then, can Nietzsche refer to the weak as weak? Either he cannot do this at all, or he must subtly elide the distinction between

15 The consignment of this triumph to "the Jews" in this passage reflects the speaker's inattentiveness to Nietzsche's remarks in the prior two aphorisms, wherein he claims that the Jewish inversion of values may have begun the slave revolt in morality but was responsible for neither its completion nor success (for these, Christianity is to blame; see *On the Genealogy of Morals* I §8–9).

16 Nietzsche, *On the Genealogy of Morals*, I §9.

17 Ibid., I §7.

18 Nietzsche, *Twilight of the Idols,* "Skirmishes of an Untimely Man," §14, entitled "Anti-Darwin."

"weak" and "slavish," the latter of which is opposed to nobility or mastery, not strength. Indeed, for Nietzsche, it is not the weakness of the weak that is contemptible but in fact their strength, which in this case functions as the name of whatever it is that allows them to triumph. Nietzsche acknowledges this distinction by qualifying the character of the strength of the weak as "spiritual," which he explicates as "care, patience, cunning, simulation, great self control," and "mimicry."[19] However, the fact that spiritual strength can triumph over physical strength leaves us with the question of what power physical strength in fact possesses if it can be vanquished by the ostensibly non-physical power of spiritual strength, and moreover raises the question once again as to why spiritual strength is contemptible if it triumphs repeatedly. As Nietzsche undermines any easy or commonsense conflation of "spirit" with mind or strength with body, the question becomes: what, in fact, does Nietzsche object to in the exercise of "strength" by the weak?

These questions are made even more confusing in the *Anti-Darwin* aphorism when Nietzsche says, "One must need spirit in order to acquire spirit; one loses it when one no longer needs it. Whoever has strength dispenses with the spirit ('Let it go!' they think in Germany today; 'the Reich must still remain to us')." While it may be the case that "whoever has strength dispenses with the spirit," Nietzsche's appending a mocking counterexample to this sentence throws that schema into doubt, insofar as the Reich's triumph — despite its indisputable strength — represents no noble victory for Nietzsche but instead the ascendance of *kleine Politik*.[20] In fact, the indisputable, physical strength of these politically victorious forces (what political scientists straight-facedly refer to as "hard power") is nevertheless not noble in Nietzsche's book, regardless of its domination *and* dispensation with the spirit. It is rather an ignoble triumph, one that (as we well know from his other writings) Nietzsche holds in contempt.

19 Nietzsche, *Twilight of the Idols,* "Skirmishes of an Untimely Man," §14.
20 Ibid., §37; Id., *The Gay Science,* §337.

Furthermore, while Nietzsche disparages the "spirit" or "spiritual" character of the strength of slavish types, he praises spiritualization itself in other places. In part, he does so because spiritualization is one of the last resorts available to modern men for their survival and flourishing in the face of modernity's demise.[21] That spiritualization "represents a great triumph over Christianity," signaling an opportunity for growth and victoriousness where, Nietzsche states, "we, we immoralists and Antichristians, find our advantage in this, that the church exists."[22] Perhaps performing his own critique that "spiritualization" is the only resource remaining to cope with a suffocating modernity, Nietzsche here credits Christianity with giving him the opportunity for enmity, the condition of his "advantage." Going even further, Nietzsche later suggests that

> The most spiritual human beings, if we assume that they are the most courageous, also experience by far the most painful tragedies: but just for that reason they honor life because it pits its greatest opposition against them.[23]

Coupled with Nietzsche's bravado-laden apologia for Christianity's existence in the first passage, this surprising defense of the most spiritual human beings as the most courageous types and the honorers of life (knowing as we do that priests are among the most "spiritual" types) suggests either that the ostensibly noble can themselves manifest the characteristics of "spirit" that Nietzsche elsewhere criticizes in relationship to the Jews and Darwin, or else that Nietzsche has ambivalent feelings about spirituality itself — namely, it can be either base or noble.[24]

21 See Daniel Conway, *Nietzsche's Dangerous Game: Philosophy in the Twilight of the Idols* (Cambridge: Cambridge University Press, 1997).

22 Nietzsche, *Twilight of the Idols,* "Skirmishes of an Untimely Man," §3.

23 Ibid., §17.

24 See, for instance, *On the Genealogy of Morals* II §6, wherein he notes that the spiritualization of cruelty "in a significant sense" constitutes the history of higher culture, and ibid., III §8, wherein he notes that "all animal being

Just as "spiritualization" cannot constitute an unconditional demarcation of weakness in Nietzsche's vocabulary, other aspects of weak people or behaviors Nietzsche condemns are nevertheless also displayed by the strong or else are appropriable by them for noble purposes. For example, slave morality is criticized for being fundamentally resentful and essentially reactive, rather than affirmative, active, and self-determining. Yet both are qualities that the nobility may also exhibit. So, first, Nietzsche acknowledges that *ressentiment* — that glowering lust for revenge that poisons all morality and may be the best candidate for what is definitively slavish in Nietzsche's view — occurs in masterful types. Of course, he hastens to note that it appears much less frequently than among slavish types, noting conditionally that "[r]*essentiment* itself, if it should appear in the noble man, consummates and exhausts itself in an immediate reaction, and therefore does not *poison*."[25] But the point is that *ressentiment* is not necessarily the monopoly of slaves. As for reactivity, that other hallmark of slavishness, Nietzsche importantly if casually observes that the creativity of slave morality emerges from the *ressentiment* of "natures that are denied the *true* [*eigentliche*] reaction, that of deeds, and compensate themselves with an imaginary revenge."[26] Here Nietzsche suggests that "deeds" — that province of the masters — may be understood as "true" reactions, thereby offhandedly acknowledging that no deed could be purely active, undetermined by any pre-existing condition or force; every action is always also reaction. If this is the case, then reactivity is not the sole province of slaves, but rather the very condition of activity itself.

This leaves us with Nietzsche offering a critique of the weak that cannot claim "weakness" to be either objectionable in itself or the definitive mark of slavishness. Although Nietzsche frequently elides the binary opposition of "strength" and "weak-

becomes more spiritual" in "good air; thin, clear, open, dry, like the air of the heights."

25 Nietzsche, *On the Genealogy of Morals,* I §10. Emphasis added.
26 Ibid. Emphasis added.

ness" with the binaries of both "master" and "slave" and "noble" and "base," it is the latter set of categories that must be primary for him, for nothing else reconciles his shifting evaluations of spiritualization, resentment, and reactivity. While Nietzsche's discussion of slave morality retains both its binary and hierarchical character, the classification he is discussing — whatever names one wants to use for it — is a consistent hierarchy of neither simply physical nor simply political power. In short, Nietzsche condemns slaves for something other than weakness and praises strength for something other than its ability to triumph.

2. Strength and Psychology

The set of qualities Nietzsche rejects as ignoble and praises as masterful are psychological in character. Master morality is better read as a paradigm of healthy psychic functioning, a kind of ethical practice of the self in relationship to itself, other(s), and activity. Slave morality, by contrast, emblematizes correlative psychic dysfunction.[27] To get at these observations, a brief examination of master and slave moralities is in order.

27 As Tracy Strong notes, it is not power that is at stake in determining who is a master and who a slave: "What counts, in both cases, is the particular relationship between one's sense of self and one's sense of others" (*Friedrich Nietzsche and the Politics of Transfiguration* [Chicago: University of Illinois Press, 2000], 239). Nietzsche repeatedly claims himself to be a psychologist; that he is so particularly in the *Genealogy* has been persuasively argued by Ken Gemes: "The point of [Nietzsche's] historical narratives is ultimately to make us aware of certain psychological types and their possible relations"; "[i]n reading Nietzsche we should follow the implied advice of looking for psychological rather than philosophical or historical insights" ("*We Remain of Necessity Strangers to Ourselves*: The Key Message of Nietzsche's *Genealogy*," in *Nietzsche's Genealogy of Morals: Critical Essays,* ed. Christa Davis Acampora [Lanham: Rowman & Littlefield, 2006], 207–8). Nietzsche's psychology seems most associated with inquiry regarding the instincts (in a proto-Freudian, depth-psychological sense) and a mocking deconstruction of the soul/subject, free will, and consciousness. While "spiritualization" sometimes names a particular psychological mechanism or process in Nietzsche (e.g., sublimation), his otherwise wide-ranging references to "spirit" (as mentioned in the previous section) seem to cover a much broader terrain than the more narrowly psychological, a tempting conflation I

As noted previously, in §10 of the first essay of the *Genealogy* Nietzsche claims that the slave revolt in morality is the by-product of persons or groups who have somehow been prevented from acting and must therefore resort to other means in order to live and flourish. Reactive from the outset, then, Nietzsche notes that slave morality always requires "a hostile external world" in order to exist at all; "its action is fundamentally reaction." This reactivity is fundamentally negative: slave morality says "no" to that hostile external world, to what thwarts its own activity and expenditure. The selfhood of the slavish type, then, comes to exist only via reference to an imposed external (set of) force(s) and can only understand and affirm itself through negation: "[S]lave morality from the outset says No to what is 'outside,' what is 'different,' what is 'not itself.'" Nietzsche calls this negative reactivity *ressentiment*; its mightiest production and primary weapon is the concept of evil: "[P]icture 'the enemy' as the man of *ressentiment* conceives him — and here precisely is his deed, his creation: he has conceived 'the evil enemy,' 'the Evil One,'" and this in fact is his basic concept, from which he then evolves, as an afterthought and pendant, a "'good one' — himself!" "Evil" is used to limit, judge, and punish those deemed to have brought about the original imposition that has so bitterly limited the activity of the weaker. This production of evil is accomplished via the fabrication of the responsible subject, the notion of an actor with the freedom and ability to do otherwise, and who thus may be held accountable for his deeds. Incapable of acting themselves, impotent to strike back at their aggressors, and condemning their imposition as the very definition of evil, slavish types valorize their own weakness and produce the unwieldy apparatus responsible-subject/moral-opprobrium/political-punishment to restrain the activity of the strong. Nietzsche is clear about the

think we must refuse. On the issues of psychology, instincts, and "the soul," see the first chapter of my monograph, *Nietzsche's Revolution: Decadence, Politics, and Sexuality* (New York: Palgrave, 2009), as well as Jacob Golomb, Weaver Santaniello, and Ronald Lehrer, eds., *Nietzsche and Depth Psychology* (Albany: SUNY Press, 1999).

effectiveness of this weapon,[28] and equally clear that it is not a weapon the strong deserve to have wielded against them. For imposition is the character of life itself. It is erroneous to think such fatality comes at one's own expense or vengefully demand that life be otherwise. Rather, "to be incapable of taking one's enemies, one's accidents, even one's misdeeds seriously for very long — that is the sign of strong, full natures in whom there is an excess of power to form, to mold, to recuperate and to forget."[29]

Noble morality, by contrast, does not emerge as the result of any necessary relationship to any other person or set of forces.[30] Instead, noble morality is cast by Nietzsche as the anti- or non-morality; it is a kind of disposition or relationship with the self that might be characterized as unselfconscious self-affirmation: "the 'well-born' *felt* themselves to be the 'happy'; they did not have to establish their happiness artificially by examining their enemies, or to persuade themselves, *deceive* themselves, that they were happy (as all men of *ressentiment* are in the habit of doing)."[31] Although slave morality, too, constitutes a kind of relationship with the self, it is nevertheless also clearly a morality in its production of the concept of "evil." But noble morality has no notion of evil (only "bad"-ness, which functions simply as the designation for whatever is not-me) and cannot even exactly be construed as a relation with the self insofar as, as we have seen, the self comes into existence, at a minimum, via reference to some competing or disparate set of others that are not oneself. Thus a masterful type becomes aware of himself[32] as a

---

28 Nietzsche, *On the Genealogy of Morals,* I §7–8.

29 Ibid., I §10.

30 Indeed, it does not seem to emerge at all, being presented by Nietzsche in *On the Genealogy of Morals* I as some sort of originary state of the healthy, more beastly version of human being. Nietzsche also encourages us to believe that slave morality emerges as a reaction to noble morality or the behavior of the nobles, a relationship that is neither necessary nor explicitly established by him (more on this in Section 3).

31 Nietzsche, *On the Genealogy of Morals,* I §10.

32 I use male pronouns because I think this is clearly to whom Nietzsche is referring. For justification, see my "Note on Citations" as well as Chapters 4–5 in *Nietzsche's Revolution.*

self-affirmer only through unpredictable and insignificant encounters with other people, forces, or things that are not himself. These phenomena are designated as "bad," which carries
no moral weight and is better thought of as empirically descriptive. Contrary to the slavish type, the masterful person regards
such encounters with foreign elements as at best unremarkable,
at worst, a negative confrontation so fleeting or light that it is
quickly forgotten or otherwise dispensed with:

> [The noble mode of valuation] acts and grows spontaneously,
> it seeks its opposite only so as to affirm itself more gratefully
> and triumphantly — its negative concept "low," "common,"
> "bad" is only a subsequently-invented pale, contrasting im-
> age in relation to its positive basic concept — filled with life
> and passion through and through — "we noble ones, we
> good, beautiful, happy ones!" When the noble mode of valu-
> ation blunders and sins against reality, it does so in respect
> to the sphere with which it is not sufficiently familiar, against
> a real knowledge of which it has indeed inflexibly guarded
> itself: in some circumstances it misunderstands the sphere
> it despises, that of the common man, of the lower orders; on
> the other hand, one should remember that, even supposing
> that the affect of contempt, of looking down from a supe-
> rior height, *falsifies* the image of that which it despises, it will
> at any rate still be a much less serious falsification than that
> perpetrated on its opponent — in *effigie* of course — by the
> submerged hatred, the vengefulness of the impotent. There
> is indeed too much carelessness, too much taking lightly, too
> much looking away and impatience involved in contempt,
> even too much joyfulness, for it to be able to transform its
> object into a real caricature and monster.[33]

Now, recalling that Nietzsche condemns slaves for something
other than weakness and praises strength for something other
than its ability to triumph, it becomes clear from this discus-

33 Nietzsche, *On the Genealogy of Morals,* I §10.

sion of master and slave morality that "strength" and "weakness" name neither physical prowess nor "spiritual" cunning but rather a set of qualities or characteristics that are better described as ethical dispositions, the content of which is twofold: 1) the order (first or second) and character (affirmative or deceptive) of self-recognition, and 2) the resulting activity in response to this self-recognition (nothing at all or revenge). So the masterful type, for instance, recognizes himself first and the other second, if at all. Indeed, "recognition" is not really the correct word here, for the masterful type is self-affirmative without necessary reference to any other being or standard of affirmation. He is first insofar as he is good, and he is good insofar as he is first. The two entail and are inextricable from one another, leaving any other person, force, or thing secondary if not irrelevant, and rendering the "first" of this formulation an erroneous, retrospective attribution.

While the masterful type is largely indifferent to the existence of others, the slavish type, by contrast, takes his existence to be founded upon and in reaction to the existence of that other or those others to whom he responds in negation and with hostility:

> This, then, is quite the contrary of what the noble man does, who conceives the basic concept "good" in advance and spontaneously out of himself and only then creates for himself an idea of "bad"! This "bad" of noble origin and that "evil" out of the cauldron of unsatisfied hatred — the former an after-production, a side-issue, a contrasting shade, the latter on the contrary an original thing, the beginning, the distinctive *deed* in the conception of slave morality — how different these words "bad" and "evil" are, although they are both apparently the opposite of the same concept "good."[34]

Therefore, these two types have very different behavioral responses to their encounter with an/other: the masterful type is

34 Ibid., I §11.

indifferent — having no reaction at all — or else is harmlessly destructive, seeking "blindly" to remove obstacles to his own existence and flourishing, which he thoughtlessly calls "bad."[35] The slavish type, by contrast, because of his derivative existence, resorts to vengefulness and resentment, for the alleged hostility experienced by the slavish type himself. Destruction and revenge, then, respectively constitute the distinctive forms of activity for the masterful and slavish type.[36]

Understanding master and slave morality from this psychological perspective makes clear what Nietzsche condemns about "weakness" and what he finds admirable about "strength." As we know, victoriousness is an insufficient characterization of strength. Instead, what *Essay* I of the *Genealogy* reveals is that the "strong" — i.e., masterful — type is strong because he affirms his own existence for no other reason than that existence itself — i.e., for no reason at all. Physicality — despite Nietzsche's rhapsodizing of its importance — is simply not what is at stake here. The strong man is affirming, honest, and unselfconsciously entitled, but physical prowess or victoriousness is neither what is distinctive about him nor plays a significant role in determining the shamefulness of his defeat. Similarly, Nietzsche critiques the "weak" because they are slavish, a consideration to which physical qualities are immaterial. Slavish types understand themselves only residually, as afterthoughts, as secondary to a

---

35 The masterful type's destructiveness is "harmless" from a perspective that is, as Nietzsche might say, beyond good and evil — outside the demands of slave morality that measures any activity's value by its effect on the weak or the many. It may be "destructive," however, precisely from the perspective of the weak or the many. Thus, reading master morality as an ethical disposition accurately describes not simply Nietzsche's fictitious prehistorical humans, but potentially also Wall Street CEOs, colleagues who refuse departmental service, or unreliable parents more interested in their own affairs than those of their children.

36 This is an approach that de-privileges "active" and "reactive" as central categories of analysis in Nietzsche's philosophy, a conclusion that follows in part from Nietzsche's important qualification of activity as "true" reaction, discussed above; cf. Gilles Deleuze, *Nietzsche and Philosophy,* trans. Hugh Tomlinson (New York: Athlone Press, 1983).

(set of) force(s) deemed primary and domineering, if not out-right hostile and oppressive. They wage war on these forces, condemning them for their "injustice," seeking to triumph over them by criminalizing their activity, without which they could not exist and against which they have come to understand themselves, even if only as a negation. Ironically, then, slaves need the external phenomena from which they claim to suffer, for without these constraints they themselves are nothing.[37] Slave morality, then, despite its critical façade, is a deeply conservative and risk-averse comportment. As Nietzsche notes, it is the instinct of self-preservation at work, the "prudence of the lowest order which even insects possess (posing as dead, when in great danger, so as not to do 'too much')."[38] The indefinite endeavor of the slaves is simultaneously to preserve the external world and demonize it, thereby maintaining themselves securely intact. As is obvious, this disposition is quite opposed to the indifferent expenditure of the masterful type, who confronts obstacles if and as they arise with the energy, awareness, and morality of

37 Wendy Brown offers a clear application of this understanding of slave mo-rality to a critique of left-leaning identity-politics in her "Wounded Attach-ments," in *States of Injury: Power and Freedom in Late Modernity* (Princeton: Princeton University Press, 1995), 52–76. However, Brown's argument paved the way for a series of critiques of feminism as a version of slave morality which, while compelling in their own right, nevertheless seem to have set an unspoken precedent that only progressive movements — or only femi-nism? — should be subjected to this particular analysis, a critique recently reincarnated in Janet Halley's *Split Decisions: How and Why to Take a Break from Feminism* (Princeton: Princeton University Press, 2008), 354–63; also see Wendy Brown, "Post-modern Exposures, Feminist Hesitations," in *States of Injury,* 30–51; Daniel Conway, "*Das Weib an Sich*: The Slave Revolt in Epistemology," in *Feminist Interpretations of Nietzsche,* ed. Kelly Oliver and Marilyn Pearsall (University Park: Pennsylvania State University Press, 1998); Rebecca Stringer, "*Nietzschean Breed*: Feminism, Victimology and Ressentiment," in *Why Nietzsche Still?: Reflections on Drama, Culture and Politics,* ed. Alan Schrift (Berkeley: University of California Press, 2000); and Marion Tapper, "Ressentiment and Power: Some Reflections on Femi-nist Practices," in *Nietzsche, Feminism and Political Theory,* ed. Paul Patton (New York: Routledge, 1993). The present paper is one attempt to disrupt this puzzling tendency in political theory scholarship.
38 Nietzsche, *On the Genealogy of Morals,* I §13.

any other force of nature — the rain, a gust of wind, the crashing of waves onto the shore.

3. Strength, Slavishness, and the War on Gaza

The reason the physical and the psychological versions of master and slave morality are so difficult to disentangle is due, in part, to Nietzsche's own incessant, pounding rhetoric of physical domination. But there is another difficulty: Nietzsche tends to suggest that master and slave morality arise in a historical, dialectical relationship with one another, such that the "others" whom the master encounters are necessarily slaves while the "others" so vehemently hated and stigmatized by the slaves are necessarily the masters, who have imposed the constraints against which the slaves protest. Yet while Nietzsche clearly presents things as developing this way, there is certainly no necessity that they do so. First, it is clear according to the psychological framework Nietzsche offers that the master sees virtually all external phenomena, insofar as they are not-himself, as that which is "lower" or not to be affirmed — regardless of whether that not-himself is "strong" or "weak." Indeed, it is difficult to imagine the masterful type even taking the time to determine the relative nobility or slavishness of the external, not-me phenomena he encounters. This is especially so when we remember that these phenomena need not be limited to other humans: the masterful type will experience everything from an avalanche to other people to the mall being closed as a kind of foreign, not-me obstacle in his path, one perhaps worth reckoning with but not otherwise worthy of extended reflection or rancor (worthy of ridicule, perhaps, but only if he happens to bother with it for that long).[39]

---

39 Thus there is also no necessity that a masterful type be an oppressor or someone with a penchant for domination. As Aaron Ridley observes, "Whether life affirmers are bound also to be murdering, rapacious, pyromaniacal torturers, however, is an entirely separate question (i.e. not one settled either way by the observation that Nietzsche prefers the original nobles, unattractive habits notwithstanding [...]) [...] You could say yes to life, that

Similarly, it is simply not the case that the "hostile external world" to which the slave objects and against which he reacts is necessarily the existence, imposition, or violence of the nobility. There are two points here: first, as is the case with the masters' not-me phenomena, there is no reason to suppose that the external impositions encountered by the slave are necessarily other humans. Second, and consequently, just because the slave perceives the external world — whether other humans or an avalanche or the mall being closed — *as* hostile does not mean this external world actually *is* hostile. Indeed, this act of projection is an essential aspect of the slave's slavishness. As Nietzsche notes,

> This inversion of the value-positing eye — this need to direct one's view outward instead of back to oneself — is of the essence of *ressentiment*: in order to exist, slave morality always first needs a hostile external world; it needs, physiologically speaking, external stimuli in order to act at all — its action is fundamentally reaction.[40]

Looking at this important sentence more closely, I would argue that there is quite a bit of difference between needing "external stimuli" — Nietzsche's *physiological* explanation of slavishness — and needing a "hostile external world" — Nietzsche's *psychological* explanation of slavishness. Given the overall dishonesty of slavish types,[41] it seems reasonable to conclude that the "hostility" of these external stimuli are not intrinsic to the phenomena themselves. A slavish type understands and experiences himself as under siege — but this is a fact about the slave, not the external world, much less the masterful type. Even if the slave *were* under siege, and by the master no less, the slave would still not be under siege in the willful or systematic sense associated with the word "oppression."

is, without being then obliged by any logical consideration to go and burn something down" (*Nietzsche's Conscience: Six Character-Studies from the Genealogy* [Ithaca: Cornell University Press, 1998], 129).

40 Nietzsche, *On the Genealogy of Morals,* I §10.
41 See, for instance, ibid., §10, §11, §14.

Nietzsche thus rhetorically conflates categories he analytical-ly distinguishes.[42] Although he seems an unequivocal advocate of strength, which seems uncontroversially to be the domain of the physically superior, domineering, and, let us acknowledge it, supremely *manly* man, there are also significant problems with taking Nietzsche at his word on these issues. So, to return to the question asked at the outset of this paper: are all expenditures of strength justifiable for Nietzsche as, simply, expenditures of strength? I think the answer to this question is no. It is possi-ble to condemn certain expressions of strength or triumphs of power while nevertheless endorsing Nietzsche's critique of slav-ishness, first, because the categories of master and slave do not correspond to obvious categories of strong and weak, and sec-ond, because Nietzsche's critique of slave morality is not, in fact, a critique of condemnations of strength *per se*. Slave morality is problematic for Nietzsche insofar as what is slavish is whatever understands itself as derivative, and subsequently seeks retribu-tion against the phenomena it believes itself to be derivative *of,* thereby preserving the antagonistic relationship in a defensive and reactionary attempt at preserving itself. Thus one can clear-ly condemn particular expenditures of strength insofar as they are slavish in this way, and condemnations of strength *per se* are not themselves slavish. Third, the victimization against which slaves identify themselves is in no way necessarily committed by the masterful or "strong." Because these categories have been adequately disentangled and their actual referents established, it becomes clear that those who are victimized are not natural vic-

---

42 Why he would do so is itself a psychological question that, while not consid-
    ered here, is crucial to any interpretation of Nietzsche that takes the form of
    his philosophy as seriously as its content (Daniel Conway's *Nietzsche's Dan-
    gerous Game* is instructive on this question; also see my own *Nietzsche's Rev-
    olution*). As Ridley notes, Nietzsche's binary categorizations in the *Genealogy*
    seem as though they function as "navigational aids" when "[i]n truth, they
    are what need to be navigated […]. To expect, in light of this, that Nietzsche's
    dichotomous pairs should function as solid path markers is to expect quite
    the wrong sort of thing. Instead, one should expect that good/bad, slave/no-
    ble, and so on would mark out fields of tension" or even "treacherous zones"
    (*Nietzsche's Conscience,* 12).

tims any more than those perpetrating the victimization cannot do otherwise than undertake it. Indeed, what Nietzsche laments in the triumph of the slave revolt in morality is the triumph of derivative, conservative, self-preservative vengefulness and the loss of mastery: honest, unselfconscious, self-affirmative activity. There is no reason to presume that those with political power are strong in this particular, psychological way, or that those who suffer from impositions of political domination are weak in this particular, psychological way, either.

In the case of the recent war on Gaza, then, I would argue that Nietzsche's categories of master and slave suggest that this particular war was in fact an exercise in slavishness, not mastery. The gratuitous and gruesome disproportion of Israel's aggression was not the indifferent destruction of a self-affirming power merely eliminating obstacles to its existence. It was instead a revenge that mistook the existence — and paltry "imposition" — of others as the source of its identity and suffering.[43] Israel's actions exemplify slavishness insofar as the justification of this war relied on a wildly inaccurate portrayal of Israeli society as a nation precariously under siege by forces that, if not immobilized, would have brought about the destruction of the state itself. This political narrative is consonant with Israel's larger justification of its existence — as the safe refuge of a people perpetually besieged by a historically variable but ever-present genocidal hatred. Without this desperately needed hostile external world, the reason for Israel's existence and the content of its national identity would evaporate.[44] This narrative of Is-

43 I recognize the difficulties involved in "psychologizing" national identities or cultures. Nevertheless, I follow Judith Butler when she claims that "when we are speaking about 'the subject' we are not always speaking about an individual: we are speaking about a model for agency and intelligibility, one that is very often based on notions of sovereign power" (*Precarious Life: The Powers of Mourning and Violence* [London: Verso, 2004], 45).

44 As President Obama has put it, "America's strong bonds with Israel are well known. This bond is unbreakable. It is based upon cultural and historical ties, and the recognition that the aspiration for a Jewish homeland is rooted in a tragic history that cannot be denied" ("Text: Obama's Speech in Cairo," *The New York Times,* June 4, 2009). As Melanie Kaye-Kantrowitz puts it,

rael's existence is long-standing: it was essential to its historical founding and continues to be used to defend Israel's otherwise indefensible activities — such as, in this case, *Operation Cast Lead* — to this day.[45] The endurance of this narrative, however, does not make it any the more true.[46] Like all adherents of slave morality, then, Israel will continue to constitute itself in relation to an ever-shifting constellation of hostile enemies,[47] a dysfunc-

"images of male/state power are complicated inside Israel (as in Jewish communities around the world) by the excruciating history of Holocaust, manipulated to arouse shame and fear, and to blur the distinction between a period of European Jewish powerlessness, and a current reality of an extremely powerful Israeli military, complete with nuclear weapons. The Israeli/Jew is seen one minute as a sabra (native of Israel) paratrooper" ("Feminist Organizing in Israel," in *Feminism and War: Confronting US Imperialism,* ed. Robin Riley, Chandra Talpade Mohanty, and Minnie Bruce Pratt [London: Zed Books, 2008]).

45 See Hannah Arendt, *Eichmann in Jerusalem: A Report on the Banality of Evil* (New York: Penguin 1991), 10, and Idith Zertal, *Israel's Holocaust and the Politics of Nationhood* (New York: Cambridge University Press, 2005), Chapter 5.

46 As Rashid Khalidi puts it in a recent interview with the Israeli newspaper *Ha'aretz,* "Israel is always going to be stronger than everyone else [in the region] because of its nuclear arsenal, because of its conventional edge, because of its technological edge, because of its links to the United States and I can go on and on and on. The idea that Israel is under any existential danger [from Iran] is fantasy. Is that deeply implanted in many Israelis's minds because of Jewish history? Yes. Is that an irrational fear? Yes. We can talk psychology, but we're talking nuclear capabilities, actual intentions, the ideological orientation of this regime, who actually controls things — those are factual matters." Chemi Shalev, "Full Transcript of Interview With Palestinian Professor Rashid Khalidi," Dec. 5, 2011, http://www.Haaretz.com/news/middle-east/full-transcript-of-interview-with-palestinian-professor-rashidkhalidi-1.399632.

47 On Hamas as the latest incarnation of Nazism, see this production by *The David Horowitz Freedom Center,* disseminated widely during the 2008–9 Gaza massacre, which encapsulates this particular Zionist discourse of victimization, advancing the racist claim that "Arabs" irrationally hate Jewish people and seek to destroy Israel primarily for that reason: http://fun.mivza-kon.co.il/flash/video/2664/2664.html (subsequently reposted onto YouTube at http://www.youtube.com/watch?v= f81j5Zk-GSA). On Iran as the newest Nazi threat, see, for example, Natasha Mozgovaya, "Peres to Obama: No Choice But to Compare Iran to Nazis," *Ha'aretz,* May 5, 2009, http://www.haaretz.com/hasen/spages/1083222.html (cf. Zertal, *Israel's Holocaust and*

tional and tragic state of affairs that chillingly suggests that wars of the kind we recently witnessed will by no means remain either exceptional or rare.

the Politics of Nationhood on Israel's "Nazification" of Arabs — e.g., 63, and of "the enemy" in general — e.g., 174).

07

Nietzsche's *Amor Fati:*
Wishing and Willing in a *Cybernetic Circuit*

Nicola Masciandaro

NWW.IV, April 13, 2013

> *There is no sanity* [sanitas] *in anyone*
> *who is displeased with your creation.*
> — Augustine, *Confessions*[1]

> *We make doors and windows for a room;*
> *but it is these empty spaces that make the room livable.*
> — Lao Tzu, *Tao Teh Ching*[2]

This paper is commentary on *The Gay Science* §276 in light of the cybernetic.[3] The natural connection between the cybernetic and Nietzsche's *amor fati* is evident in their intersection within the principle of interface as the site of steering or helmsmanship (*kubernēsis*). Nietzsche names this love under the double sign of *Januarius* — at once the two-faced god of beginnings/doorways/

1   Augustine, *Confessions,* 2nd ed., trans. F.J. Sheed (Indianapolis: Hackett, 2006), 7.14.20. Translation modified.
2   Lao Tzu, *Tao Teh Ching,* trans. John C.H. Wu (New York: St. John's University Press, 1961), 11.
3   Friedrich Nietzsche, *The Gay Science: With a Prelude in German Rhymes and an Appendix of Songs,* ed. Bernard Williams, trans. Josefine Nauckhoff (Cambridge: Cambridge University Press, 2001).

gates and the saint whose annually liquefying blood signals the miracle of spiritual renewal — and installs it as a navigational protocol in the form of a new year's resolution: "Let that be my love from now on!" *Amor fati,* I will affirm, is the protocol for navigating interface itself, a *pure cybernetic law* that steers steering *per se* around the radically immanent negative interfacial pole of looking away: "Let *looking away* be my only negation!" Love of fate, the positive formulation of not worrying, is a prosthetic intrinsically necessary for manipulating the inoperability of interface, its being "a medium that does not mediate."[4] Far from representing an immaterial or merely subjective affect, *amor fati* enjoys a terrifying invisible positive traction and inescapable occult influence upon all interfaces. Why? Because its own inoperativity, the workless work of "the thought [which] shall be the reason, warrant, and sweetness of the rest of my life," is nothing less than *the true will of the cybernetic sign* — namely, that for which "the internal, coded level can only be fully experienced by way of the external, expressive level [...] [and] what goes on at the external level can be fully understood only in light of the internal."[5] Like a magic non-medium at play between the solid of being and the liquid of thought, love of fate realizes the cybernetic nature of life itself, its weird double intrinsicity or "unique dual materiality,"[6] and is thus the singular way to "to 'politicize' the 'natural sweetness' of *zoē*" and realize the "politics [...] already contained in *zoē* as its most precious center."[7] Neither inaction nor action, *amor fati* is the ground of the authenticity of both, preserving the good against all perversions of justification. A supremely proper and scientific form of self-control, precisely because it requires no self at all, love of fate is an infinitely powerful protocol that one never need worry about, a perfectly implementable and unprogrammable rule whose ful-

4   Alexander R. Galloway, *The Interface Effect* (London: Polity Press, 2012), 52.
5   Espen J. Aarseth, *Cybertext: Perspectives on Ergodic Literature* (Baltimore, MD: Johns Hopkins University Press, 1997), 40.
6   Ibid.
7   Giorgio Agamben, *Homo Sacer: Sovereign Power and Bare Life,* trans. Daniel Heller-Roazen (Stanford, CA: Stanford University Press, 1998), 11.

fillment passes freely within and without the imprisoning walls of false power, above all the narrow circle of demands upon reality that maintains the world, individually and collectively, as not paradise. *Amor fati*'s cybernetic truth is inarguable and unassailable. All objection to it is direct demonstration of the sheer insanity and psychic sickness of doing otherwise: your inane insistence on being something that cannot not fret, worry, fear.

I. *For the New Year.*

The chronic newness of the calendar year is null and void without the affirmation of ontological newness. The year is not new unless there is something new *for* it and something new that it is *for*. This newness is provided through the topology of the wish which, in fulfillment of the polysemy of the preposition *zum,* traces the shape of the heart: interface of soul and body, thought and being — at once the place from which wishes spring and the place where one is oneself. "My heart," expertly glossed by Augustine as "*ubi ego sum quicumque sum* [where I am whoever or whatever I am],"[8] is exactly what holds the non-difference between *with* and *to,* being and doing. Here is the dynamic threshold and creative limit carrying the apocalyptic secret of newness — "Behold, I make all things new."[9] Newness is wish before and after any object, affirmation without anything *to* affirm, the hopelessly helpless *yes* eternally in advance of all *no,* that is, the purest most perfect *no* of all, the one that says no first to itself. Whence the excellent negativity of newness, newness as wholly not what has been before, as expressed in Nietzsche's later comment, in a letter to Franz Overbeck, on the verse which opens this book of *The Gay Science*: "I have crossed a tropic. Everything that lies before me is new, and it will not be long before I catch sight also of the *terrifying* face of my more distant

8   Augustine, *Confessions*, 10.3.4.
9   Rev 21:5.

task."[10] The new is produced in the occult wish of an open *no*. "Whoever seeks or aims at *something*," writes Meister Eckhart, "is seeking and aiming at nothing, and he who prays for something will get nothing."[11] And Meher Baba says, "I may give you more, much more, than you expect — or maybe nothing, and that nothing may prove to be everything."[12]

II.   I'm still alive; I still think.
*   I must still be alive because I still have to think.*

The perfectly operative unworkability of the interface, a unilateral duality of thought and life, exposes the terribly unending and inescapable suddenness of being trapped alive in consciousness, of finding oneself (to be) something like an always improper sum of thought and being. Thought proves life and life proves nothing, nothing but itself, which is present to but not found in thought. This is the inverse of Descartes' dubious *ergo*: there is thinking, therefore there is not a thinker, therefore the thinker *is not*. The thing that seems to be thinking, that thinking supposedly presupposes, is impossible to face, being a kind of divinely stupid, supra-cogitational, immediate intelligence, wholly coincident with the inevitable impossibility or substantial negativity *that* one is. It is the immanent thing always already specularly on both sides of the thought–being dyad, independent of any communication between them whatsoever, and thus no thing at all.

III.   Sum, ergo cogito; cogito, ergo sum.

Nietzsche's new year starts with returning to the scene of modern philosophical decision in order to reopen the wound it hastily

10 Friedrich Nietzsche, *Select Letters of Friedrich Nietzsche,* ed. and trans. Christopher Middleton (Indianapolis: Hackett, 1969), 193.
11 Meister Eckhart, *Complete Mystical Works,* trans. Maurice O'Connell Walshe (New York: Herder & Herder, 2009), Sermon 68.
12 Meher Baba, quoted in C.B. Purdom, *The God-Man: The Life, Journeys and Work of Meher Baba with an Interpretation of His Silence and Spiritual Teaching* (Crescent Beach, SC: Sheriar Press, 1964), 296.

bound, to let it, like the blood of Saint Januarius, heal in bleeding anew. Curing by cutting the Cartesian suture of thought and being means melting reason's freezing of their relation, returning it to the sanifying upsurge of living intelligence or *analogos,* as figured in the beginning verses: "You who with the flaming spear split the ice of my soul and make it thunder down now to the sea of its highest hope."[13] The doubling of Descartes' equation across the consequential preposition exposes the interface that philosophy claims to operate and occupy as a site of steering. The anti-philosophical lesson of this non-mediated mutualizing of thinking and being is that in truth the correlation has no helmsman, because *there is no correlation* properly speaking, because being's belonging to thought and thought's belonging to being are not relative. Rather, thought and being are found here and now to have neither no relation (equivocity) nor total relation (univocity) but the intelligible obscurity of some relation (analogy). Note that the concept of *analogy* has an important temporal dimension, the prefix meaning "up, anew, upon" — think time as tree, a movement of upward supplanting[14] — so that the concept of analogy itself explicates the triangularity of *amor fati* as a form Nietzsche constellates from the points of thought, being, and time. The generative leap of analogy traces without tracing how a being is new thought and a thought new being. Like a non-anatomizable nerve in the brain of Janus Bifrons, like the whatever-works mix of supplication and insult that makes the martyr's dry blood liquefy, thought and being are involved with each other, just not in a way that could ever be sorted out *within* time, not in a way that can be reduced to process. Thought and being are interfacial. Neither steers, or can be steered by, the other. And it is the fatal delusion of assuming so that *amor fati* essentially refuses, the sheer ignorance of trying to steer life in positions of identification with thought and/or being. Such is the delusion of mistaking

13 Nietzsche, *Selected Letters,* 212.
14 Cf. Dante Alighieri, *Paradiso,* trans. Charles S. Singleton (Princeton: Princeton University Press, 1975), 27.118–20.

interface for steering wheel, of remaining the one who, thrown by birth into the alien space ship of oneself, never stops saying, amidst constant accidents and crashes, "Hey, I can drive this thing!" What navigation of interface requires, what interface itself, as manifestation of the cybernetic sign, is desperately wishing for, is to steer steering. This is the paradox which weakness, wanting to be *in* power rather than power itself, wanting to *have* freedom rather than be freedom itself, paradoxically wants not to be true. Interface cannot be steered, yet it is all the more intimately and precisely steered, not by simply not steering it, but by a not-steering that steers steering itself.

IV. *Today everyone allows himself*
     to express his dearest wish and thoughts.

The allowing of wish-expression both underscores and overcomes the principle of wish-secrecy, establishing its truth in the neither diachronic nor synchronic space of the present's dilation beyond past and future. The time of wish corresponds with the time of fulfillment — "today you will be with me in paradise"[15] — wherein future stretches into present. Thus wish-expression is a kind of anagogical exercise or test, a suspension of the hiddenness which holds and ensures a wish's futurity, so that the wish can indeed come true, even if what is wished-for does not happen — the inverse of the common fear of wishing uncarefully. For the authentic or do-it-yourself truth of a wish is never something that can simply occur or arrive circumstantially, being a movement deeper than the wisher as such, bigger than the self-image of the wish. A wish is not satisfied, but fulfilled, precisely because it is founded on a non-relating relation, an interfacial non-mediating mediation — wishing "upon a star," throwing a coin into a fountain, putting a wish "out there." A real wish manifests the weird will of its interface, attempts to realize the non-arbitrariness of what one is facing in the moment of wish. Correlatively, the new year's wish, a sacrificial

15 Luke 23:43.

breaking of the taboo against speaking one's wish, occupies the strange planned spontaneity of a convergence of licitness and self-permission. Speaking a wish on this day works like a ritual destruction of wish that preserves it simultaneously against the perversity of the selfishly occult wish and the superficiality of merely wishing. Voicing wish, passing it through the threshold of the mouth, enacts at once the sympathetic foretaste of its fulfillment, a word-binding of its truth, and the renunciation of the wish as wish, a letting-go of the wish so that it may be, mysteriously at the moment of destruction, already true. For every wish must be ruined, not simply in the logical sense that a fulfilled wish would no longer be wished, which is wrong anyway given that will persists in infinite excess of want — "as love grows [...] the search for the one already found become[s] more intense,"[16] but in the deeper sense that the true wish can never properly be wished, cannot be a literal wishing, because wish itself is an improper translation of will into want. Whence the link between wish and resolution. As will is never reducible to personal want, to the parameters of desire within life, so the fulfillment of a true wish, as the *dying wish* inversely exposes, necessarily brings the wisher to the threshold of life: "[N]ow lettest thou thy servant depart in peace."[17] The anagogic game of the wish, wherein will is constrained to playing the role of want, is won by the one who, sensing the consequent impossibility of wishing, nevertheless wishes all the more intensely in a manner that spontaneously manifests will's negative essence as the ground of paradise, of all that one could ever desire being even now positively true. Knowing that a true wish cannot be spoken, such a one paradoxically becomes in the speaking of wish a perfect wisher, one who, not being above falling for having something to wish for, still ascends, by wishing beyond wishing, into the perfection of wishing nothing by wishing a wish that is its own fulfillment.

16 Augustine, *Expositions on the Psalms,* 6 vols., trans. Maria Boulding (Hyde Park, NY: New City Press, 2003), 5.186.
17 Luke 2:2.

v. *I, too, want to say what I wish from myself today*
    and what thought first crossed my heart.

Amor fati is found in open consciousness of heartfelt first-
ness — a simple and not so simple matter, this clear knowing
and seeing of what comes first, without the screen of any fear
that would interrupt, avert, or ignore its arising. Everyone is ter-
rified of doing this, petrified to the point of not being able to do
it at all. Proof: if there were freely offered, right now, a delicious
and absolutely trustworthy candy that would immediately and
forever cure you of all worry, how many of us would, without
hesitation, swallow it whole? No, Nietzsche has your number:

> I find those people unpleasant in whom every natural incli-
> nation immediately becomes a sickness something disfigur-
> ing or even contemptible [...].There are enough people who
> could well entrust themselves to their inclinations with grace
> and without care, but who do not for fear of the imagined
> "evil essence" of nature! *That* is why there is so little nobility
> among human beings; its distinguishing feature has always
> been to have no fear of oneself, to expect nothing contempt-
> ible from oneself, to fly without misgivings wherever we're
> inclined — we free-born birds![18]

vi. *What thought shall be*
     the reason, warrant
     and sweetness
     of the rest of my life.

The first thought is now rigorously decided and distinguished,
via the decision itself, from fleeting impulse. Yet even the decision is not, being already decided, of a piece with the simple wish to speak the wish, which carries its will in advance
of expression into its expression's future, like the way a vow is
made before it is said, the way crossing a threshold requires, be-

18 Nietzsche, *The Gay Science*, §294.

fore crossing, that it be already crossed. *What will be already is* — where insanity sees this fact as foreclosure, sanity seizes it as the very source of openness, the ground of passing beyond what is, or better, living on the yonder side of end (in both senses). "In the Original Unity of the First Thing," says Edgar Allan Poe, "lies the Secondary Cause of All Things, with the Germ of their Inevitable Annihilation."[19] The anticipatory terms of the wish ("reason, warrant, and sweetness") here confirm its identity both with its own event — the love of fate as a form of first thought — and its expression: affirmation of wish as an instance of loving fate. Furthermore, these terms restore wishing itself to its original auto-teleological unity, as shadowed in the etymology of the word (*Wunsch*), cognate of *venerate* and *win,* whose root signifies both desire and satisfaction, to strive for and to gain. *Amor fati* is a winning wish, the wish of wish itself that needs no other. Binding oneself to this wish, making it the law of one's life, fulfills the point of identity between law and sweetness lost in the splitting of life into *bios* and *zoē.* Love of fate directly fulfills the sweet bare promise of law itself, as what binds one to truth–beauty–goodness, without binding life to a ground or reason. Over and against the "natural sweetness [γλυκύτητος φυσικῆς]" according to which "men cling to life even at the cost of enduring great misfortune,"[20] *amor fati* finds the higher sense of an willful not-clinging that releases a new sweetness sweeter still, an always fresh taste for things that makes everything possible by virtue of the non-difference between love — "Love and do what you will [*Dilige et fac quod vis*]"[21] — and detachment: "Do everything, but don't worry. Worrying binds."[22]

19 Edgar Allan Poe, *Eureka: A Prose Poem* (New York: Putnam, 1848), 8.

20 Aristotle, *Politics,* III.6, in *The Basic Works of Aristotle,* ed. Richard McKeon (New York: Random House, 1941), 1184.

21 Augustine, *Tractates on the Gospel of John 112–24,* trans. John W. Rettig (Washington, DC: Catholic University of America, 1995), 223.

22 Meher Baba, quoted in Ivy O. Duce, *How a Master Works* (Walnut Creek, CA: Sufism Reoriented, 1975), 582.

VII. I want to learn more and more how to see
   what is necessary *in things as what is* beautiful *in them.*
   Thus I will be one of those who make things beautiful.
   Amor fati: *let that be my love from now on!*
   I do not want to wage war against ugliness;
   I do not want to accuse;
   I do not even want to accuse the accusers.
   Let looking away be my only negation!

Like the visual interior of turning the other cheek, looking away is forgiveness without false humility and immediate fulfillment of will-to-power — the only way to evade Narcissus's fate and not die in one's sleep, or in the terms of Marshall McLuhan media-theory reading of the myth, in the middle of being a numb servomechanism of the image. Turn away, the world is strangling you in the loop of your own feedback — the seeing of this *is* turning away. No one really wants to hear it, above all the only part of you worth listening to. The specular spell is broken as interface is unveiled to be mirror, a reflecting pool of a weird ungraspable kind that cannot itself be wielded or turned as such, a multidimensional mirror in which the image is also always looking out. Continuous with the mirror's inversely representational operation, the minimum spontaneous negation of looking away is in fact a maximum exercise of intelligent strength, of being-in-control. Conversely, whoever fears, worries, frets, over ANYTHING, is in fact an imaginary steerless nothing, an evil inexistent imp who merely wants to rule, likes the idea of it, but *will* not. Power is rather where one *does not look,* as Nietzsche explains: "I have found strength where one does not look for it: in simple, mild, pleasant people, without the least desire to rule [...]. The powerful natures *dominate,* it is a necessity, they need not lift one finger."[23] By virtue of this same principle, it is futile to request any justifying, legitimizing, or calculative account for

---

23 Friedrich Nietzsche, *Gesammelte Werke,* x.412, quoted in Walter Kaufman, *Nietzsche: Philosopher, Psychologist, Antichrist,* 4th ed. (Princeton: Princeton University Press, 1974), 252.

loving fate, any reason for it that would delimit or define its telos. I leave that misfortunate task to progressivism and so-called positive thinking. However, one may understand the invisible radical power of *amor fati,* the farsightedness of its headless helmsman, in a manner that acknowledges the substantiality of its force without attempting to mediate its intrinsic worth (and in this setting I suppose we must). This *prosthetic* understanding, which preserves one against what McLuhan identifies as the autoamputative seductions of the interface, must be sought with respect to both the active and passive principles of *amor fati.* Toward the first, there is William Blake's vision of the reproductivity of perception:

> If Perceptive Organs vary: Objects of Perception seem to vary: / If the Perceptive Organs close: their Objects seem to close also: / Consider this O mortal Man! O worm of sixty winters said Los / Consider Sexual Organization & hide thee in the dust […] Then those in Great Eternity who contemplate on Death / Said thus. What seems to Be: Is. To those to whom / It seems to Be, & is productive of the most dreadful / Consequences to those to whom it seems to Be: even of / Torments, Despair, Eternal Death.[24]

Toward the second, there is Meister Eckhart's symmetrically specular articulation of the negative agency of spiritual withdrawal, which immediately permits the operation of an infinite immanent intelligence:

> [God] need not turn from one thing to another, as we do. Suppose in this life we always had a mirror before us, in which we saw all things at a glance and recognized them in a single image, then neither action nor knowledge would be any hindrance to us. But we have to turn from one thing to another, and so we can only attend to one thing at the ex-

24 William Blake, *The Complete Poetry and Prose,* ed. David V. Erdman (New York: Doubleday, 1988), 177–79.

pense of another [...] [But] when a man is quite unpreoc-
cupied, and the active intellect within him is silent, then God
must take up the work [...].The active intellect cannot give
what it has not got: and it cannot entertain two images together; it has first one and then the other [...]. But when God
acts in place of the active intellect, He engenders many images together in one point.[25]

In other words, whenever Narcissus recognizes that his gaze is
a cybernetic sign, at once the world and himself are something
they never were, nor could ever have been, before.

VIII. And, all in all and on the whole:
    some day I want only to be a Yes-sayer!

25   Meister Eckhart, *Complete Mystical Works,* Sermons 2–3.

o8

Outing the "It" that Thinks:
On the Collapse of an Intellectual Ecosystem

R. Scott Bakker
NWW.III, October 1, 2011

> *Psychology is now once again the road to the fundamental problems.*
> — Nietzsche, *Beyond Good and Evil*[1]

1. *The Soul-Hypothesis*

Who kills Hector in *The Illiad*? The easy answer is: Achilles. After all, he was the one who drove his spear through Hector's neck, who gloried over his dying form, then proceeded to desecrate his corpse. But if you read Homer carefully, you see that the death of Hector is in fact a *corporate* enterprise. We are told shortly after the duel that death and fate seized him and dragged him down. And, even more curiously, we learn that Hector was "struck down *at* Achilles' hands *by* blazing-eyed Athena."[2]

The ancient Greeks, it seems, saw themselves — or their heroes, at least — as conduits, as prone to enact the will of more shadowy, supernatural agencies as to act on their own. Perhaps

---

1   Friedrich Nietzsche, *Beyond Good and Evil,* trans. R.J. Hollingdale (New York: Penguin Books, 1990), 54.

2   Homer, *The Iliad*, trans. Robert Fagles (New York: Penguin Books, 1990), 556.

it was the exigencies of their lives, the sense of powerlessness that comes with living at the whim of organized violence and random scarcity. Perhaps it was simply a misplaced humility, or a cunning moral prophylactic, a reluctance to take credit for what could turn into an obligation. Whatever the reason, they were disinclined to see themselves as the *sole* authors of their thoughts and actions. The way we are taught to see ourselves. The way I saw myself up to the age of 14, the age my mother made the mistake of buying me an old manual typewriter at a local yard sale. I made the mistake of *using* it, you see, not just to type out adventures for my weekly *Dungeons and Dragons* sessions, but *to think things through*.

I really can't remember much of those musings: I like to think that they were packed with the kind of accidental profundity you often find in your student's naïve musings, but I really have no way of knowing. All I know for certain is that my thoughts eventually fastened on the concept of *cause*. Its ubiquity. Its explanatory power. And at one point, I typed the following:

Everything has a cause.
A → B → C
A = *outer* event
B = *inner* event
C = this very thought *now*!!!!!!

I had stumbled across determinism. The insight had the character of a religious revelation for me, quite literally. I even wept, realizing not only that everything I had been taught was a lie, but that *I was myself* a kind of lie. I was an illusion weeping at my own illusoriness. How mad was *that*? Whenever I got high alone, I would listen to Pink Floyd or some such and just sit staring at my experience, trying to will my way *through* it, or daring it to show its paltry hand. I became a kind of naïve nihilist, blowing away my buddies and alienating all the babes at parties with my arguments against the freedom of will. I would always finish the same way, swinging my arms wide and saying "It's *all* bullshit. *All* of it. It can't be and yet it is. *Bullshit,* through and through!"

Of course, I never stopped believing in the bullshit, as I called it. I was, if anything, quite strident in my moral declarations, and extremely possessive of my "choices." But nevertheless, a ribbon of despair continually floated in and out of the obscurities that hedged my daily life. I would sigh and look away from all the looked-at things, out a window, or through the fingers of a tree, and just exist in momentary impossibility. A vacancy absorbing space, as Helen Keller would say.

Later, while at university, I read Heidegger's *Being and Time* in an effort to understand deconstruction and Derrida, whom I thought just *had* to be wrong, whatever it was the crazy bastard was saying. This would be my second religious revelation — one that would ultimately lead to my disastrous tenure as a Branch Derridean. The facticity of my thrownness made a deep impression on me. As did the ontological difference. I realized my earlier revelation was simply that of a naïve fourteen-year-old, one who had been brainwashed by the *Encyclopedia of Technology and Innovation* that I'd received for Christmas when I was 8. I had made a fetish out of science, failing to see that science had its own historical and conceptual conditions, that it was a skewed artifact, part of the dread "metaphysics of presence." Aristotle, man. Had to go and ruin it for everybody.

It was a joyous, heady time for me. Suddenly the world, which had been little more than a skin of mammalian lies whenever I looked with my theoretical eyes, became positively soupy with meaning. Sure, thanks to *différance,* I could never nail that meaning down with representation, but it was the oh-so-Western *urge to nail* that was the problem. I had been the proverbial man with a hammer — of course I had seen all questions as ontic nails! At long last I could set aside the conceptual toolbox I had inherited from his well-intentioned, but ultimately deluded Euro-fathers. Of course, I still waved my arms at parties, but this time the *babes seemed to listen*. I stared in the mirror saying, "*Je ne sais quoi…*" I cursed myself for hating French when I was in public school. I began practicing my Gallic shrug. I openly envied the children of diplomats and rued my own backwater upbringing.

Since I had read Derrida and Heidegger, I had no choice but to read Descartes. How could I carry on the critique of metaphysics unless I immersed myself in the Western Tradition? Know thy enemy, no? This led me to ponder the famous Frenchman's infamous *cogito,* "I think, therefore I am," Descartes' attempt, given the collapse in confidence wrought by the new science of the seventeenth century, to place knowledge on a new, secure, *subjective* foundation. Just who did the guy think he was fooling, really?

To show just how hopeless Descartes was, I began returning to Nietzsche again and again and again in all of my undergraduate papers. I was all, like, *Beyond Good and Evil,* like. I continually paraphrased Nietzsche's famous reformulation of the Cartesian *cogito.* I would always write, using a double hanging indent for dramatic purposes, *it* thinks, therefore *I am.* Of course, the "it" simply had to be italicized, if only to underscore the abject impersonality at the root of subjectivity. Even though we like to think our thoughts come from our prior thoughts, which is to say, from ourselves, the merest reflection shows this cannot be the case, that each thought is dropped into consciousness *from the outside,* and that hence the "I" is born *after the fact.*

Then, the following academic year, I came across Sartre's reformulation of the *cogito* in *Being and Nothingness.* Combining the two, the Sartrean and Nietzschean, I arrived at a reformulation that I thought was distinctly *my own*: *it* thinks, therefore I *was.* Here, I would tell people, we see how well and truly fucked up things are. Not only do our origins congenitally outrun us, we continually outrun ourselves as well! We're an echo that knows itself only as an echo of this echo. Or, as I used to joke with my in-the-know friends, we're "Umberto squared." In my papers, I started using this final formulation to describe Derrida's self-erasing notion of *différance* as applied to subjectivity, the way all reflection is in fact a species of *deflection.* My professors lapped it up. On my papers I would find comments like "Excellent!" or

"Great stuff!" or, more exciting still, "What would Freud make of this?" scrawled in red pen.

The formula became my mantra, my originary repetition, even though it took quite some time to realize just how originary it was. For some reason, it never dawned on me that *I had come full circle* — that at twenty-eight I had yet to take a single step beyond fourteen, intellectually speaking. I had literally kept typing the same self-immolating thought through fourteen years and two life-transforming revelations. It. Me. Nobody. Over and over again. It would be a poker game, of all absurdities, that would bring this absurdity to light for me. At this particular game, which took place before the hysterical popularity of Texas Hold'em, I met a philosophy PhD student from Mississippi who was also an avowed nihilist. Given my own heathen, positivistic past, I took it upon myself to convert the poor fool. He was just an adolescent, after all — time to set aside childish thoughts! So I launched into an account of my own sorry history and how I had been saved by Heidegger and the ontological difference.

The nihilist listened to me carefully, interrupting only to clarify this or that point with astute questions. Then, after I had more or less burned through my batteries, the nihilist asked: "You agree that science clearly implies nihilism, right?" — "Of course." "Well… it's kind of inconsistent, isn't it?" — "What's inconsistent?" A thoughtful bulge of the bottom lip. "Well, that despite the fact that philosophy hasn't resolved any matter with any reliability *ever,* and, despite the fact that science is the most powerful, reliable, theoretical claim-making institution *in human history,* you're still willing to suspend your commitment to scientific implications on the basis of prior commitments to *philosophical* claims about science and this… ontological difference." Tortured syntax aside, I understood exactly what the nihilist meant: Why believe Heidegger when you could argue almost *anything* in philosophy? I had read enough by now to know this was the only sure thing in the humanities. It was an uncomfortable fact: outside the natural sciences there was no way short of exhaustion or conspiracy to end the regress of interpretation. Nevertheless, I found myself resenting that bottom lip. "I don't follow." "Well," the nihilist said, making one of those pained *correct-me-if-I'm-wrong* faces, "isn't that kind of like using Ted Bundy's testimony to convict Mother Theresa?" — "Um," I replied, my voice pinched in *please-no* resignation, "...I guess?" So, back to the "bullshit" it was.

I should have known. After all, I had only spent *fourteen years* repeating myself.

2. *The New Mistrust*

When I was fourteen, I had understood the "it" that comes before in naïve *causal* terms — probably because of the pervasiveness of the scientific worldview. I lost my faith in intentionality. Heidegger changed my life because he convinced me that this was a *loaded* way of looking at things, that it begged apparently indefensible assumptions — and most importantly, a certain destructive *attitude* toward being and life *as it is lived.* I regained my faith in intentionality. Even though I qualified that faith with Nietzsche, Sartre, and Derrida — particularly when it came to *agency* — my renewed faith in intentionality remained unquestioned.

What I had done, I now realize, is reconsider the same problematic in intentional terms. My adolescent horror, that I wasn't *originary,* had become my adult preoccupation. The problem of *it* had become *safer,* somehow, less conceptually corrosive. I became quite fond of my fragmented self hanging out in the grad pub with all my fragmented friends. My old causal way of looking at things, it seemed to me, was juvenile, the presumption of someone bound in the ontic blinders of the scientific worldview. I even told the story I told above, the way I imagine born-again Christians are prone to tell stories of their youthful cognitive folly to fellow believers. "*Science....* Can you imagine?" Then I had to go play poker with a bloody nihilist.

...Let's make up a word: *determinativity.* Determinativity is simply the degree of determination, the hot potato of efficacy. So let's say that I have the determinativity at this moment, that I'm dictating the movements of your soul in the course of verbalizing these marks on the page. Or let's say the *marks themselves* have the determinativity, they write you and I simply vanish into them, a kind of Foucauldian sham meant to impose order on an unruly world o' texts. Or let's say that *you* have the determinativity, that you take the words, make of them what you will. Or let's say *your unconscious* has the determinativity, that you're simply the aporetic interstice between the text and some psychodynamic subtext. Or let's say *history* has the determinativity, or that *culture* or *society* or *God* or *language* has the determinativity. Can we say that all of these things possess determinativity? None of them? Sure. We can mix and match, recast this and tweak that, and come up with entirely new theoretical outlooks if we want. Spin the academic bottle. The bottom line is that we really don't know what the hell we're talking about. For better or worse, the only kind of determinativity we can follow with enough methodological and institutional rigor to actually resolve (as opposed to exhaust) interpretative disputes is *causality* — whatever the hell *that* is. As Richard Dawkins is so fond of pointing out in interviews, scientists — unlike us — can actually *agree* on what will change their minds. And this, as the past five centuries have amply demonstrated, is a powerful thing.

Grasping a problem or a theory or a concept is never enough. Like the blind gurus who confuse the elephant for a snake, tree, and rope because they each only feel its trunk, leg, or tail, you have to know just where you're grasping *from*. By some astounding coincidence, I had relegated science using precisely the same self-aggrandizing theoretical tactic used by all my friends. (Amazing, isn't it?, the way groups of thinkers magically find themselves convinced by the same things — how, as Nietzsche puts it, "under an invisible spell they always trace once more the identical orbit."[3]) The second flabbergasting coincidence was the way these commitments had the happy consequence of rendering my discursive domain *immune* to scientific critique, even as it exposed science to my theoretical scrutiny. I mean, who did those scientists think they were, waving around their big

3   Nietzsche, *Beyond Good and Evil,* 50.

fat language game like that? They were so obviously blind to the *conditions* of their discourse…

In other words, I had used my prior commitment to *What Science Was* — a social construct, a language game, an expression of the metaphysics of presence — to condition my commitment to *What Science Does*, which is explicate natural phenomena in causal terms. My domain was nothing less than the human soul, and the last I checked, science was the *product* of human souls: if anything, science was a subset of *my domain,* not vice versa. So I once believed, more or less.

Two kinds of ignorance, it now seems to me, are required to make this family of assumptions convincing (beyond the social psychological dimensions of belief acquisition, such as the hunger for belonging and prestige). First, you need to be unaware of what we now know about human cognition and its apparent limitations. Second, you need to know next to nothing about the *physiology* of the human soul.

3. The New Psychologist

The first ignorance, I have come to think, is nothing short of *astounding,* and demonstrates the way the humanities, which are so quick to posture themselves as critical authorities, are simply of a piece with our sham culture of pseudo-empowerment and fatuous self-affirmation. For decades now, cognitive psychologists have been dismantling our flattering cognitive assumptions, compiling an encyclopedic inventory of the biases, fallacies, and outright illusions that afflict human cognition. Please bear with me as I read through the following (partial!) list: actor–observer bias (fundamental attribution error), ambiguity effect, anchoring effect, asymmetric insight illusion, attentional bias, availability cascade, availability heuristic, the bandwagon effect, Barnum effect, base-rate neglect, belief bias, black swan effect, choice bias, clustering illusion, confirmation bias, congruence bias, consensus fallacy, contrast effect, control bias, cryptonesia, deprivation bias, distinction bias, Dunnig-Kruger effect, egocentric bias, exception bias, expectation bias, exposure effect, false memory, focusing effect, framing effect, future discounting, gambler's fallacy, halo effect, hindsight bias, impact bias, ingroup bias, just-world illusion, moral credential effect, moral luck bias, negativity bias, omission bias, outcome bias, outgroup homogeneity bias, planning fallacy, *post-hoc ergo propter hoc, post-hoc* rationalization, projection bias, observer-expectancy effect, optimism bias, ostrich effect, pareidolia, pessimism bias, positive outcome bias, positivity effect, primacy effect, reaction bias, recency effect, regression neglect, restraint bias, rosy retrospection effect, selective perception, self-serving bias, Semmelweis reflex, social comparison bias, status-quo bias, stereotyping, suggestibility, sunk-cost bias, superiority illusion, trait ascription bias, transparency illusion, ultimate attribution error, unit bias, wishful thinking, zero-risk bias…. Tedious, I know, but some cognitive shortcomings, such as the Semmelweis reflex (where paradigm-incompatible evidence is rejected out-of-hand) or exception biases (where individuals think themselves immune to the failings of others), need to be bludgeoned into submission.

This inventory of cognitive foibles has lead many psychologists, perhaps not surprisingly, to rethink the function of reason and argumentation. The traditional view of reason as a cognitive instrument, a tool we use to produce new knowledge out of old, has been all but overturned. The story has to be far more complicated than mere cognition: even though evolution has devised many, many imperfect tools, rarely do the imperfections line up so neatly. All too often, reason seems to fail precisely where and when *we need it to.* Earlier this year, the *Journal of Behavioural and Brain Sciences* devoted an entire issue to Dan Sperber's *Argumentative Theory of Reason* (sparking enough interest to warrant an article in *The New York Times*).[4] According to Sperber, the primary function of reason is to facilitate argumentation

4   Patricia Cohen, "Reason Seen More as Weapon Than as a Path to Truth," *The New York Times,* June 14 2011, http://nytimes.com/2011/06/15/arts/people-argue-just-to-win-scholars-assert.html (print version published June 15, 2011 on page C-1 of the New York edition with the headline "People Argue Just to Win, Scholars Assert").

instead of cognition, to win the game of giving and asking for reasons rather than get things right. Far from a "flawed general mechanism," he argues that human reasoning "is a remarkably efficient specialized device" when viewed through the lens of social and cognitive interaction.[5] And though this might prove to be an epistemic disaster at the individual level, he contends the picture is not "wholly disheartening"[6] when viewed in a larger social context. As bad as we are when it comes to producing arguments, the research suggests that we are not *quite* so bad when it comes to evaluating them, "provided [we] have no particular axe to grind"[7] — an important proviso to say the least.

My own reservations with *Argumentative Theory of Reason* stem from a failure to discriminate between various contexts of reasoning, or to consider the role played by ambiguity. In either case, my guess is that balance between the epistemic and the egocentric dimensions of reasoning varies according to social and semantic circumstances. Human reason evolved in social conditions far different than our own, at a time when almost all our relationships were at once relationships of material interdependency — when our lives literally depended on *face-to-face* consensus and cooperation. Given this, it stands to reason that the epistemic/egocentric emphasis of reasoning will vary depending on the urgency of the subject matter, whether we are arguing about the constitution of the moon, or the direction of a roaming pack of predators. Based on the work of David Dunning, *Self-Insight*,[8] I also think that the epistemic/egocentric emphasis is indexed to the relative clarity and ambiguity of the subject matter, that reasoning is more knowledge-prone when the matter at issue is proximal and practical, and more display-prone when it is distal and abstract. Anyone who has rescued any kind of relationship knows something of the way circumstances can induce us to "check our ego at the door."

5   Ibid.
6   Ibid.
7   Ibid.
8   David Dunning, *Self-Insight: Roadblocks and Detours on the Path to Knowing Thyself* (New York: Psychology Press, 2000).

Either way, we now know enough about reasoning to assert that we are, as the ancient Skeptics argued so long ago, theoretical incompetents. (And if you think about it, this really isn't all that surprising, insofar as science counts as an accomplishment, something humanity had to discover, nurture, and defend. Human theoretical incompetence actually *explains* why we required the methodological and institutional apparatuses of science to so miraculously transform the world.) If the first ignorance pertains to the *how* of theory in the humanities, the *thinking*, the second concerns the what — the "it" that thinks. As much as cognitive psychology has problematized reasoning, cognitive neuroscience has all but demolished the so-called "manifest image," consciousness as it appears to introspection and intuition.

Consider the "feeling of certainty" that motivates not just some, but all of your beliefs. Short of this "sense of rightness," it's hard to imagine how we could commit to any claim or paradigm. And yet, as neurologist Richard Burton has recently argued, "certainty and similar states of 'knowing what we know' arise out of involuntary brain mechanisms that, like love or anger, function independently of reason" — which is to say, independent of any rational warrant.[9] And the list of "debunked experiences" goes on. You have Daniel Wegner arguing that the "feeling of willing," far from initiating action, is something that merely accompanies behavior;[10] Daniel Dennett contending that *qualia* — the much-vaunted "what-it-is-like" of experience — do not exist; Thomas Metzinger arguing much the same about agency and selfhood[11]; Paul and Patricia Churchland arguing the wholesale replacement of "folk psychology" — talk of desires, beliefs, affects, and so on — with a more neuroscientifically adequate vocabulary.

9   Richard Burton, *On Being Certain* (New York: St Martin's Press, 2008).
10 Daniel Wegner, *The Illusion of Conscious Will* (Cambridge, MA: MIT Press, 2002).
11 Thomas Metzinger, *Being No One* (Cambridge, MA: MIT Press, 2003).

None of these theories and arguments command anything approaching consensus in the cognitive neuroscience research community, but each of them represents an attempt to make sense of a steadily growing body of radically counterintuitive data. Though we cannot yet say what a given experience "is," we can say that the final answer, like so many answers provided by science, will lie far outside the pale of our intuitive preconceptions — perhaps incomprehensibly so. In my own view, this is precisely what we should expect. We now know that only a fraction of the estimated 38,000 *trillion* operations per second processed by the brain finds its way to consciousness. This means that experience, all experience, is profoundly privative, a simplistic caricature of otherwise breathtakingly complex processes. We *want* to think that this loss of information is synoptic, that despite its relative paucity, experience nevertheless captures some functional kernel of its correlated neurological functions. But there are telling structural and developmental reasons to think otherwise. The metabolic costs associated with neural processing and the sheer evolutionary youth of human consciousness suggest that experience should be severely blinkered: synoptic or "low resolution" in some respects, perhaps, but thoroughly fictitious otherwise. (The fact that these fictions appear to play efficacious roles should come as no surprise, since they need only be systematically related to actually efficacious brain functions. Since they constitute the sum of what we experience, they will also constitute the sum of "understanding," albeit one which is itself incomprehensible.) This second ignorance, you might object, is anything but problematic, since the human soul has always been an open question. But this is precisely what I'm saying: *the human soul is no longer an open question*. It has become an empirical one.

One of the great paradoxes of human cognition is the way ignorance, far more than knowledge, serves as the foundation of certainty. For years I had tackled the question of the human soul using the analytic and speculative tools belonging to the humanities — and I had done so with absolute confidence. Sure, I knew that reason was "flawed" and that the soul was "problematic." Sure, I felt the irony of clinging to my interpretations given the "tropical luxuriance" of the alternatives. Sure, I realized that there was no definitive way to arbitrate between alternatives. But I had embraced a theoretical outlook that seemed to make a virtue out of these apparent liabilities. Even more importantly, I had secured a *privileged social identity*. I… was the radical one. I… was the one asking the difficult questions. I… was the *truly critical one*. I understood the way my subject position had been culturally and historically conditioned. I realized that all theory was *laden,* warped by the weight of innumerable implicit assumptions. And because of this, I was "enlightened" in a way that scientific researchers (outside of France, perhaps) were not. Where scientists (and, well, every other human on planet) were constrained by their ignorance of their assumptions, unwitting agents of a benighted and pernicious conceptual status quo, I understood the oh-so-onerous burden of culture and history — and so thought I could work around them, with a little luck.

In other words, I believed what pretty much every human being (not suffering clinical depression) believes: that I had won the Magical Belief Lottery, that my totalizing post-structuralist/ contextualist/constructivist theoretical outlook really was "just the way things were." Why bother interrogating it, when all the critical heavy lifting had already been done? Besides, I *wanted* to think I was a non-conformist contrarian iconoclastic radical. I needed an outlook to match my culture-jamming T-shirts. But the ugly, perhaps monstrous, fact remains. If the cognitive psychologists are right and reasoning — outside of a narrow family of contexts — is profoundly flawed, far more egocentric than epistemic, then the humanities are stranded with a box of broken tools. If the eliminativists and revisionists are right and consciousness is itself a kind of cognitive illusion, then the *very subject-matter* of the humanities awaits scientifically legitimized redefinition. If these two ignorances were all that kept us safe, then we are about to become extinct.

4. Inventing the New

Which brings me back to the remarkable exception that is Nietzsche.

Neither of the ignorances described above, I think, would surprise him in the least. The notion that reasoning is motivated is a pervasive theme throughout his work. Like Sperber, he believes reason's epistemic presumption is largely a ploy, a way to gain advantage. Where the philosophical tradition assumed that intuition, observation, and logical necessity primarily motivated reason — he proposes breakfast, weather, cleanliness, or abode.[12]

Nietzsche commonly employs what might be called a *trans-categorical* interpretative strategy in his work. He likes to peer past the obvious and the conceptually contiguous to things un-likely — even inhuman — and so regularly spins outrage and revelation out of what other philosophers would call "category mistakes." To this extent, contemporary cognitive neuroscience would not shock him in the least. I'm sure he would be delighted to see so many of his counter-intuitive hunches reborn in empirical guise. As he famously writes in *The Antichrist*: "our knowledge of man today is real knowledge precisely to the extent that it is knowledge of him as a machine."[13]

For the longest time I read Nietzsche as a proto-post-struc-turalist, as *the* thinker of the so-called "performative turn" that would come to dominate so much twentieth-century philoso-phy. Now I appreciate that he is so very much more, that he was actually thinking *past* post-structuralism *a century before it.* And I realize that his continual references to *physiology* — and other empirical wheels that never seemed to turn — are in fact every bit as central as their frequency suggests. Consider the following quote, one which I think can only be truly appreciated *now*:

12 Nietzsche, *On the Genealogy of Morals and Ecce Homo,* trans. Walter Kauf-mann (New York: Vintage Books, 1989), 236–58.
13 Nietzsche, *Twilight of the Idols and The Anti-Christ,* trans. R.J. Hollingdale (New York: Penguin Books, 1990), 136.

But the road to new forms and refinements of the soul-hypothesis stands open: and such conceptions as "mortal soul" and "soul as multiplicity of the subject" and "soul structure of the drives and emotions" want henceforth to possess civic rights in science. To be sure, when the *new* psychologist puts an end to the superstition which has hitherto flourished around the soul-idea with almost tropical luxuriance, he has as it were thrust himself out into a new wilderness and a new mistrust — it may be that the older psychologists had a merrier and more comfortable time of it; ultimately, however, he sees that, precisely that act, he has also condemned himself to *inventing* the new — and who knows? perhaps to *finding* it.[14]

The anachronistic timeliness of this statement is nothing short of remarkable. Nietzsche was as much futurist as intellectual historian, an annalist of endangered and collapsing conceptual ecosystems. He understood that the Enlightenment would not stop exploding our ingrown vanities, that sooner or later the *anthropos* would fall with the anthropomorphic. When I first read this passage as a young man I thought that I was one of the new psychologists, that I was the one "condemned" to be so cool. Sure, the terms "science" and "psychologist" made me uncomfortable, but certainly Nietzsche was using these terms in their broadest, Latin and Ancient Greek, senses — *scientia, psukhē,* and *logos*. He couldn't mean *science* science, or *psychologist* psychologist, could he? Noooo…. Yes? Of course he did.

I thought, the way so many others thought, that Nietzsche had glimpsed *post-modernity,* that his "deconstruction of the subject" was far more post-structural than Humean. Now I'm convinced that *this* is the moment he had glimpsed, however obscurely: the moment when our methods crumble, and our discursive domain slips away — when *science* asserts its problematic cognitive rights.

14   Id., *Beyond Good and Evil,* 43–44.

My strategy here has been twofold: First, to offer this thesis within a biographical context, to demonstrate the powerful way path-dependency shapes our theoretical commitments. So much of what we believe is simply a matter of who or what gets to us first. And second, to introduce you to the "new psychologists," the ones that are "outing" the "it" that thinks — and unfortunately (though not surprisingly) showing that monsters hide in the closet after all. The goal of this strategy has been to show you the cognitive fragility of your ecosystem, and thus your inevitable demise as an intellectual species.

So here's the cartoon I want to offer you: The sciences have spent centuries rooting through the world, replacing anecdote and apocrypha with quantitative observation, and intentional, anthropomorphic accounts of natural phenomena with functional explanations. During this time, however, one stubborn corner of the natural world remained relatively immune to this process simply because of the sheer complexity of its functions: the human brain. As a result, the discursive traditions that took the *soul* as their domain were spared the revolution that swept away the old, anthropomorphic discourses of the physical world. Though certainly conditioned by the sciences, the humanities have flourished within what might be called an "intentional game-preserve." Motivated reasoning means that we can make endless conceptual hash of ambiguity. So long as the causal precursors of thought remain shrouded, *anything goes,* theoretically speaking. Instead of saying "Here be dragons," we say "Here be the *Will to Power,* the *Id, différance, virtualities, normative contexts,* the social *a priori,* and so on."

We make the very mistake that Spinoza accuses naïve Christians of making in his letters: we conceive of the condition in terms *belonging to the conditioned.* So, where naïve Christians anthropomorphize God, theorists in the humanities *anthropomorphize* (albeit in a conceptually decomposed form) the "darkness that comes before" thought: we foist *intentional* interpretations on the conditions of the soul. Where the ancient Greeks said "Athena struck down Hector by Achilles' hand," we say "The social *a priori* struck down Hector by Achilles' hand," or "The unconscious struck down Hector by Achilles' hand." Thanks to the obduracy of the brain, scholars in the humanities could safely expound on the "real" "it" without any knowledge of natural science — let alone respect for its practices. As the one family of interrelated domains where intentional speculation retained something of its ancient cognitive *gravitas,* the humanities provided a discursive space where specialists could still intentionally theorize without fear of embarrassing themselves. So long as we discharged our discursive obligations with domain-specific erudition and intelligence, we could hold our heads up high with in-group pride.

The humanities have remained, in a peculiar way, "pre-scientific." You might even say "ancient." How times have changed. The walls of the brain have been overrun. The intentional bastions of the soul are falling. Taken together, the sciences of the mind and brain are developing a picture that in many cases out-and-out contradicts many of the folk-psychological intuitions that underwrite so much speculation within the humanities. Unless one believes the humanities magically constitute a "special case," there is no reason to think that its voluminous, armchair speculations will have a place in the "post-scientific" humanities to come.

09

All for *Naught*

Eugene Thacker
NWW.IV, April 13, 2013

In the 1830s, fleeing a cholera epidemic in Berlin, Schopenhauer writes the following in his notebook:

> When I was seventeen, without any proper schooling, I was affected by the misery and wretchedness of life, as was the Buddha when in his youth he caught sight of sickness, old age, pain and death [...] the result for me was that this world could not be the work of an all-bountiful, infinitely good being, but rather of a demon who had summoned into existence creatures in order to gloat over the sight of their anguish and agony.[1]

Now, Schopenhauer was no Buddha, but the passage reveals something at the core of his thinking, and that is the dual origin of pessimism. On the one hand, pessimism is conditional, it stems from observation and experience, but also from inclination and predilection — maybe you're stressed out, maybe you're feeling under the weather, maybe something somewhere hurts. This conditional pessimism can be found in Pascal, Lichtenberg, the French moralists, and it surfaces in Schopenhauer's many

---

1   Arthur Schopenhauer, *Manuscript Remains*, Vol. 4, ed. Arthur Hübscher, trans. E.F.J. Payne (Oxford: Berg, 1990), 119.

grumblings concerning humanity, caught as it is in the pedantic, existential metronome of boredom and striving.

But Schopenhauer also makes reference to another origin of pessimism that is unconditional, a kind of metaphysical suffering that is tantamount to existing itself, regardless of our attempts to tailor everything to the sufficient reasons that form the bedrock of philosophy and its realist impulse — all forms of access are at best shadow plays that, in the end, mock the human form. But this metaphysical pessimism must fail — by definition — and Schopenhauer is forced to digress either into grumpy rants, or obscure evocations of the *nihil negativum*.

If Schopenhauer's philosophy is pessimistic, it is because pessimism is caught somewhere between philosophy and a bad attitude, the syllogism entombed in the morose refusal of everything that is, a starless, luminous refusal of every principle of sufficiency — the futility of philosophy, in the key of philosophy. In one of his last notebooks — to which he gave the title "Senilia" — Schopenhauer writes, "I can bear the thought that in a short time worms will eat away my body; but the idea of philosophy-professors nibbling at my philosophy makes me shudder."[2]

*

In one of his letters, Nietzsche details how, in October of 1865, he discovered Schopenhauer's book *The World as Will and Representation* in a used bookstore in Leipzig. He writes:

> One day I found this book in a second-hand bookshop, picked it up as something quite unknown to me and turned the pages. I do not know what demon whispered to me "Take this home with you." It was contrary to my usual practice of hesitating over the purchase of books. Once at home, I threw

2   Ibid., 393.

myself onto the sofa with the newly-won treasure and began to let that energetic and gloomy genius operate upon me.[3]

For Nietzsche, the spell was to last for some time. So great is his enthusiasm that he will even attempt to convert others to Schopenhauer's philosophy, often unsuccessfully. Later, Nietzsche regarded pessimism as something to be overcome, a saying "yes" to this world as it is, unfortunate, indifferent, tragic. Nietzsche often names this horizon a "Dionysian pessimism." One is tempted to call it a pessimism of joy. But the stakes are high, perhaps too high — even for Nietzsche. There is a sense in which the entirety of Nietzsche's philosophy is a sustained, concerted attempt to shake pessimism.

What I've always wanted to know is who sold back those volumes of Schopenhauer to that used bookstore? One usually sells a book back out of disappointment. Occasionally, one sells a book back out of enthusiasm.

∗

There is no philosophy of pessimism, only the reverse.

∗

A Manual of Style: the bad joke, the "to do" list, the epitaph.

∗

Dare one hope for a philosophy of futility? Phosphorescent, moss-ridden aphorisms inseparable from the thickness and ossification of our own bodies, inseparable from the stillness of breathing.

∗

3 R.J. Hollingdale, *Nietzsche: The Man and His Philosophy* (Baton Rouge: Louisiana State University Press, 1965), 43–44.

Schopenhauer, using the metaphors of astronomy, once noted that there were three types of writers — meteors (the flare of fads and trends), planets (the faithful rotation of tradition), and the fixed stars (impervious and unwavering). But in Schopenhauer's own writing — aphorisms, fragments, stray thoughts — one is acutely aware of the way that all writing ultimately negates itself, either to be forgotten or to have been so precise that it results in silence. Was Schopenhauer aware that he himself was a fourth type of writer... the black hole?

*

Nietzsche once lauded the value of the "incomplete thought" for philosophy. If we were to take this up, perhaps the best place to look for incomplete thoughts would be in the notebooks of philosophers. Nietzsche himself was a fastidious user of his notebooks, often writing on the right-hand side only and then flipping the notebook over, allowing him to fill notebooks front-to-back and back-to-front. This economy of the page was, perhaps, offset by Nietzsche's notoriously unreadable handwriting.

Schopenhauer, no less fastidious than Nietzsche, preferred to keep several notebooks going at once, notebooks of all sizes and types — octavo, quarto, folio, bound and unbound. Some notebooks remained fixed on his desk at home, while others could be taken with him on walks, and still other notebooks were reserved for traveling. And then there is Cioran, that gloomy prowler of the Latin Quarter, who was fond of the bright, multi-colored, spiral notebooks used by students.... It's almost as if the notebook mitigates against the book, if the former is not, in the end, negated by the latter. As Nietzsche notes, the incomplete thought "displays the most beautiful butterfly wings — and it slips away from us."[4] I'm assuming that Nietzsche distinguishes the incomplete thought from the merely lazy thought — though I'm rarely able to do so myself.

4   Friedrich Nietzsche, *Human, All Too Human,* trans. Gary Handwerk (Stanford: Stanford University Press, 1995), I, 139.

*

Kierkegaard: life is a jump-rope.

Nietzsche: life is a tight-rope.

Kafka: life is a trip-rope.

Schopenhauer: life is a noose.

Cioran: life is a noose, improperly tied.

*

Sometime around 1658, Pascal conceived of an ambitious work of religious philosophy, to be called *Apology for the Christian Religion*. The work was never completed, cut short by Pascal's death four years later. What remains of the work — now known as the *Pensées* — is perhaps one of the most unfinished books in the history of philosophy.

Admittedly, Pascal is partially to blame for the confusion. He wrote his many fragments on large sheets of paper, separating each by a horizontal line. When a sheet was full, he would then cut the paper along the horizontal lines, so that each fragment was self-contained on a strip of paper. These strips of paper where then grouped into piles. Pascal then poked a hole in the top corner of each of the strips and joined them by running a thread through the hole, forming a bundle. Many of the bundles were thematically grouped — for instance, fragments on human vanity, or boredom, or religious despair were each sewn together. But other bundles don't appear to have any thematic grouping, and many of the fragments are not sewn together at all. What the reader confronts is a book that is, in every way, unbound.

What strikes me is the care Pascal put into his bundles, threading them together like fabric, or like a wound. On the evening of November 23, 1654, Pascal had what scholars refer to as his "second conversion." It is recorded in a short text known as "The Memorial." Composed of terse, mystical visions of fire and light, it was written by Pascal on a tiny piece of paper. The paper was sewn into the inside of Pascal's coat, so that it was always near his heart, and it was discovered on him when he died.

I don't know why, but part of me is secretly disappointed that Pascal didn't actually sew "The Memorial" directly into his flesh, perhaps threading it just below his left nipple. There it might fester and flower forth from his chest in lyrical, tendril-like growths of unreflective black opal, gradually submerging his entire body — and later his corpse — into so many distillate specks of ashen thought.

∗

In his last productive year, Nietzsche looked back at this first book, noting how, in his words, "the cadaverous perfume of Schopenhauer stuck to only a few pages."[5] A critique, a confession.

∗

Schopenhauer's *The World as Will and Representation* is one of the great failures of systematic philosophy. What begins with the scintillating architectonics of Kant ends up crumbling into dubious arguments, irascible indictments against humanity, nocturnal evocations of the vanity of all being, and stark, aphoristic phrases entombed within dense prose, prose that trails off in meditations on nothingness. Perhaps, counter to what the scholars say, Schopenhauer was right about Buddhism, though his is a funereal Buddhism, in which sorrow and a silent smile seamlessly overlap. Schopenhauer, the *depressive* Kantian.

∗

5   Nietzsche, *On the Genealogy of Morals / Ecce Homo*, trans. Walter Kaufmann (New York: Vintage, 1969), 270–71.

A philosophy exists between the axiom and the sigh. Pessimism is the wavering, the hovering.

*

The notion of an American pessimism is an oxymoron, which is as good a reason as any to undertake it.

*

Nietzsche uses several techniques in his aphorisms. For instance, there are Nietzsche's spells of enthusiasm, which suddenly burst through the layers of irony and sarcasm he has so carefully constructed. For instance, following a weighty critique of morality, we get this: "[F]orward on the track of wisdom with a firm step and a steady confidence! Whatever you are, serve as your own source of experience! Throw off the dissatisfaction with your nature, pardon yourself for your own self, for in every case you have in yourself a ladder with a hundred rungs,"[6] and so on.

As a student, when I first read such passages, I wanted to jump up with Nietzsche in affirmation. Now, rereading them, I almost look down in embarrassment. How should one balance the stark, cynical critique of the human condition with such explosions of sincerity? — The fault is mine, I'm sure, not Nietzsche's. I have, it seems, become immune to his enthusiasm.

*

Philosophers are often book-lovers, though not all book-lovers are alike. The distance that separates the bibliophile from the bibliomaniac is the same distance that separates the optimist from the pessimist.

*

6   Nietzsche, *Human, All Too Human*, I, 194.

> As the strata of the earth preserve in their order the living creatures of past epochs, so do the shelves of libraries preserve in their order the past errors and their expositions.[7]

Schopenhauer's words are uniquely expressed in a place like Angkor Wat — the temple city whose main entrance houses two massive libraries, now empty. Standing in them today, one feels one is inside a tomb.

*

Do philosophers also die philosophically? Nietzsche and Schopenhauer provide what are, arguably, the two poles in this debate. Nietzsche's end is filled with great drama — it is even melodramatic, filled with so many scheming characters and plot twists that it seems tailor-made for modern-day television. His now mythical mental collapse in Turin, while embracing a flogged horse; the numerous attempts to "cure" him — including one by an art therapist (which failed); the short, effusive, *Wahnbreife* or "madness letters" that constitute his last writings; the menacing care of his sister, dressing him up in priestly white robes so that fawning followers could make pilgrimage to the "mad philosopher"; the eleven ensuing years of illness, paralysis, silence, before his death on August 25, 1900. And Nietzsche's death was just the beginning, for his manuscripts were about to be published....

By contrast, Schopenhauer's death was both undramatic and uneventful. He simply passed away in his sleep on the morning of September 21, 1860. A few months earlier, Schopenhauer had written to a sickly friend with some advice: "Sleep is the source of all health and energy, even of the intellectual sort. I sleep 7, often 8 hours, sometimes 9." This, of course, from the philosopher who wrote that "death is to the species what sleep is to the individual"....

7   Schopenhauer, *Essays and Aphorisms,* trans. R.J. Hollingdale (New York: Penguin, 1970), 209.

Which death, then, is the more "philosophical"? Perhaps neither. A third option presents itself — that of the eighteenth-century French aphorist Nicolas Chamfort, a writer admired by both Schopenhauer and Nietzsche for his pessimistic outlook on life. On the evening of September 10, 1793, Chamfort was about to be imprisoned for his criticisms of the French government. Rather than be taken prisoner, he resolved to kill himself. According to a friend, Chamfort calmly finished his soup, excused himself, and went into his bedroom, where he loaded a pistol and fired it at his forehead. But he missed, injuring his nose and blowing out his right eye. Grabbing a razor, he then tried to slit his own throat — several times. Still alive, he then stabbed himself repeatedly in the heart, but to no avail. His final effort was to cut both wrists, but this again failed to produce the desired effect. Overcome with either pain or frustration, he cried out and collapsed into a chair. Barely alive, he reportedly said, "What can you expect?.... One never manages to do anything successfully, even killing oneself."

The pessimist, who fails to die....

10

A Horse is Being Beaten: On Nietzsche's "Equinimity"

Dominic Pettman

NWW.IV, April 13, 2013[1]

In Turin on 3rd January, 1889, Friedrich Nietzsche steps out of the doorway of number six, Via Carlo-Alberto. Not far from him, the driver of a hansom cab is having trouble with a stubborn horse. Despite all his urging, the horse refuses to move, whereupon the driver loses his patience and takes his whip to it. Nietzsche comes up to the throng and puts an end to the brutal scene, throwing his arms around the horse's neck, sobbing. His landlord takes him home, he lies motionless and silent for two days on a divan until he mutters the obligatory last words ["Mother, I am dumb"], and lives for another ten years, silent and demented, cared for by his mother and sisters. We do not know what happened to the horse.

These are the introductory titles at the beginning of Béla Tarr's film, which picks up the narrative immediately after these events. The film is a meticulous, monotonous, mesmerizing depiction of the life of the driver of the cart — not actually a hansom cab, in fact — his daughter, and (to a lesser degree) the horse (*fig.* 1).

1   An alternate version of this essay can be found online at *NECSUS: European Journal of Media Studies*; see Dominic Pettman, "When Lulu Met the Centaur: Photographic Traces of Creaturely Love" (Spring 2015), http://www. necsus-ejms.org/When-Lulu-Met-the-Centaur-photographic-traces-of-Creaturely-Love/.

Fig. 1. Film still from Béla Tarr, *A Torinói Ló* (*The Turin Horse*) (Másképp Alapítvány Cirko Films, 2011).

We can only speculate what it was that triggered this event (and of course the debate continues concerning the extent to which it really happened or is purely apocryphal). In any case, this story has become such a primal scene for Western philosophy because it rests on a fatal or poetic irony: Nietzsche, the great Zarathustrian warrior of the right and mighty, is undone by a tsunami of pity inspired by a single beast. (Had not the same man, in a book called *Genealogy of Morals,* warned against such tender sympathies as a Trojan Horse, bearing yet more moralistic slaves into the city?[2]) How to read this anomolous moment of empathy and compassion in the light of his un-Samaritan perspective on ethics?

Did he empathize with the horse, seeing its will-to-power bridled and injured so? Did he see the creature as a proxy for his own imminent fallen and harassed state? Was there pure projection, or some kind of mutual communication? Was there a telescoping of his vivid past onto the agoraphobic present, linking

2   Friedrich Nietzsche, *On The Genealogy of Morals* (New York: Dover Publications, 2003).

173

the mounted cavalry with his own pagan Calvary? Such questions haunt the margins of Béla Tarr's film.

Nietzsche's work has a strong totemic aspect to it, enlisting figural and symbolic animals for his counter-moral system — eagles, lions, asses, and so on. Interestingly, given the ostensible source of his meltdown, horses did not feature, even though they seem readymade to serve as avatars of nobility and transcendence, leaping over old resentments and kicking slave-mentality in the teeth.

However, there are a few cameo moments when horses appear in his life and writing. In 1867, for instance, Nietzsche signed up for one year of voluntary service with the Prussian artillery division in Naumburg. He woke up at 5:30 every morning to muck out the manure in the stables and groom his own steed. In a letter to a friend penned at this time, Nietzsche writes: "I like the riding lessons best. I have a very good-looking horse, and people say I have a talent for riding. When I whirl around the exercise area on my Balduin, I am very satisfied with my lot."[3] However, in March of the following year, the young man had a riding accident, leaving him exhausted and unable to walk for months, and subsequently returned to the library chair, rather than the saddle.

Later, in *Human, All Too Human,* Nietzsche would write, "A good posture on a horse robs your opponent of his courage and your audience of their hearts — why do you need to attack? Sit like one who has conquered!"[4]

In the same text, Nietzsche represented the historical will, inspired by "the light of genius," as a horse ready to "break out and leap over into another domain"[5] (just as Kant did before, in a different register, namely artistic genius).

Fusing these two comments together is a third observation, also in *Human, All Too Human,* which reads:

3 Nietzsche, *Selected Letters of Friedrich Nietzsche,* ed. and trans. Christopher Middleton, (Chicago: University of Chicago Press, 1996), 32.
4 Nietzsche, *Human, All Too Human: A Book for Free Spirits,* trans. R.J. Hollingdale (Cambridge: Cambridge University Press, 1996), 292.
5 Ibid., 111.

Genius of culture. — If anyone wanted to imagine a genius of culture, what would the latter be like? He would manipulate falsehood, force, the most ruthless self-interest as his instruments so skilfully he could only be called an evil, demonic being; but his objectives, which here and there shine through, would be great and good. He would be a centaur, half beast, half man, and with angel's wings attached to his head in addition.[6]

So clearly Nietzsche did, at least on occasion, identify himself and his philosophical hero with a horse, or centaur, or horse-like being.

Of course that other giant of Germanic letters, Freud, also viewed the horse as a totemic creature, which often featured in neurotic or psychotic narratives revolving around what he called "anxiety-animals."[7] In the famous case of Little Hans, who was five years old, the paralyzing fear of horses stemmed — or so Freud insisted — from displaced ambivalence concerning the father and his intimidating "widdle." The father-horse chimera is at once magnificent, dreadful, enviable, and fascinating. This case prompted Freud to look at children's self-representation in an entirely new light, via modern-day totemism, inflected through the Oedipus Complex.

Ultimately, Freud would use the horse as his own symbol for the id itself: a powerful yet unruly animal, requiring the ever-straining harness of the superego to function with disciplined direction. For Freud, then, *all* humans are in fact centaurs. Thus, there is something inherently erotic or libidinal about actual horses, in the eyes of humans, given that the animalistic "lower" half is powered by the id. We might say, then, that if *Schadenfreude* is the perverse, neurotic pleasure one gets from seeing others fail or suffer, then *Schadennietzsche* is the healthy,

6 Ibid., 115.
7 For a more detailed discussion of the ways in which totemic thinking and symbolism continues to inform the twenty-first century mediascape, see my recent book, *Look at the Bunny: Totem, Taboo, Technology.*

noble glow one gets from seeing others rejoice and overcome. It logically follows that someone who experiences the latter would also be more distressed at the scene of suffering than someone more inclined to the former.

In any case, according to the ongoing mythology, the horse is at once master and mastered. This dual nature in respect to humans has gendered repercussions: for proto-men, who must embody the horse in order to become full sexual beings, and inchoate women, who often fall in love with horses long before they look adoringly at boys or other playmates. Or so the story goes. Horses are one of the primary totems of libidinal economics.

In fourteenth-century Europe, a horse was the equivalent of a sportscar, only much more so, since if a young peasant could secure one — by, say, ambushing a knight in the woods — then he was granted access into a world of prestige, privilege, and relative power. Ownership of such an animal, no matter how obtained, allowed instant upward mobility, at least for a time. It also inspired Denholm-Young's dictum, "[I]t is impossible to be chivalrous without a horse."[8]

The great invention that enabled the rise of this new class of socio-economic centaurs was the stirrup. Both McLuhan and Deleuze had much to say about this new technology, which created an unprecedented inter-species war-machine. The horse-human-armor-lance assemblage became one lethal galloping event. "Few inventions have been so simple as the stirrup, but few have had so catalytic an influence on history," writes McLuhan. "Antiquity imagined the Centaur; the early Middle Ages made him the master of Europe."[9]

It is arguable that the horse is the second cyborg, after humans, given that we find evidence of equine armor over 4000

8   Noah Efron, "Without a Horse: On Being Human in an Age of Biotechnology," in *Human Identity at the Intersection of Science, Technology and Religion,* ed. Nancey Murphy and Christopher C. Knight (Farnham: Ashgate, 2010), 196.

9   Marshall McLuhan and Quentin Fiore, *War and Peace in the Global Village* (San Francisco: Hardwired, 1997), 33.

years ago in Persia. Medieval horses lugged as much metal as their riders did during battle. And of course the horseshoe allowed horses to haul their loads far longer than previously possible, enhancing the animal for trade and industry. (As Desmond Morris noted, perhaps courting controversy, "If a dog is man's best friend, the horse has been man's best slave."[10]) Indeed, whenever we "harness" the power of Nature, we unconsciously figure the forces of *phusis* as equine in character.

For Deleuze, however, a horse is not merely a *stable* entity — if you excuse the pun — which is used for this or that purpose. On the contrary, for him a draft horse and a racehorse are almost different species, by virtue of a revised taxonomy which takes into account experience and context more than morphology or genetics. "Their affects are very different," he writes; "their maladies are absolutely different, their capacities of being affected are completely different and, from this point of view, we must say that a draft horse is closer to an ox than to a race-horse."[11]

Horses were, of course, one of the main engines helping humans move from feudal to more modern social and economic structures, up until the invention of the automobile (whose engine is still measured in "horsepower," as if the car is a mechanical descendent of this same animal). Speaking of the political aspect of ongoing industrial process, Nietzsche writes,

That which now calls itself democracy differs from older forms of government solely in that it drives with *new horses*: the streets are still the same old streets, and the wheels are likewise the same old wheels. — Have things really got less perilous because the wellbeing of the nations now rides in *this* vehicle?[12]

10 Desmond Morris, *Horse Watching* (New York: Crown Publishers, 1989), 1.

11 Gilles Deleuze, "Spinoza's Concept of Affect," lecture transcripts, Cours Vincennes, Paris, France, Jan. 24, 1978, https://archive.org/stream/mybooks/DeleuzeSpinozaAffect_djvu.txt.

12 Nietzsche, *Human, All Too Human,* 384.

Which is not to say that horses became obsolete; just that their presence and power became more ambient, figural, and cultural. The erotic aura of the knight, for example — witnessed by his starring role in chivalry and romance — returns in the form of the cowboy and polo champion. We call a sexually potent man a *stud* or a *stallion*. Indeed, French branding expert Clotaire Rapaille dramatically increased sales of the Jeep, or so he claims, when he changed the front headlights from square to round, after divining that the "cultural code" of this iconic vehicle for American consumers is the horse.[13]

But I digress.

Horses are the third member of the holy trinity of "companion species." Haraway has her dog. Derrida had his cat. And those who live with horses also look into the eye of this intimate stranger and try to initiate authentic communication across species lines. As John Jeremiah Sullivan notes, "Today in Greece you can walk by a field and hear two farmers talking about an *alogo,* a horse. An *alogos.* No *logos,* no language. That's where one of their words for horse comes from. The animal has no speech; it has no reason. It has no reason because it has no speech."[14] (Which recalls Count Vronsky, who notes to himself in *Anna Karenina,* admiring his ride Frou-Frou, "In her whole figure and especially in her head there was a distinctly energetic and at the same time tender expression. She was one of those animals who, it seems, do not talk only because the mechanism of their mouths does not permit it."[15])

But perhaps we are not becoming increasingly civilized in relation to horses, but merely *rediscovering* a lost kinship, which perhaps the riders of old took for granted. Consider, for example, the fact that many horses were hanged and killed, along

---

13 Clotaire Rapaille, *The Culture Code: An Ingenious Way to Understand Why People Around the World Live and Buy as They Do* (New York: Broadway Books, 2006), 2.

14 John Jeremiah Sullivan, "One of Us," *Lapham's Quarterly* 6.2 (Spring 2013), http://www.laphamsquarterly.org/animals/one-us.

15 Leo Tolstoy, *Anna Karenina,* trans. Richard Pevear and Larissa Volokhonsky (New York: Penguin Books, 2000), 182.

with the highwaymen who rode them, in eighteenth-century Europe. Jean Baudrillard argues that this in fact demonstrates a genuine respect for the animal, as co-conspirator of equal ontological significance, preferable in his view to the precious patronage of something like PETA.[16] (A controversial but productively provocative point, as is consistent with this neo-Nietzschean thinker.)

Given the ongoing energy crisis and pressing ecological questions of sustainability, one wonders if the second half of the twenty-first century will witness a return to actual horse power, when the oil inevitably runs out. Perhaps our streets will be covered with horse dung once more, and the car alarm will be replaced by the cracking of the whip as the most vexing sound for sensitive ears and nerves. (Schopenhauer dedicated an entire article to this sonic urban problem, since "noise is a torture to intellectual people."[17])

If this scenario does indeed come to pass, no doubt we will see a new generation taking up Nietzsche's cry for mercy (a cry echoed by Dostoevsky, Nijinsky, and no doubt many others). This returns us full circle to Béla Tarr's film, which provides a visceral understanding of what the director calls the "unbearable heaviness of being."[18] Despite the title, there is little of the horse itself. As is usually the way, it moves off-screen, and human drama (or lack of) takes center stage. The unknowability of the horse conditions and limits not only this film, but our own relationship with this exceptional companion animal. We can "tell" horses where we want to go, and at what speed, but the conversation goes in one direction (beyond messages of hunger and fatigue).

Bresson perhaps made the most valiant effort to convey the phenomenological experience of a horse-like creature: in his

16 Jean Beaudrillard, *Symbolic Exchange and Death: Theory, Culture & Society,* trans. Iain Hamilton Grant (London: Sage Publications, 1993), 166–67.
17 Arthur Schopenhauer, "On Noise," *Studies in Pessimism,* trans. Thomas Bailey Saunders (New York: The Macmillan Co., 1908), 127.
18 Alex Barrett, "EIFF 2011: The Turin Horse," June 25, 2011, http://www.directorsnotes.com/2011/06/25/eiff2011-the-turin-horse/.

Fig. 2. Lou Salomé, Paul Rée, and Friedrich Nietzsche with Horse-Cart, 1883
(photo by Jules Bonnet)

case the cousin of the horse, the donkey. And as a friend of a friend said about this director, every film in his oeuvre essentially says, "Life sucks. Then you die." However, in the case of Balthazar, there is a caveat: "Life sucks, then you die. But you're a donkey."

Here we have a remarkable photo of Nietzsche (*fig.* 2), seven years before his public breakdown, pretending — somewhat self-consciously — to be a horse whipped by his Lou Salomé and seemingly "owned" by the poet Paul Rée. More than an uncanny foreshadowing of his collapse in Turin, this image also serves to highlight the cybernetic arrangement of the horse-and-cart, and the multiple vectors of command, control, and communication it requires. If Ms. Salomé whips the Professor — as the staging suggests — he will respond as a beast does, enmeshed in one of *the* machines of nineteenth-century motion. In its own awkward and whimsical way, this photograph thus anticipates Norbert Wiener's decisive and epoch-changing observation that "the fact that the signal [...] has gone through a machine rather than through a person is irrelevant and does not in any case greatly change my relation to the signal. Thus the theory of control in engineering, whether human or animal or mechanical, is a chapter in the theory of messages."[19] No doubt we are tired of being reminded that "cybernetics" traces its name and mission back to the Greek word for *steersman, pilot, government,* or *rudder.* And yet, keeping a ship or a horse — and certainly a country — on an even keel is no small matter. (Let us not forget that Neptune was worshipped by the Romans as a god of horses and horse racing, *Neptunus Equester.*) Whether on land or sea, the cybernetic imperative is to harness an assemblage of elements into what is in effect a single distributed being, which can then move over the surface, or through the environment, with purpose and grace: or, in a word, equanimity.

Equanimity is the enviable state embedded in its etymology: *aequus,* "even" + *animus,* "mind." If you respond to an event

19 Norbert Wiener, *The Human Use of Human Beings: Cybernetics and Society* (New York: Da Capo Press, 1988), 16–17.

Fig. 3. Boston Dynamics' BigDog.

with equanimity, then you do so on an even keel, and with measured affect. Nietzsche, in contrast, greeted the spectacle of a beaten horse with *equinimity*: a horse-like mind, wild, kicking, unbridled — yet because of this, more sensitive to alterity, and capable of responsible response. The common hierarchical parsing of species-based ontologies is thus dispelled for an intense form of intersubjective feedback: a negative and diminishing spiral which inverts the disciplined joy in things which Nietzsche sought in his less stricken days. A profound cosmic pathos is belatedly discovered; a kind of "sorrowful science" which complements and complicates his more celebrated gay or queer one. Instead of the Passion of the Christ, the compassion of the anti-Christ.

Allow me to finish now with a contemporary descendent of the Turin Horse — a robotic creature assembled by the military contractors Boston Dynamics known as BigDog (*fig.* 3), not to be confused with my two-legged namesake Petman, fashioned by the same company. The makers take great pleasure in kicking the headless robotic quadruped, and watching it steady itself; running ever forward, over snow, rocks, and ice, all while making a sound like a giant angry gnat — a sound as annoying as it is plaintive. Even so, the determined acephalic entity

continues, as if on a quest, obeying the codes of this unprecedented, sadistic form of dressage (or what McLuhan might call
"spastic equilibrium"[20]). But who will throw their arms over *this*
mechanical animal, and protect it from its brutish and brutal
owners?

Boston Dynamics' new cyber-dog-*cum*-horse is a perfect il-
lustration of what we might consider Nietzsche's warning to us
from Turin. If we approach the world with a will-to-equanimity,
then we are not involved in its (often brutal) unfolding. Instead,
we are transfixed by our own sovereign sillage: the vapor trails
of entitled existence. We have bracketed ourselves off from inconvenient entanglement — mentally, spiritually — so we can,
amongst other things, extract secret self-satisfaction from the
trials and tribulations of others. Indeed, we might reach the
stage (as we have today) where we rewire the world, and its abject inhabitants, for a banal instance of the eternal return. So
that others may topple over and then immediately bounce back
from our violent acts — all the better to be beaten back once
more.

To err is human, the older Nietzsche tells us. To forgive,
equine.

20 McLuhan and Fiore, *War and Peace in the Global Village.*

11

The Rope-Dancer's Fall:
"Going Under" as Undergoing
Nietzscheo-Simondonian Transindividuation

Sarah Choukah
NWW.IV, April 13, 2013

The transindividual relation is that between Zarathustra and his disciples or that between Zarathustra and the rope-dancer who fell to the ground in front of him and was abandoned by the crowd of onlookers. The crowd appreciated the funambulist only for his function, abandoning him when — deceased — he ceased to exercise his function; Zarathustra on the contrary feels himself a brother to this man, and carries the latter's cadaver so as to give him a proper burial. It is with and in solitude that Zarathustra, in the presence of the deceased comrade abandoned by the crowd, that the ordeal of transindividuality commences. What Nietzsche describes here […] is the act of every man who undergoes the ordeal of solitude to discover transindividuality.[1]

I initially marveled at Simondon's exemplification of transindividuation through Zarathustra's experience of the rope-dancer's death in *Also Sprach Zarathustra*. Transindividuation — a be-

---

1   Gilbert Simondon, *L'individu à la lumière des notions de forme et d'information* (Grenoble: Editions Jérôme Millon, 2005), 280. All translations of Simondon by the editors.

ing's passage from psychic to collective existence — operates through affects and emotions that express a lack, a void, a gap in the fabric of its interrelation with others. A prior state of things having seemingly little to do with the end result is necessary for collective modes of existence to emerge. The perspective is sobering, especially in comparison with an overoptimistic but all too common view of the formation of networked collectivities. Such contemporary ideologies of the good tell us innate properties of contemporary information networks improve knowledge production and sharing, communication, and, by implication, human culture.[2]

This brings Simondon and Nietzsche in close proximity as thinkers able to situate values and norms on compatible planes: an ontogenetic one for the former, and a genealogical one for the latter. Both tell us individuality cannot be understood through an account of an individual's condition in a particular slice of time or space, that it is impossible to examine in isolation. Nietzsche posits eternal recurrence — a lived experience — as a path toward becoming individual. Simondon fully engages those who ask about individuation by making them part of the problem itself. "Beings may be known by the subject's knowledge, but the individuation of beings can only be grasped by the individuation of the subject's knowledge."[3]

It struck me that there was more work to do with respect to the interrelation of Nietzschean and Simondonian thought and its relevance to contemporary conditions of "networked subjectivity," or being "more-than-one" self, as Simondon would say.[4] This "more-than-one" — an amplification of Parmenides' unity of being — still stands as an underappreciated proposition in

2   Examples of this kind of reasoning can be found in Clay Shirky, *Here Comes Everybody: The Power of Organizing Without Organizations* (New York: Penguin, 2008); Kevin Kelly, *New Rules for the New Economy: 10 Radical Strategies for a Connected World* (New York: Penguin, 1999); and Yochai Benkler, *The Wealth of Networks: How Social Production Transforms Markets and Freedom* (New Haven: Yale University Press, 2006).

3   Simondon, *L'Individu à la Lumière des Notions de Forme et d'Information*, 36.

4   Ibid., 327.

philosophy. It is still waiting for a wider introduction to the field of media studies, in particular to researchers and thinkers concerned with ontologies of media, of information and networks.[5] Here I wish to provide a small contribution by asking how this "more-than-one" can be understood without reducing it to a "plurality," an "excess," or an attribute shared by either a "self" or a late-modern "network." To start this exploration I'll use Simondon's passage on the rope-dancer's fall to amplify some of its aspects in Nietzsche's poem. I'll then conclude with a suggestion about the ways in which Nietzsche's "overman" and "will-to-power" can be understood through a Simondonian lens.

My point of departure in this exploration helps us foreground reticulation and networks as points of emergence for specific acts of information. It would be far too ambitious to give an exhaustive idea of Simondon's far-reaching and finely detailed concept of information in this text. But for present purposes I'll clarify a dimension of the concept of information in relation to another term that can guide us: that of *amplification*. As a term inspired by electrical engineering and combined with general systems-theory, cybernetics, and physics,[6] amplification's most basic instantiation in Simondon's philosophy is the functioning of a *relay*. "The relay is a triodic mechanism by which *low*

---

5   Researchers who have firmly engaged with this exploration, especially with regards to media studies, include Mark B. N. Hansen, "Engineering Preindividual Potentiality: Technics, Transindividuation, and 21st-Century Media," *SubStance* 41.3 (2012): 32–59; Scott Wark and Thomas Sutherland, in their co-edited work on a special issue on Simondon in *Platform: Journal of Media and Communication* 6 (2015): 4–10; Justin Clemens and Adam Nash, "Being and Media: Digital Ontology After the Event of the End of Media," *The Fibreculture Journal* 24: Images and Assemblages (2015): 6–32.

6   Simondon was a great polymath in addition to being a philosopher. In "Informational Ontology: The Meaning of Gilbert Simondon's Concept of Individuation," *Communication +1* 2.5 (2013), A. Iliadis notes that "Simondon was incredibly well-versed in fields that lay beyond the ken of most practicing philosophers. In a brief interview he conducted with the French magazine *Esprit* late in his life, he spoke about his philosophical approach, yet the interview is peppered with references to a diverse array of scientists, engineers, and inventors, including Albert Ducrocq, James Clerk Maxwell, Allen B. DuMont, Robert Stephenson, Michael Faraday, and others" (2).

energy acting on an input (and generally bearing information) governs and apportions *high energy* available to it and thereby permits the latter to actualize itself through the output as *work*."[7] Simondon applies this notion of information, also termed an "occasional cause,"[8] to all modes of existence ("[t]he technical relay can serve as a model to understand a wide variety of technical, natural or physiological operations," he writes[9]). This allows Simondon to theorize the way events of great magnitude can be triggered by relatively little quantities of energy across a wide spectrum of phenomena. Reproduction among living beings is described as amplification in his thesis *L'information à la lumière des notions de forme et d'information*.[10] Other instances, such as the way a flock of birds reacts to a predator, infections turns into epidemics, and how certain kinds of content "go viral" online, also come to mind.

Amplification is thus caused — albeit not *directly* — by a difference in potential between two different kinds of input. When these inputs enter in communication together, their differences in energy actualize into a transformed — Simondon would say "transduced" — system. One finds this exemplified in various ways throughout both Simondon's and Nietzsche's works, perhaps most clearly in a section of Simondon's thesis on individuation called "The Problem of Reflexivity in Individuation."[11] Here Simondon exemplifies what he calls the "transindividual" with relations emerging "between Zarathustra and his disciples or [...] between Zarathustra and the rope-dancer who fell to the ground in front of him and was abandoned by the crowd of onlookers."[12] Zarathustra's encounter with the rope-danc-

---

7 Simondon, *Communication et information. Cours et conférences* (Chatou: Editions de la Transparence, 2010), 179.
8 Ibid., 28.
9 Ibid., 179.
10 Here it is hard to convey the polysemy the French term *sens* might have provided, as it can designate all of these instances of amplification.
11 Simondon, *L'individu à la lumière des notions de forme et d'information*, 276–84.
12 Ibid., 380.

er comes early on in the first part of *Also Sprach Zarathustra*. Nietzsche opens his poem by telling us about Zarathustra's ten years of solitude in the mountains, talking to the sun and having a serpent and eagle as companions. Zarathustra gets "weary" of his wisdom, having "hands outstretched to receive it." To "receive it" he "goes under" and "descends to the depths."[13] This is where the reader finds one of the first amplifications at work in Zarathustra. The philosopher's descent is best understood not only as a displacement but also as a change in desire and vital inclination. Life calls on Zarathustra to break free from his former bounds, horizons, and haunts so that new situations and novel terms can emerge. From a Simondonian perspective, going "under" or "over" would not be a matter of differentiation or identity, but rather — as an amplification — it would instead involve an irreversible transformation of available energies into something much greater than their simple addition. Available energies (here the philosopher's temperament, his accumulated weariness or *ennui* as predisposition) correspond to an individuation process's preindividual state and its phase changes: "This is why preindividual being can be perpetuated only by dephasing. The notion of dephasing, which in thermodynamics indicates a change in state of a system, becomes the term for becoming in Simondon's philosophy."[14]

There are many such instances of amplification to be found in Nietzsche's *Zarathustra*. Each is composed equally of directions (up and down, with special attention provided to sky and ground), motions, and differential affects and meanings[15] corresponding to much greater orders of magnitude. Zarathustra's going under coincides and resonates with the rope-dancer's fall from on high, right after Zarathustra offers to teach the overman to the villagers for the first time. Zarathustra's burying of the rope-dancer with his own hands makes him further "go under"

---

13   Friedrich Nietzsche, *Thus Spoke Zarathustra: First Part,* trans. Walter Kaufmann, in *The Portable Nietzsche* (New York: Penguin Books, 1954), 122.

14   Muriel Combes, *Gilbert Simondon and the Philosophy of the Transindividual,* trans. Thomas LaMarre (Cambridge, MA: MIT Press, 2012), 4.

15   Simondon, *L'individu à la lumière des notions de forme et d'information,* 174.

in various ways: under earth's surface to bury an outcast, under as an excluded stranger himself, warned that he should not come to the village again, under or over the appearances of the herd's baseness and fear he encountered. Each time the theme of isolation couples itself with that of a subterranean depth, an undergoing, an undoing, where possibilities for a different kind of individuation are found.[16]

After spending the night near the rope-dancer's corpse hidden in a hollow tree, Zarathustra sees a "new truth." "An insight has come to me," he says:

> Let Zarathustra speak not to the people but to companions. Zarathustra shall not become the shepherd and dog of a herd. To lure many away from the herd, for that I have come. The people and the herd shall be angry with me: Zarathustra wants to be called a robber by the shepherds.[17]

As a communicational act, Zarathustra's insight sits far from the well-meaning, idealistic representation of openness and sharing that can be found in contemporary techno-optimistic accounts of the liberating power of information networks. This insight is nevertheless thoroughly reticular. If a particular communicative form could describe Zarathustra's wish to "lure as many away

16 Here again "Man hitherto [...] [is,] as it were, an embryo of the man of the future; [and] all the form-giving forces directed toward the latter are present in the former; and because they are tremendous, the more a present-day individual determines the future, the more he will suffer. This is the profoundest conception of suffering: the form-giving forces are in painful collision. — The isolation of the individual ought not to deceive us: something flows on *underneath* individuals. That the individual feels himself isolated is itself the most powerful goad in the process toward the most distant goals: his search for his happiness is the means that holds together and moderates the form-giving forces, so they do not destroy themselves" (Nietzsche, *Will to Power,* trans. Kaufmann [New York: Random House, 1968], 365). This passage is exemplified in an unequaled manner in Dostoyevsky's *Notes from Underground,* which Nietzsche found through "an accidental reach of the arm in a bookstore." See his "Letter to Overbeck," in *The Portable Nietzsche,* 454.

17 Nietzsche, *Thus Spoke Zarathustra,* 135.

from" the herd, to "be called a robber by the shepherds," it would be that of an emerging contagion or a contamination ripe for the happening, a continuous injunction calling itself through each of its iterations, amplifying itself as it grows.

Zarathustra's initiating transduction started taking form, reached critical thresholds and expanded "from place to place."[18] Internal resonances created within this network of thought irreversibly inform action to come. Zarathustra worries at this point about receivers being able to stand the signification of new knowledge, not in the least about how to transmit a message put in a different way. The philosopher wants to address individuals concerned with their collective becoming, not a population rounded up for yet another communications campaign or only wanting to hear the good news.

This brings us to another of Simondon's concepts, and one that functions along similar lines: *transduction*. Simondon uses it in a specific and very extensive way throughout his work. It denotes the operation whereby two domains of reality, which previously didn't communicate, form a new metastable system together and allow for further individuations to take place.[19] Every domain of being (physical, living, psychic, and collective) gets informed this way, taking each previous domain's remaining potential energy as a starting point. The reason why this wouldn't be the case is simple enough to start with: for Simondon, a system that exhausted all of its potential energy is a dead system.[20]

---

18 Simondon, *L'individu à la lumière des notions de forme et d'information*, 32.
19 Here is Simondon's definition: "By transduction we mean an operation — physical, biological, mental, social — by which an activity propagates itself from one element to the next, within a given domain, and founds this propagation on a structuration of the domain that is realized from place to place: each area of the constituted structure serves as the principle and the model for the next area, as a primer for its constitution, to the extent that the modification expands progressively at the same time as the structuring operation" ("The Position of the Problem of Ontogenesis," trans. Gregory Flanders, *Parrhesia* 7 [2009]: 4–16).
20 Simondon, *L'individu à la lumière des notions de forme et d'information*, 213.

Amplification can take place without transduction, but transduction needs amplification to extend from a domain of reality to another, initially incompatible one. Both amplification and transduction help account for the terms that constitute an act of individuation. Transduction is situated within a transformative process; it would be hard to find in an object or being bounded once and for all by interiors and exteriors, inputs and outputs, addition or subtraction. Similarly, space and direction in Zarathustra are not presented as absolutes, but rather as the grounds on which values can be examined, worked through, and transformed.[21] As we indicated above, if "going under" doesn't refer to a spatial orientation with prescribed value, it corresponds to something akin to a necessary period of undoing. A "phase shift" (*déphasage*) of sorts which, as it initiates the incursion of something entirely different, allows for inversions of outer and inner limits at the same time: transvaluations of values.

In this regard, Simondon's philosophy is all about individuation rather than individuals for good reasons. He doesn't so much focus on what would be thought as the stability of beings but on their "metastability." Muriel Combes explains:

Before all individuation, being can be understood as a system containing potential energy. Although this energy becomes active within the system, it is called potential because it requires a transformation of the system in order to be structured, that is, to be actualized in accordance with structures. Preindividual being, and in a general way, any system in a metastable state, harbours potentials that are incompatible because they belong to heterogeneous dimensions of being.[22]

---

21 "Tell me, my brothers: what do we consider bad and worst of all? Is it not *degeneration*? And it is degeneration that we always infer where the gift-giving soul is lacking. Upward goes our way, from genus to over-genus. But we shudder at the degenerate sense which says, 'Everything for me'. Upward flies our sense: thus it is a parable of our body, a parable of elevation. Parables of such elections are the names of the virtues" (Friedrich Nietzsche, *Thus Spoke Zarathustra: First Part*, 187).

22 Combes, *Gilbert Simondon and the Philosophy of the Transindividual*, 3–4.

The term *preindividual* denotes that state of potential energy that a system has prior to its actualization. Nature in *Zarathustra* is the field of potential energy actualizing under and beyond him. The apparent exteriority of nature is only a moment in space and time. As it is involved, involuted in a further individuation process, its exteriority (ground, soil, trees, and skies alike) becomes part of a transformed interiority in Zarathustra.

Psychic and collective domains of life, for their part, aren't autonomous or closed domains of being for Simondon either. In other words, preindividuality, the potential energy contained in both the charged systems of nature and Zarathustra, can be further located in the affective dimensions of psychic and collective life. For Simondon, two different modes of resolution present themselves to the problem these latter dimensions pose. One is through the experience of what can be translated as anxiety (*angoisse*), the other is through the undergoing of a trial of solitude.

Anxiety in Simondon can be described as a destructive experience wherein the subject tries to resolve a charge of potential contained in him all by himself, without reaching out to the collective dimensions of being. The obverse experience of the process of anxiety (which Combes refers to as an "inverted reflexion"[23]) is that of solitude. Zarathustra experiences that solitude, Simondon writes, as a trial.[24]

First, the trial unravels as such in light of an exceptional event, the rope-dancer's fall in this case. And that exceptional event, although common for most, will prove itself to be exceptional as it presents itself with the character of a revelation.

Additionally, the trial doesn't refer to the undergoing of a passion for the sake of redemption. We should rather make sense of it, as Muriel Combes suggests, as a sign of the potential already contained in the individual for transindividuality want-

23 Combes, *Gilbert Simondon and the Philosophy of the Transindividual*, 36.
24 The french term *épreuve* which Simondon uses to qualify this process conveys a slightly different meaning in comparison to its English translation: that of something or someone undergoing a particular kind of experience, or an experimentation aiming to bring up qualities in something or someone.

ing to reach out to its actualization. More like "a call for a response than an announcement," "more like the wave of a hand than a premonitory sign."[25]

Here the whole notion of "undergoing" and going under can be interpreted pretty far from banal uses and coincides well with Simondon's meaning. What in his work resonates about this conception of transindividuality is that the process of undergoing solitude is independent of any of the reassurances a religion or pre-existing organized belief could give. It is a process situated prior to what institutionalized, organized religion does with it in other cultural contexts. Zarathustra's trial is a quest for a new *milieu,* that is, for the capacity of a nonetheless spiritual life to grow somewhere other than in its own, familiar environment. This quest is set out as a condition of possibility for amplification and transduction processes to occur. For this event to become meaningful, living information, Zarathustra has to modulate into its point of reception, its percipient.

This helps locate another point of resonance between Simondon and Nietzsche's philosophies. For Simondon, the terms "interindividual" and "transindividual" denote different available modes of individuality, for the first term, and individuation, for the second term. The domain of interindividual life acts as a kind of register of "social images" that are shared by individuals and allow for self-identification within a more stable set of "simple relationships."[26] The domain of transindividuality, for its part, acts as another kind of *milieu.* It allows for a loosening of the communitarian bonds formed in the interindividual domain (Zarathustra's solitary retreat away from the "herd"). Transindividuality thus gets constituted through the charge of preindividuality not solved by the transaction of "social images" and social functions. It acts as a *milieu* allowing the discovery of new meanings in collective life. We could say in the case of

25 Combes, *Gilbert Simondon and the Philosophy of the Transindividual,* 35.
26 Simondon, *L'individu à la lumière des notions de forme et d'information,* 279–80; Combes, *Gilbert Simondon and the Philosophy of the Transindividual,* 37.

Nietzsche the overman could equally be considered as such a *milieu,* and not a substantive kind of being.

Zarathustra's relation to his animals, the snake and the eagle, is information amplifying the *milieu*: a transindividuality that outdoes the bonds of interindividuality. They are the ones who sing to him: "In every Now, being begins, round every Here rolls the sphere There. The center is everywhere."[27] Nature is informing and informs the *milieu* that is the overman who also teaches eternal recurrence.

In this way, Nietzsche's expression of the overman is cast in a different light, on a different kind of stage. The sign that calls for the trial of solitude leads to an altogether different mode of being when it is answered to. A mode of being that wouldn't be considered as "superior" to the previous incarnations of man in Nietzsche's philosophy, and a mode of being that wouldn't be necessarily considered a progression. Thus in addition to making the overman into a *milieu,* I suggest to understand its process of becoming as phase shifts. As a phase shift occurs on the basis of a state of matter's relation to another state, their differentiation isn't so much the result of their succession or ordering in time. Their quality lies in how a state, reaching a critical threshold under certain conditions, turns into another.

As Keith Ansell Pearson notes, it is easy to associate the figure of the overman with that of technologically augmented, enthusiastic, and somewhat naïve forms of transhumanism.[28] Such an association would follow from an underlying view of progress from simple life forms to more and more "perfected" or "adapted" ones. If we follow a bit of what Thomas LaMarre — following Alberto Toscano — calls Simondon's "energetics" (and not what we would initially be tempted to call a biological or a technical determinism) as we did, we'll be less tempted to make such a move.[29] I'd like to propose a phased and dephased mode of

27 Nietzsche, *Thus Spoke Zarathustra,* 330.
28 Keith Ansell-Pearson, *Viroid Life: Perspectives on Nietzsche and the Transhuman Condition* (London: Routledge, 1997).
29 Combes, *Gilbert Simondon and the Philosophy of the Transindividual,* 83.

constitution of ourselves with the world in this regard. It would eschew technologically determined views of a gradual, and still ongoing, networked collective becoming by not forcing us to oppose technology and nature while making the argument.

As a kind of individuation, it takes other life forms and modes of reality to amplify and transduce into meaningful acts. An incidental difference, however small, can only become information in a specific system that acts as its receiver (Simondon also calls this specificity *haecceity*[30]). This, as we have seen, implies for the receiver to set himself apart from the group in which he belongs, and while this process can have disastrous outcomes (a lonely death apart from the herd that we were part of), it also carries with it the potential to transduce the individual and his *milieu* into an altogether new set of relationships.

It would seem more fitting to see the overman as somewhat of a figure better able to make new sense of its environment instead of being "more technologically fit" in a sense often conflated with a kind of biosocial Darwinism Nietzsche is ignorantly taxed with. In the field of media and communication studies, another version of this conflation consists in reducing amplification and networks to the organization of patterns of late modern commodities of information and communication in which "information is free" insofar as it represents the most advanced commodity and means of evolution our species disposes of.

And in this sense, there is a possibility here to understand *networking,* as Simondon suggests, as an ethical act. We can think of movements of affirmation and negation in Nietzsche as relations dynamically informing, involuting, excavating the self's modes of existence. The eternal return could be considered as a special instance of amplification instead of repetition, a self-awareness constantly *out of phase,* unmade, yet ready to undergo its very own individuation.

30 Simondon, *L'individu à la lumière des notions de forme et d'information,* 49.

12

The Will to Obsolescence:
Nietzsche, Code, and the Digital Present

Jen Boyle

NWW.IV, April 13, 2013

1. Code

> *The Writing-Ball is a thing like me, made of iron, yet easily twisted*
> *on journeys. Patience and tact are required in adbundance,*
> *as well as fine fingers, to use us.*
> — Friedrich Nietzsche[1]

This small love-poem written by Nietzsche in 1882 celebrates his acquisition of the Malling-Hansen Writing-Ball, a machine that would — for a time at least — offer prosthetic assistance for Nietzsche's failing vision (*fig.* 1). In various letters, he expresses his delight with a device for writing that is "guided only by a sense of touch" and which no longer requires "the eyes to do their work."[2] Friedrich Kittler juxtaposes Nietzsche's sentiments on the definitively tactile power of the Writing-Ball with frag-

---

1 Cited in Friedrich Kittler, *Gramophone, Film, Typewriter,* trans. Geoffrey Winthrop-Young and Michael Wutz (Stanford: Stanford University Press, 1999), 207.
2 Kittler, *Gramophone,* 201–8.

Fig. 1. The Malling-Hansen Writing-Ball (1878 model).

ments from Heidegger's essay on "The Hand and Typewriter" to write:

> Man himself acts [*handelt*] through the hand [*Hand*]; for the hand is, together with the word, the essential distinction of man. Only a being which, like man, "has" the word (μύθος, λόγος), can and must "have" "the hand." Through the hand occur both prayer and murder, greeting and thanks, oath and signal, and also the "work" of the hand, the "hand-work," and the tool. The handshake seals the covenant.[3]

3   Ibid., 198–200.

"The handshake seals the covenant." The work of the hand is thus a form of action in the present, a making of "essential distinction"; but it is also a prolepsis, a contract with the future, a covenant. In this sense, the *technē* of the hand and the "handshake" (Nietzsche's encounter with the Writing-Ball) can be understood as a form of "code" as we have come to understand it in the digital present (the digital: "of or pertaining to a digit or finger"[4]). Digital code operates as a series of procedures and performatives of conversion that depend upon discrete digits (0s and 1s) as opposed to continuous data, quantities, and flow. The "digit" in the digital is a procedural counting and action that begins anew with each instance of its unfolding. As Bradley Bryan frames it, "code is the command of the not-yet. The digital relies on the opening of time made possible by code."[5] The "work" of the hand for Nietzsche, then, is not just the emanation of automatic writing (Friedrich Kittler dubs Nietzsche the first "automated philosopher") but also the touch of the machine as a differently "digital" procedural calculus: its pressures back, its resistance to complying with a predetermined arc of writing. Nietzsche's style would fundamentally change with his use of the Writing-Ball, his writing transforming from longer prosaic elements to aphoristic and telegraphic epigrammatics.[6] The work of the hand and the machine is a covenant of code, an action in the present and the opening of time made possible by the not-yet.

The protocol of the hand or handshake that conducts Nietzsche through the machine and the machine through Nietzsche is intensive but halting. The hand's touch to the twisting iron of the Ball's keys, Nietzsche's play on the required "tact" in dealing with what is often an unpredictable encounter, and his twisting

4   *Oxford English Dictionary* (Oxford: Oxford University Press, 1989).
5   Bradley Bryan, "Code and the Technical Provenance of Nihilism," in *Code Drift: Essays in Critical Digital Studies,* ed. Arthur and Marilouise Kroker (May 6, 2010), http://www.ctheory.net/articles.aspx?id=643.
6   It is during this time, due explicitly to the mechanical restrictions of working with the Malling-Hansen Writing-Ball, that Nietzsche takes up aphoristic and epigrammatic prose.

of himself as a "thing" like the machine, comprise an event at once historically distinct — so much so that it lends itself to Kittler's quasi-genealogical reading — but also indistinct, not fully formed, a transformation that is both an intensity in the moment and an unfolding pressure toward the future.

The Writing-Ball is a media-machine that Kittler takes interest in as well — not just because it serves as a vital material remnant of (as Nietzsche put it) "how these machines are working on our thoughts," but because it hovers as a kind of remainder to the techno-exuberance of Weimar Germany — one might even say, as an obsolete memory. These machines expressed at their moment materialized acceleration, reproducibility, simultaneity, and, most significantly for Kittler, a break with the Symbolic and language, where writing is no longer conducted through the hand (as in Heidegger's formulation). But such machines also promised a speeding acceleration through and away from a just post-war Europe. The Writing-Ball is coded as present action and future promise. The media machine's action as past *technē* is obsolete (its impressions marked and even quickly discarded). Its future promise, however, is a matter of obsolescence.

2. Obsolescence

The Writing-Ball embodies obsolescence. Not just because it outlines the past in anticipation of our "new" digital present, nor because it could only be "a thing like" Nietzsche for a brief moment; but because, like many of the tools we employ in our digital present (for the busy work of mining, digging, excavating — all of the hand!), it is an embodiment of what Gilbert Simondon would call arrested "individuation."[7] That is, the machine transitions to no longer be a vital site of events and processes of becoming (becoming history; becoming machine;

7   Gilbert Simondon, "The Genesis of the Individual," in *Incorporations,* ed. Jonathan Crary and Sanford Kwinter (New York: Zone Books, 1992), 297–319; see also Steven Shaviro, "Simondon Individuation," *The Pinnochio Theory,* http://www.shaviro.com/blog/?p=471.

becoming human) but suddenly, violently, grasped as an ima-gething of the dead object. And yet, like all media machines, it persists and flourishes as a placeholder for the "next" *technē,* the next opening for the fulfillment of being human against or for the machine ("Machines will liberate us!" "Machines are coming for us!"). Thus, we end up with a powerful paradox of obsoles-cence — one very Nietzschean in its form: the dead media ma-chine, on the one hand, and the too vital remainder that lurks in anticipation of the next afterlife, on the other.

The dead machine is perhaps the more recognizable aspect of this dyad of obsolescence. This half of machine obsolescence has become a symptom of a new form of historicism that seizes upon the materiality of media objects as epistemic breaks within a linear chronology of history. It is the case, for example, that some quarters of the Digital Humanities have now become places where traditional, even conservative historicisms flourish again under the guise of new accelerations or "access," exploit-ing a nostalgic and utopian promise of "the next." By contrast, the second aspect of obsolescence, the too vital threat to human power, is a shape that outlines some interesting pressures and potential energies of a competing encounter with the digital.

Gilbert Simondon has offered media ecology a direction for negotiating models of becoming over being ("technicity").[8] Si-mondon's technicity casts mediating *technē* as functionally ac-tive entities that do not just mediate modes of being but which actively re-organize the potential of states of being and becom-ing. In this sense, media objects are not static entities or con-duits of human action but act entirely as "genetic" energies that convert the encounter between human action and mediator into new virtualities. This is a mode for re-imagining the assemblag-es that form between human and non-human agents. Technicity is a perceptual framing that obscures a focus on slowed-down representations and conceptualizations, while illuminating en-

8   Gilbert Simondon, "The Essence of Technicity," trans. Ninian Mellamphy, Dan Mellamphy, and Nandita Biswas Mellamphy, *Deleuze Studies* 5 (2011): 406–24.

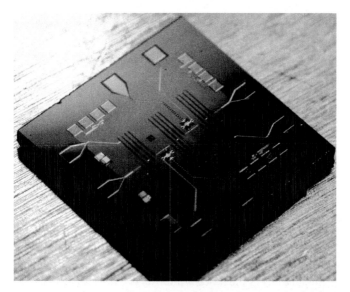

Fig. 2. Superconducting quantum integrated circuit.

counters with the energies of transduction: powers that materialize across macro and micro scales and in between form and matter (*fig.* 2). These are processes of reproduction and movement that reanimate rigid actualizations and representational stasis.

Simondon's transduction, in particular, conceives of new structural couplings of environments and agents as a matter of relations rather than the elements related. Transduction requires that we turn our attention away from the predispositions of what things are and toward how unities transformatively "become" as transfers of scale and pattern within a given medium and from one medium to another. Here, the organic and inorganic, the material and immaterial, scale and movement, intensity and actualization unfold as active relations. Obsolescence as a term in Simondon explicitly returns us to a biological (and geological) model where the obsolete is what is left to pre-actualization as a force, a power, an energy that is virtual and vestigial in its potency. This model of obsolescence conceives of not just an even-

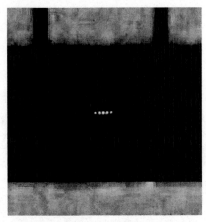

Fig. 3. Ions changing phase-state captured on lithograph.

tual "dead end" to a given species, media or form, but embraces the phantasms of the nascent traces of a given organism or energy field, some of which completely atrophy, some of which may flourish as vestigial new starts, hovering with potential to become something else (traits or characteristics quivering with the potential to flourish anew) (*fig.* 3).

Micro- and macro-protocols of bits and pulses, whose packets and flows accelerate and change form, genetically and differentially, across fiber-optic cables, through air, bending across circuits of human and non-human apprehension, forming "handshakes" between human and machine, surging intensities, quantum entanglements, as Karan Barad describes it, these processes scream out for explorations that return to protean flows and energies. These becomings deny an ontology of conceptualization and epistemic stasis.

I turn now to David Link's "Poetry Machine" from 2001–3, an event that amplifies in the present the significance of media obsolescence and code on the order of Nietzsche's Malling-Hansen Writing-Ball Machine:

There is certainly a species of automatic writing at play here, and the scene is set forth as an assemblage of human and machine language. The absent presences are the most interesting to the extent that they invoke phantasmically the "handwork" of writing and semantic ontologies. Less so the handwork of a Heideggerian losing touch, however, than of Nietzsche's brushes with the indirect and direct pressures of the hand as the not yet protocol of code.

The keys, absent a hand, go up and down as Link states it, "as if someone was typing."[9] The "as if" here working creatively as an assemblage of human and machine language, ghosting the simultaneity and distinctiveness of their transducing energies. Yet, this shaping present defies full actualization or articulation. The coherence of the "flows" and "energies" of this event are poetically and generatively compelling. They offer a kind of promise for the future. As Link puts it, "because the system is all the time searching, there is something like a political actuality there."[10] The somethings, the someones, the *as ifs*, all work indirectly as "powers of the false," shadowing the event. Powers of the false are pressures that exert influence on an event without assuming the shape of full representations. Powers of the false are alignments that come short of full phenomena, but which emerge as differing intensities, and ones that can call forth past, present, and future while persisting within an ecology of flows, flows both quantum and perceptible.[11] The "next" oil spill and the "last" September of terrorist attacks are all vestigial and active on the same plane of flows.

9   David Link, "Poetry Machine 1.0," filmed August 2002, YouTube video, 4'33". Posted August 2010, at https://www.youtube.com/watch?v=u2muCBXw-Z8.
10 Ibid.
11 "The power of the false is the potential of that which is merely simmering in a formation; it is not implicit in the sense of tending on its own to become only one thing. The powers of the false refers to that which quivers with a potential that can be defined authoritatively only after the fact of its emergence and evolution" (Jane Bennett and William Connolly, "The Crumpled Handkerchief," in *Time and History in Deleuze and Serres*, ed. Bernd Herzogenrath (London: Continuum, 2012), 153–73.

3. The Promise

> *Promises are the uniquely human way of ordering the future.*
> — Hannah Arendt[12]

> *The best way to promise: When a man makes a promise it is not
> merely the word that promises but what lies unexpressed behind the
> word. Words indeed weaken a promise by discharging and using up
> a power which forms part of that power which promises. Therefore
> shake hands when making a promise, but put your finger on your
> lips. In this way you will make the safest promises.*
> — Friedrich Nietzsche[13]

As Hannah Arendt states it, the promise is the "uniquely human way of ordering the future" because it is (through action) imminent in the materiality of memory of the past and the potential (through time) of the performative in the future. In many ways, this defines the very possibility of affective action in the polity for someone like Arendt.[14] However, as Nietzsche's encounter with the Malling-Hansen Ball and David Link's automated performances with the Poetry Machine make clear, promising is an enactment of the human–media performative as well — particularly as it is inheres in a specific perspective on the digital and code.

Both Arendt and Nietzsche embrace the "unexpressed" in the function of the promise. That is, its potential to retain a power not fully discharged in the first instance. In Nietzsche we see this potential engaged most vibrantly in his encounters with the Writing-Ball. With each strike of the finger on the key, Nietzsche's "twisting journey" through and between the machine and his text re-animates his actions with greater *potentia,* an unfolding that desires to be something other than a fulfilled and fully

---

12   Hannah Arendt, "Civil Disobedience," in *Crises of the Republic* (New York: Mariner Books, 1972).

13   Friedrich Nietzsche, *Daybreak: Thoughts on the Prejudices of Morality,* trans. John McFarland Kennedy (New York: Macmillan, 1911), IV §350.

14   See Vanessa Lemm, "Memory and Promise in Arendt and Nietzsche," *Revista de ciencia politica* 26 (2006): 161–73.

executed expression in the present. Nietzsche's encounters with this media *technē* anticipate digital code. This is not, however, the automatic writing of an inert and dead machine, but the obsolescence of code, the will and "command of the not-yet." Like Link's Poetry-Machine, the assemblage of Nietzsche and the Malling-Hansen deepens our engagement with the power of the false. And both mediated encounters engage with a kind of "political actuality," as Link demonstrates.

From the standpoint of the digital present, Nietzsche offers a different perspective on the power of digital code and *technē*. The digging and excavating of Big Data within specific configurations of the Digital and the Digital Humanities materialize as projects that reproduce the phantasy of "the next," simultaneously ordering a clean epistemic break with and a lucid projection of the past. Such projections require an inert framing of the past and the present: the past exists only to be excavated by and through the fulfillment and perfection of the machine. For Nietzsche this model of digital *technē* is commensurate with a historical culture that "wills" that we become "thinking, speaking, writing machines."[15] Such projects also resist attention to code as anything other than a mysterious translation of data into the fully "discharged" expression of conceptual meaning — a promise unfulfilled in its insistence on the code understood *as* the word. Clare Colebrook has referred to this emergence as the kind of "post-human landscape in which there is one general dynamic system with animals, machines and digital codes all woven together to constitute a single ecology. [...] What is not considered are radically differing intensities."[16]

The political actuality of the above configuration resonates as well with Nietzsche's notion of the "abuse of history": an inert framing of the present as the past, described at one point by Nietzsche as a lifeless bodymachine: "So cold, so icy that one

---

15 Friedrich Nietzsche, *Thoughts Out of Season,* trans. Adrian Collins (Stony Brook, NY: Bottom of the Hill Publishing, 2012), 12.
16 Claire Colebrook, "Post-human Humanities," in *The Death of the Post-Human: Essays on Extinction,* Vol. 1 (London: Open Humanities Press, 2012).

burns one's fingers on him! Every hand is startled when touching him. — And for that very reason some think he glows."[17]

But Nietzsche's digital coupling with the Writing-Ball requires more than a capitulation to lifeless machinations. Indeed, it is in Nietzsche that we find a competing perspective on digital code in the present. Countering the sterile and obsolete materializations of the digital machine which offer only a Heideggerian "losing touch," Nietzsche's experimentations with digital coding point us to an entirely other dimension of the promise of human–machine performatives. His encounter with the automated media machine is a past-present glimpse at what the digital might promise if we were to redirect our perceptions toward the micro and macro entanglements and intensities made possible by its procedures. Here we would find not the sterile actualizations of Digital Data writ large, but the unexpected and unpredictable unfolding that accompanies the opening of time around code, around the action of the not-yet. Here too we see Nietzsche's clairvoyance on the enactments between the quantum and the perceivable that code deploys, actions, and outcomes that are conjoined to the hand's "fine fingers," twisting keys, morphing ions, and the imperceptible powers of the false that persist through the obsolescence of media and mediation. Nietzsche's "twisting journey" offers up a different kind of promise on the political actuality of the digital.

17 Friedrich Nietzsche, "Beyond Good and Evil, § 91," in *Basic Writings of Nietzsche,* trans. Walter Kaufmann (New York: Modern Library, 2000), 272.

13

Farmville, Eternal Recurrence, and the *Will-to-Power-*Ups

Dylan Wittkower

NWW.IV, April 13, 2013

Was heißt Gamification? That is: what is called gamification? — but also, what calls upon us to gamify? What is it, in our age, that is such that gamification should emerge within it, should be called forth by it?

I hope, most centrally, to ask the last of these questions, but the way we build in our questioning cannot but pass through the other questions as well. Still, since this last concern is my focus, we will begin with Heidegger's use of Nietzsche in his attempt to understand our technological age, in which we are called upon to gamify.

1. Heidegger's View of Nietzschean Eternal Recurrence

In Lecture X of *Was Heißt Denken?*, Heidegger claims that eternal recurrence, encapsulated in *Will to Power* §617 ("That everything recurs is the closest approximation of a world of Becoming to the world of Being"[1]), remains "wrapped in thick clouds" not due to "any inability in Nietzsche's own thinking,"

---

1   Friedrich Nietzsche, *The Will to Power,* trans. Walter Kaufmann and R.J. Hollingdale (New York: Vintage Books, 1968), 330.

but because "it is the matter itself which is named by the term 'the eternal recurrence of the same' that is wrapped in a darkness from which even Nietzsche had to shrink back in terror."[2] He goes on to caution us not to dismiss eternal recurrence as "a mystical fantasy," commenting that "the coming age, in which the essence of modern technology — the steadily rotating recurrence of the same — will come to light, might have taught man that a thinker's essential thoughts do not become in any way less true simply because we fail to think them."[3]

Eternal recurrence, then, is shrouded in darkness because it is a kind of expression or reflection of the essence of modern technology, which Heidegger would elsewhere call "Enframing."[4] To reinforce this connection, we might note the parallel between Heidegger's phrase in these passages, "the steadily rotating recurrence of the same [*die ständig rotierende Wiederkehr des Gleichen*]," and Nietzsche's phrase, "the eternal recurrence of the same [*der ewigen Wiederkehr des Gleichen*]." This is no illusion of translation! We see also, in "Who is Nietzsche's Zarathustra," where Heidegger again warns us not to think of eternal recurrence as "a mystic phantasmagoria," a further comment that "a look at the present age might well teach us a different lesson — presupposing of course that thinking is called upon to bring to light the essence of modern technology," followed by the rhetorical question, "what else is the essence of the modern power-driven machine than one offshoot of the eternal recurrence of the same?"[5]

The difference, then, between eternal recurrence and the darkness of the steadily rotating recurrence, corresponds to the transformative and nihilistic responses to "the greatest weight" — that is, the gap between "[e]verything recurs, it de-

2   Martin Heidegger, *What is Called Thinking?*, trans. John Gray and Fred Weick (New York: Harper and Row, 2004), 108.

3   Ibid., 109.

4   Martin Heidegger, *The Question Concerning Technology and Other Essays*, trans. William Lovitt (New York: Harper & Row, 1977).

5   Martin Heidegger, *Nietzsche: Volumes I & II*, trans. David Farrell Krell (San Francisco: Harper, 1991), 233.

pends on each moment, everything matters — it is all alike," and "[e]verything is naught, indifferent, so that nothing is worth-while — it is all alike."[6] Nihilism, however — exemplified by the last man, who says "we have achieved happiness" and blinks — is not easily marked by awareness of nihilism but (as in "the danger") may be accompanied by a lack of awareness that there are alternate, life-affirming forms of valuation, valuation which is true to the earth.

What could be a more perfect, complete, and literal version of this steadily rotating recurrence, this nihilism that does not know it is a nihilism, than gamification?

Consider the closed system of *Farmville* in which clicks plant fictional seeds upon which we must wait to harvest fictional crops to get coins so that we can continue to click and to buy decorations to give us something to look at while we cycle from clicking to waiting captured in a circuit of drive[7] to play out capitalist accumulation serving nothing but the exchange of real time and money for fictional time and money — and in which the "fiction" has little in the way of story, characters, or other compelling elements of fiction!

Consider the economies of *World of Warcraft,* in which we grind and level, paying for the ability to toil alongside Chinese gold farmers in offline sweatshops.

Is this not hatred of the earth in practice if not in thought?

2. Gamification: A Post-Nietzschean Definition

For further analysis, we need some discussion of definitions and examples of gamification. But this is itself fraught with difficulties! Gamification is an ill-defined process. Those things that characterize games need not be present in the gamified — for example, that games are fun, at least in principle — and even games can be gamified, as in fantasy football, or in the simple case of betting.

---

6   Ibid., 182.
7   Jodi Dean, *Blog Theory* (Malden: Polity Press, 2010).

Gamification, like the term "game" itself,[8] is likely a family-resemblance term. How then shall we define it in a manner sufficient to ask what, in our age, calls gamification forth?

A merely descriptive definition may not get us to the heart of the matter, given the family-resemblance use of the term, and so we will begin from a core starting point, and then put forth a prescriptively-oriented definition. This will allow us to identify forms of gamification not commonly discussed as such, and to discard false positives as well. And where better to turn for a starting point than to business research on effective gamification?

In her article "Seven Examples: Put Gamification to Work," Debra Donston-Miller draws upon a definition from Gartner Research Inc., where gamification is characterized by:

1. Accelerated feedback cycles: Gamification increases the velocity of feedback loops to maintain engagement.
2. Clear goals and rules of play: Gamification provides clear goals and well-defined rules of play to ensure players feel empowered to achieve goals.
3. A compelling narrative: Gamification builds a narrative that engages players to participate and achieve the goals of the activity.
4. Tasks that are challenging but achievable: Gamification provides many short-term, achievable goals to maintain engagement.

A prescriptive definition departing from this might then be that gamification is a kind of exploit[9] of fundamental intra- and interpersonal drives, to achieve effects external and accidentally related to the natural outcomes of their means,[10] thereby con-

---

8   Ludwig Wittgenstein, *Philosophical Investigations,* trans. Gertrude Anscombe (Oxford: Basil Blackwell, 1986), 32, §67.

9   Alexander Galloway and Eugene Thacker, *The Exploit: A Theory of Networks* (Minneapolis: University of Minnesota Press, 2007).

10 Rather than true ends, which are consummatory fulfillments of their means (John Dewey, *Experience & Nature* [New York: Dover Publications, 1958], 366).

stituting, rather than a "magic circle,"[11] a simulacral realm[12] of false needs[13] which may or may not coincide with the realization of true needs. Accelerated feedback cycles hack into circuits of drive established originally with relation to actual life goals within personal narratives, displacing our will to power from the world into a safer, more empowering, more predictable, more structured false world — compelling, clear, challenging, rewarding, and tidy.

This definition should be sufficient to apply to a variety of clear cases of gamification, and to identify the structure of gamification in systems not normally described as "gamified." The MMORPG presents us with a clear case, as do social games, such as *Farmville* — with social games presenting a more unalloyed form of the gamified game, since, unlike MMORPGs, they do not contain structures that lead easily to actual robust interaction between players and friends.

As Bogost demonstrated in his *Cow Clicker reductio*,[14] the fundamental structure at work in many social games is one in which each action is valorized by its enabling of further actions within the closed system, and the sheer fact of delay, coupled with arbitrary and isolated, in-world valorized reward structures, is sufficient to generate the exploit of our psychological reward structures. This simulacral growth and progress is often enough accompanied by a simulacral sociality, as Losh demonstrated in her analysis of the antisociality of "social games,"[15] whether friends appear as assets as in *Mafia Wars,* in leaderboards as in the iOS *Game Center,* or as nominal interactants as in *Farmville*. In social games, just as play is reduced to the

11 Johan Huizinga, *Homo Ludens: A Study of the Play-Element in Culture* (Boston: Beacon Press, 1955).

12 Jean Baudrillard, *Simulacra and Simulation,* trans. Mark Poster (Ann Arbor: University of Michigan Press, 1994).

13 Herbert Marcuse, *One-Dimensional Man,* trans. Douglas Kellner (Boston: Beacon Press, 1964).

14 Ian Bogost, "Cow Clicker: The Making of Obsession," July 21, 2010, http://www.bogost.com/blog/cow_clicker_1.shtml.

15 Elizabeth Losh, "With Friends Like These, Who Needs Enemies?," in *Facebook and Philosophy,* ed. Dylan Wittkower (Chicago: Open Court, 2010).

mere disconnected simulacral image of the ludic, sociality is reduced to its mere disconnected simulacral image of sociality as well — we "play" in the mode of machine operators, as we "interact" with "friends" in the mode of network administrators. In this kind of "whatever" gaming,[16] content, story, gameworld, and fellow players are reduced to mere moving parts to be manipulated; intensity, degree, and function rather than content, meaning, or enjoyment. We play *Candy Crush Saga* in a mode of disguised self-hatred even as we continue to play it, a "regressive gaming" parallel to the "regressive listening [...] always ready to degenerate into rage" that Adorno described in relation to fashionable jazzed-up music[17] — we know it to be false and empty even as we cannot but be captured in its orbit.

But of course it is not only games which are gamified. Consider badging, barnstars, and Employees of the Month. Consider the similar drives in the schoolchild's fundraiser sales of chocolate bars, in which points are earned and trinkets given. Consider the elevation of couponing into a robust life practice in which "savings" — the shadow-world capital accumulation of merely counterfactual exchange values — are accumulated, producing as a secondary effect the piling-up of less-than-freely chosen consumer goods, which then need to be consumed in order to valorize the counterfactual shadow-wealth accumulated in their purchase. Consider No Child Left Behind, under which we have codified the movement in educational practice wherein learning and understanding are pursued in schools only in so far as they can be adequately captured within empirical and standardized assessments in regular feedback cycles — the crudest form of logical positivism, but applied not to metaphysics but instead to human growth and the enlightenment ideal.

In the broadest sense: Consider "saving time" and the cult of busyness. We have exported the corporate and capitalist con-

---

16 After Jodi Dean's "whatever blogging" (*Blog Theory*).

17 Theodor Adorno, "On the Fetish Character in Music and the Regression of Listening," in *The Culture Industry*, ed. Jay Bernstein (New York: Routledge, 1991).

cerns with cost-saving measures into our existential engagement — just as businesses seek to minimize capital outlay in
the conduct of business, so too do we seek constantly to reduce
time spent on both necessary and voluntary tasks. In business,
the capital accumulated in this manner can be used to expand
the business or can be treated as simple profits made. In our
lives, however, time "saved" cannot be accumulated, and we
cannot expand into additional lives or acquire other persons
through hostile take-overs. Instead, time "saved" will automati-
cally dissipate — will be "wasted," as it seems we cannot avoid
thinking — unless it is "spent." Just as the machines must be kept
running in order to maximize the profitability of constant capital — as Marx said, the factory left idle at night could be just as
easily used during that time to gain further surplus value from
variable capital[18] — we must keep ourselves running at full tilt,
lest the sacrifices we have made to quality of life in order to ac-
cumulate the counterfactual time we have "saved" should go to
"waste."

In this way, we see a logic of gamification at work in our most
basic Enframing: we valorize our life through its ordering as
standing-reserve, which ordering has value through its expenditure — but this expenditure must itself be productive, and we
have little notion left of productivity other than the generation
of further standing-reserve. When we fall under the sway of the
cult of busyness, we live in the constant sacrifice of the quality
of the present in the service of maximizing the quantity of the
future. The system holds together only through the ideological
projection of another form of valuation: "quality time" — as if
other time is to be without quality!; is it then merely quantity
time? Surely this would fit well enough with Heidegger's notion
of "calculative thought,"[19] and this is the mode in which we think

18 Karl Marx, *Capital, Volume One,* trans. Samuel Moore and Edward Aveling
    (Moscow: Progress Publishers, 1887), http://www.marxists.org/archive/
    marx/works/download/pdf/Capital-Volume-I.pdf.
19 Martin Heidegger, *Discourse on Thinking,* trans. Hans Freund and John An-
    derson (New York: Harper & Row, 1966).

of ourselves as a set of time-resources to be responsibly allocated.

What could be a clearer nihilism than the reduction of our own self-regard to merely quantitative valuation? What could be a greater form of hatred of the earth? Here, we devalue life not in order to sacrifice it to another life to follow, and we treat this world as false not by comparison to some true noumenal or post-mortem world, but instead treat it as a false version of nothing more than itself. The True World? Perhaps we have abolished it, but the world in which we live remains to us mostly an illusion; a series of mere passings-through *en route* to catch the will-o'-the-wisp of the True World: Quality Time, Hobbies, and Retirement.

Thankfully, we are not so foolish as to actually live by our rhetoric. Although we have difficulty avoiding viewing ourselves as standing-reserve and falling into a gamification of life, we often enough cannot but take pleasure in the world. We may speak of going to the gym in mechanistic terms of creating health, and our minds may disappear into televisions while on the machines so that the time can be "spent" in the body's self-manufacturing without our having to be present for the whole tedious affair, but we still take pleasure both in the strengthening of our bodies and in the ache of overworked muscles. We keep at our tasks and seek efficiency as if an intrinsic good, but we still enjoy our distractions and find we have somehow "made" time (out of what?) for hallway conversations and extra afternoon cups of coffee.

3. *Towards a Gamification That Is True to the Earth*

But through the danger, the saving power also grows. If the danger is that Enframing should crowd out all other modes of the revealing of Being, and if gamification is a sort of Enframing, then what, in the spread of gamification, can we identify as a new Clearing? In what ways can gamification stay true to the earth, reveal to us forms of value which lead us away from the nihilism of closed systems of in-game reward structures back to true needs and a real world? Let's look at some cases that may indicate a pathway.

Consider the Toyota Prius dashboard display. It gives us a fast cycle of change and reward, training us to think effectively about MPG rates as we drive. This structure hooks up directly to a set of concerns that motivate us to engage in this gamification, and the reward structures correspond to actual effects realized through the gamified set of actions. The skills and habits generated through this practice are, furthermore, transferable — those value-motivated practices trained through gamification can be utilized with other vehicles, and can become part of our habits such that we can continue to realize those goals through our activity when we are not paying attention to the display, but are instead listening to music, speaking with passengers, or simply engaged in driving itself.

Consider *Zombies, Run!* — an iPhone ARG (alternate reality game), *Zombies, Run!* creates an audio environmental overlay in which the long-term reward structures of running are replaced by a fast cycle of danger and achievement, through simulating a pack of zombies whose moans and shuffling come ever closer. We choose to enter its gamified environment in order to provide a proxy set of motivations for an activity towards which we have a second-order desire:[20] we do not wish to run, but we wish that we did wish to do so, and through this second-order desire choose to supplant our first-order desires with those brought upon us within the game world. The effects achieved are not isolated to the game world, but also produce desired real-world effects, and do so in a way which generates independence from the game-world: as we run more, and as we run more more often, we train and reconstitute our bodies into those which are more well-fitted to the first-order desires we wished we had initially. A non-runner who acquires something closer to a runner's body and a runner's habits is more likely to become a runner.

20 Harry Frankfurt, "Freedom of the Will and The Concept of a Person," *The Journal of Philosophy* 68 (1971): 5–20.

Consider *Superbetter*. Through the use of rapid cycling rewards corresponding to real world behaviors, activities of health and recovery can be given proxy motivations, as in the previous case, and can result in new and transferable habits and behavior, as in the first case. By folding in social networks in a robust and interactive way, the gamified sociality of social games is also brought in, but is brought in in a way which generates real bonds and support networks, by asking users to actually correspond with and create meaningful connections with friends designated as supporters in their processes of health and recovery.

Through these examples, we can begin to generate a principle of gamification that remains true to the earth. Gamification creates a system of false needs and rewards short-circuiting the will to power, capturing it in the will to power-up. This can be life-affirming when 1) actions result in outcomes that escape recapture, that extend beyond the game system; when 2) those actions are adopted by players as a reason for play; and when 3) due to the game-exterior connection, a natural end is reached, allowing intrinsic reward structures to properly motivated desired game-exterior activity. Or — perhaps — when the game is, in fact, fun.

14

Aesthetic States of Frenzy:
Nietzsche's Aesthetic Palimpsest

Joseph Nechvatal
NWW.IV, April 13, 2013

*If there is to be art, if there is to be any aesthetic doing and seeing,
one physiological condition is indispenable:* frenzy.
— Friedrich Nietzsche, *Twilight of the Idols*[1]

The realm of aesthetics holds for Friedrich Nietzsche a position of supremacy. For Nietzsche, art is the unique offset to prevailing forms of nihilism. The basic role of art in Nietzsche's philosophy is that of establishing a counter-movement to nihilism, because art both destroys handed-down nihilistic values and creates novel aesthetic values that allow for our inner intensity to flourish. This paper will address what Nietzsche called the *aesthetic state* — a state of being that is achieved through the *intelligent sensuality* of art — through a body of work that I executed in 2012–13 called the *Odyssey Palimpsest*.

For Nietzsche, the aesthetic state is an altered state of consciousness achieved through an artistic transcendental aesthetic. This aesthetic is the highest form of human activity, because in certain works of art opposites are conjoined. And it is through

---

1 Friedrich Nietzsche, *Twilight of the Idols,* in *The Portable Nietzsche,* trans. Walter Kaufmann (London: Penguin, 1982), 518.

Fig. 1. Joseph Nechvatal, *Dark Bacchae Palimpsest* (2014).

the majesty of such conjoined art that we find an optimistic path out of nihilism and toward our own aggrandizement. So we artists and thinkers need Nietzsche now more than ever — because there is so much to be nihilistic about in our mad and tragic world. Consequently, I am interested in Nietzscheian tragic aesthetic when Nietzsche emphasizes affective states — states of mind/body that we may enter into as a form of creative expression of our will to power in art.

Today the meeting of neuroaesthetics and information technology is one of the vital and pleasurable arenas in which interesting currents align for art. My endeavor in this paper shall be to give evidence of this pleasurable meeting through my recent meshwork series called *Odyssey Palimpsest* — work that returns us symbolically to Homer's lost hero. I will place this somewhat odd odyssey in relationship to Nietzsche's affirmation of life and in line with his development of the tragic hero in *The Birth of Tragedy* (1872). His doctrine of tragedy is based in the fundamental knowledge of the oneness of everything and of art as the joyous hope that the spell of false individuation may be broken in the interests of a consciousness of restored oneness. Thus it is an affirmation of the mystery of everything.

Odyssey Palimpsest is a highly elaborated ornamental scene sequence that embodies primordial joyful frenzy and primordial pain. The lyric poet that you will see in *Odyssey Palimpsest* identifies himself with the pain of the world and merges into the unification of the world. But perhaps it is necessary to comment briefly on two of Nietzsche's well-known aesthetic formulations: Dionysus (the god of intoxication, orgies, forces of nature, and music) and Apollo (god of individuation, illusion, form, and order). This use of the concepts of the Apollonian and Dionysian is famously linked to Nietzsche, where he wants to bring to our attention the way in which the development of art is bound up with the duality of the Apollonian and Dionysian. As you know, Nietzsche's aesthetic usage of these concepts, which was later developed philosophically, first appeared in *The Birth of Tragedy*. His premise there was that the fusion of Dionysian and Apollonian artistic impulses are needed to form artistic tragedies. It is through a dialectical interplay of these two opposing — and at the same time complementary — aesthetic elements that my art owes its continuous allegiance to Nietzsche.

Nietzsche famously assimilated the Apollonian and the Dionysian together under the name of an *experience* of art. *Odyssey Palimpsest* attempts an equivalent, as it fuses chaotic disturbance with classical beautiful forms. It is an attempt at situating us somewhere between the surface of empirical diverse reality and the chasm of shattering incoherence, where we must each pick through the meshwork and recover figurative meaning out of entangled ground. This approach relates to my book *Immersion into Noise,* where I have mapped out a broad spectrum of aesthetic activity I call the art of noise by tracing its past eruptions where figure/ground merge and flip the common emphasis to some extent. *Immersion into Noise* concludes with a look at the figural aspect of this aesthetic lodged within the ground of consciousness itself.[2]

But we must address noise aesthetics and the art context within our broad-spectrum data-monitoring info-economy environment of background machine-to-machine gigabyte[3] communication murmur — and think through and deploy noise art as an embedded subject within the larger environment of ubiquitous computing cognitive capitalism.[4] To do so, I will be examining *Odyssey Palimpsest* along with some trends and vivid prospects for what I have been speculatively calling noise art — that is, visual art as compared to noise music.[5]

In brief, noise-art aesthetics is an unbound zone — where qualitative shifts of coordinates take place — in which it is possible to carry out art experiments that would be unachievable in a different place. What noise-art aesthetics has to offer is the possibility to understand things in a different way, shifting boundaries, departing from established functions.

Of course art itself has recently ossified into some established functions that might provoke a nihilistic response. For example,

2   This involves a question of the *qualities and levels of awareness of our own consciousness* within aesthetic realms which we are capable of attaining through noise art. See Joseph Nechvatal, *Immersion into Noise* (Ann Arbor: Open Humanities Press, 2011), 210.

3   Data storage is measured in bytes. A gigabyte is a billion bytes of information. The New York Stock Exchange produces up to 2,000 gigabytes of data per day that must be stored for years.

4   Stupendous amounts of data generated by nearly one billion people are set in motion each day as, with an innocuous click or tap, people download movies on iTunes, check credit card balances through Visa's website, send e-mail with files attached, buy products, post on Twitter, or read newspapers and art theory papers online.

5   Noise music in general traffics in dissonance, atonality, distortion, incidental composing, etc. This music begins with Russolo, Luigi's *reti di rumori* (networks of noises) music that he performed on his intonarumori noise instruments, and his text "The Art of Noises: Futurist Manifesto," in *Audio Culture: Readings in Modern Music,* ed. Cristoph Cox and Daniel Warner (New York: Continuum, 2004). For more of the history of noise music, see Paul Hegarty, *Noise/Music: A History* (New York: Continuum, 2007), and Nechvatal, *Immersion into Noise,* 39–47.

I have been following the public proclamations on art of The New School philosopher Simon Critchley. Critchley described in 2010 contemporary art's dominant trend as an inauthenticity of "mannerist situationism" based in rituals of reenactment.[6] Critchley goes on in 2012 to describe the circumstances further, as the "cold mannerist obsessionality of the taste for appropriation and reenactment that has become hegemonic in the art world."[7] So things have gotten no better. Clearly something deep-seated must be reevaluated. And art aesthetics is more interesting when it does the work of shifting meaning. So I am declining here Critchley's urging for contemporary art to focus in on the *monstrous,* as, in my opinion, that parody of gloomy general dystopia only plays into the extreme spectacle aspect of mannerism. To be fair, Critchley doesn't explain what or who he means by the monstrous,[8] but when I think of the monstrous today I think of the high visibility of Lady Gaga (and her little monsters), extreme Hollywood lowbrow movies, and grotesque far-right political claims and postures. And in art (commodified and co-opted by the socioeconomic system that is its life blood) we have had the work of Eduardo Kac, Jake and Dinos Chapman, Orlan, and Paul McCarthy.

No, here I am only interested in a new contemporary aesthetic labor based in a certain exquisite untouchablity and unseeablity — a *monstre sacré* affinity of disconnectedness that focuses on an impregnable diva-like commitment to a nihilistic aesthetic of *becoming imperceptible.*[9] I am interested in an ex-

6   At his talk "The Faith of the Faithless, Experiments in Political Theology at the "Dance Politics & CoImmunity Workshop" in Giessen, Germany, Nov. 12, 2010.

7   Simon Critchley, "Absolutely-Too-Much," *Brooklyn Rail* (Summer 2012), http://www.brooklynrail.org/2012/08/art/absolutely-too-much.

8   Given his age and Englishness I would guess Throbbing Gristle.

9   "Although all becomings are already molecular, including becoming woman, it must be said that all becomings begin with and pass through becoming-woman. It is the key to all the other becomings. […] If becoming-woman is the first quantum, or molecular segment, with the becomings-animal that link up with it coming next, what are they all rushing toward? Without a doubt, toward *becoming-imperceptible.* The imperceptible is the immanent

quisite *monstre sacré* aesthetic (where personal anthropomorphic eccentricities and indiscretions are tolerated) that is bent on combining the neo-materialist[10] vibrant world with a wider vision of political awareness, including private spiritual, ecstatic, or numinous themes accessible through the generative subjective realm of each individual; an aesthetics of perception politics based on *resonance,* not a politics of *visibility* — which reveals in minute particulars the full spectrum of the extensive social-political dimensions.

This *monstre sacré* affinity is a materialist nihilism of no that (if it goes far enough) can transform a metamorphosis (subject to the flickering formative forces of emergence)[11] into an all-embracing yes of delicate abhorrence. So I am advocating here with *Odyssey Palimpsest* not the passive and thus incomplete nihilism of form, but a generative and virulent and curative nihilistic frenzy that unleashes forces of reverberation to emerge and resonate like a web of interconnected, molecular, and viral relational affects and intensities of dissonance, deviation, and the incidental. I believe this to be in accordance with Nietzsche's *aesthetic state.*

Such noise-frenzy makes use of the key notion of eternal return — an access to an appreciation of the eternal through analogy — that is at the heart of great art and enables art to express hope within the reality of current tragedy. It is, indeed, the access to the eternal that is the key motif of *The Birth of Tragedy,*

end of becoming, its cosmic formula" (Gilles Deleuze and Félix Guattari, *A Thousand Plateaus: Capitalism and Schizophrenia,* trans. Brian Massumi [Minneapolis: University of Minnesota Press, 1987], 279).

10 Manuel DeLanda coined the term *neo-materialist* in a short 1996 text "The Geology of Morals: A Neo-Materialist Interpretation" where he treats a portion of Deleuze and Guattari's *A Thousand Plateaus* in order to conceptualize geological movements. For more on neo-materialism, see Manuel DeLanda's interview in Rick Dolphijn and Iris van der Tuin, *New Materialism: Interviews & Cartographies* (Ann Arbor: Open Humanities Press, 2012), 38.

11 In philosophy, systems theory, science, and art, emergence is the way complex systems and patterns arise out of a multiplicity of relatively simple interactions. Emergence is central to the theories of integrative levels and of complex systems.

as is suggested when Nietzsche writes that any artwork is worth only as much as it is able to press upon experience a stamp of the eternal.

My project *Odyssey Palimpsest* is situated in my immersive noise theory of turmoil exchanges of figure/ground relationships: an agile art that emphasizes human and non-human entanglements. This is an art that depends on playing out nihilistic negativity by intensifying its forces into an affirmative nihilism. This nimble nihilist bracketing pushes us toward open defamiliarizations, challenging us to think outside of the normal system of human consciousness. So *Odyssey Palimpsest* as nimble frenzy is implicated in the very type of problematic instability that the "self" undergoes in Nietzsche's thought: the cohesiveness of the culture/state distinction, like the cohesiveness of the "self/other" distinction, disintegrates with the ontological instability produced by the annihilation of the real as distinguishable from the illusory. With a nimble art of noise — based in the distinction between active nihilism and passive nihilism (or monstrous nihilism) — *Odyssey Palimpsest* can depict the underground vigor of form as an active verve that can only be speculated at by thinking beyond the discursive. And that enacts a shift away from the subject–object dualism that is currently much lauded by object-oriented ontologists.

The embeddedness of our inner world — the life of our imagination, with its intense drives, suspicions, fears, and loves — guides our intentions and actions in the political-economic world. Our inner world is the only true source of meaning and purpose we have, and exquisite frenzy-gazing[12] (that involves self-investigation) is the way to discover for ourselves this inner life. So we might consider now that, in contrast to our frenzied data market surveillance culture,[13] that which trains us

---

12 *Gaze*: to look long and intently. Gaze is often indicative of wonder, fascination, and revelation.

13 For example, take the fact that now under construction by contractors with top-secret clearances is the blandly named Utah Data Center, being built for the National Security Agency. A project of immense secrecy, it is the final piece in a complex puzzle assembled over the past decade. Its purpose: to

to fear the atrocious eyes of outer perception, a protracted gazing art practice based in absorption could encourage the development of agile clandestine exchanges based on the embedded individual intuitive eye in conjunctive contact with an abundant *optical-mnemonic commons* (not cloud)[14] that shares a sensibility for building a defensive force.

Of course this sphere of anti-purist gazing commons (essentially a cooperative rejection of the tyranny of labels, essential identities, privileged abstractions, and fixed ideas) is what allows art to construct unstable distinctions between subjects and objects that embraces the entire spectrum of imaginary spaces, from the infinitude of actual forms to formless voids of virtuality. Subsequently, *Odyssey Palimpsest* requires a challenging exchange of the hierarchy of figure and ground (figure and abstraction) through a struggle between noise[15] and invisibility.[16]

intercept, decipher, analyze, and store vast swaths of the world's communications as they zap down from satellites and zip through the underground and undersea cables of international, foreign, and domestic networks. The heavily fortified $2 billion center should be up and running in September 2013. Flowing through its servers and routers and stored in near-bottomless databases will be all forms of communication, including the complete contents of private emails, cellphone calls, and Google searches, as well as all sorts of personal data trails — parking receipts, travel itineraries, bookstore purchases, and other digital transactions. It is, in some measure, the realization of the Total Information Awareness program created during the first term of the Bush administration — an effort that was killed by Congress in 2003 after it caused an outcry over its potential for invading Americans' privacy. For more on this trend see James Bamford, *The Shadow Factory: The Ultra-Secret NSA from 9/11 to the Eavesdropping on America* (Norwell, MA: Anchor, 2009).

14 The term *cloud* is often generally used to describe a data center's functions. More specifically, it refers to a service for leasing computing capacity.

15 As I have done with my own work while also collecting examples of many other artist's work that can be placed in this continuum.

16 Perhaps this should not be surprising given that the hidden complexity of a basic internet transaction is a mystery to most users: sending a message with photographs to a neighbour could involve a trip through hundreds or thousands of miles of Internet conduits and multiple data centers before the e-mail arrives across the street.

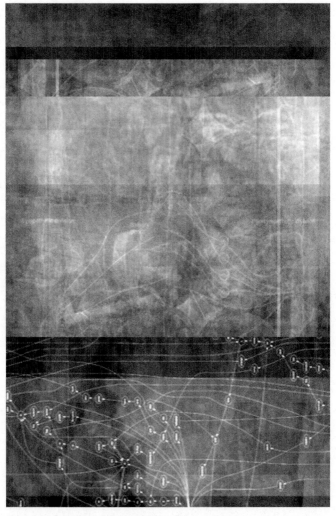

Fig. 2. Joseph Nechvatal, *Drifting Telemachus* (2014).

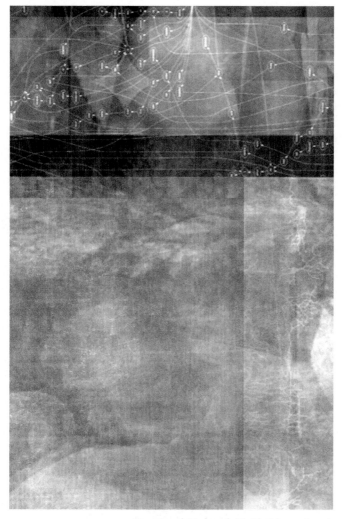

Fig. 3. Joseph Nechvatal, *Nimble Odysseus* (2014).

So I want to argue for an agony of style of logo-invisibility — and the importance that should be given noise art aesthetics.

The principle of constructing patterns of infinite becomings is perhaps inherent in avant-garde artistic tradition (avant-garde values). But this avant-garde now, I think, should be considered in terms of noisy invisibility, not ontology, as deviating from the regularities of visible normality provides the avant-garde new sources for artistic production. Certainly, the values of the avant-garde have always been interfering with the channels of artistic production and reception — and these values are responsible for expanding the forms and definitions of art itself.[17] But like in nature, noise in art plays a productive role in the invisible life of a system when it stresses becoming-imperceptible.

But a becoming-imperceptible/invisible *monstre sacré* today can no longer be a form of *enfant-terrible* withdrawal akin to Marcel Duchamp's strategic invisibility,[18] but rather a phantasmagorical plunge into what Félix Guattari expresses as the *chaosmosis*.[19] *Odyssey Palimpsest* marks such a qualitative transformation into a non-place where being and non-being reverse into each other, unfolding out and enfolding in their respective outsides. This short-circuit causes a creative conflagration typical of the art of noise.

Let's consider the difference between noise art (based on an individual's inner vision) versus the monstrous mass-machine

---

17 For more on this, read my essay "Viractuality in the Webbed Digital Age," in *M/E/A/N/I/N/G* Online #5 25th Anniversary Edition (2011), http://www.writing.upenn.edu/pepc/meaning/05/meaning-online-5.html#nechvatal.

18 Duchamp's entire artistic activity since the "definitive incompletion" of the *Large Glass* in 1923 was an exercise in strategic invisibility, giving rise to objects and events which — because they were apparently too impermanent or unimportant or insubstantial, or because they eluded established genre conventions, or because they confused or diluted authorial identity — evaded recognition as "works of art."

19 Félix Guattari said that "the work of art, for those who use it, is an activity of unframing, of rupturing sense, of baroque proliferation or extreme impoverishment that leads to a recreation and a reinvention of the subject itself" (*Chaosmosis: An Ethico-Aesthetic Paradigm* [Bloomington: Indiana University Press, 1995], 131).

data market,[20] with its digital functionalism. For me the difference is in looking *into* and projecting *onto* something — thereby discovering an emerging manifestation based in invisibility — as opposed to looking *at* something. In that sense it requires an active slow participation on the part of the viewer — and the noise style of *Odyssey Palimpsest* demands as much. For me this requires use of hidden mental participation and, as such, is now essential in our climate of monstrous mass media (mass-think) in that it plays against the grain of given objective consensus visibility. In that sense *Odyssey Palimpsest* is more like a service product (or a server).[21]

However, my main interest in invisibility with *Odyssey Palimpsest* lay in a texture of emerging claims of art-as-politics — with its emphasis on the production of individuality based in a political physiology (a political function of living systems) with a strong proposition of emergence as the key aspect. So, I will continue the work done in *Immersion into Noise* by looking at the art of noise as an emergent property rooted in obscurity. This comparison relates to my palimpsest work as an indeterminacy-based noise artist.

Now I would like to look more specifically at the possibility of further developments in noise-art aesthetics concerning where becoming-imperceptible and becoming-perceptible nimbly interact. As sketched out in my book *Immersion into Noise,* the evolution of visual noise-art develops from certain prehistoric cave areas and baroque grottoes, to certain levels of mannerist and counter-mannerist complexity, to noisy spatial renderings in various exuberant architectural styles, then into cubism, futurism, Dada, Fluxus, and other twentieth-century avant-garde

20 To support all that digital activity, there are now more than three million datacenters of widely varying sizes worldwide.

21 A server is a sort of bulked-up desktop computer, minus a screen and keyboard, that contains chips to process data. For security reasons, companies typically do not even reveal the locations of their data centers, which are housed in anonymous buildings and vigilantly protected. Each year, chips in servers get faster, and storage media get denser and cheaper, but the furious rate of data production goes a notch higher.

movements, into the screech of technological noise art, and into the softness of software noise-art aesthetics.

As noted above, what is important in the art of noise aesthetics is its intentional and elongated invisibility[22] and enigma. That is why this subject is so hard to write about. The very topic is a difficult one to pin down and make intelligible for good reason. The art of noise is an art of disbelief in habitual codes of practice and understanding. You must take the art of noise on its own terms or risk doing violence to the art.

Noise art is not a set of homogeneous practices, but a complex field converging around perceived weaknesses in the art system. Such a noisy hyper-cognitive stance[23] happens when the particular of electronic connectivity is seen as part of an accrual total system by virtue of its being connected to everything else — while remaining dissonant. Noise aesthetics is a complex and ambiguous political gazing, and its theory of an art of resistance and investigation would be increasingly valuable to an analytical social movement based on skepticism while undermining monstrous market predictabilities, as it strengthens unique personal powers of imagination and critical thinking. This is so as it counters the effects of our age of simplification: effects which have resulted from the glut of consumer-oriented entertainment messages and political propaganda, which the monstrous mass media feeds us daily in the interests of corporate profit and governmental psychological manipulations.

The noise-art aesthetic of *Odyssey Palimpsest* is that of dissonant immersion into a maelstrom of glossolaliaic unintelligibility, chaos, and exaltation. Such an art of noise style is a way of seeing that reverses the order of figure/ground[24] to ground/fig-

---

22 This parallels the fact that in many data facilities, servers are loaded with applications and left to run indefinitely, even after nearly all users have vanished or new versions of the same programs are running elsewhere. At a certain point, no one is responsible anymore, because no one, absolutely no one, wants to go in that room and unplug a server.

23 Nechvatal, *Immersion into Noise*, 32.

24 It is noteworthy that the characteristic organization of perception is into a figure that *stands out* against an undifferentiated background, e.g., a printed

ure. It collapses being into non-being (ontological implosion). It creates ambivalent aleatory[25] processes that are true to our inner essential world: dynamic pools of expansion and disintegration.

Odyssey Palimpsest refuses easy consumption then and encourages love, because a love for visual noise art will make perturbing events in your life more tolerable. It will make you able to see more and make you more adaptable to disturbances, rather than being torn up about them. It will help you to avoid psychic ossification by your loving the space of latent expanse. This is what suggests referring *Odyssey Palimpsest* to the aesthetics of the *sublime,* which, in the eighteenth century, was linked to the grandness of natural phenomena. But *Odyssey Palimpsest* is an innovative version of the sublime in which, for the first time, the embeddedness that we recognize ourselves in concerning nature matches up with our subliminal inner orb. This embedded awareness can be suggested and promoted by noisy artistic becomings such as *Odyssey Palimpsest* — as its generative aspect serves to produce unpredictable results based on arithmetic instructions contained in its code.

Poetically, the hyper-noise-dense texture of *Odyssey Palimpsest,* along with its uniform rhythms, suggests to me a possibility of connecting ourselves psychically to the great chain of being (that which precedes us and of which we are a part). However, this requires an active imagination that is aided by the visualization properties offered up. Perhaps *Odyssey Palimpsest* then is a psychotic outburst that disrupts smooth image operations with an explosion of buried visual hysteria that promises a highly diverse world. Its incomprehensibility by design connects the commons to unconscious frenzy through what I think to be a

word against a background page. What is figural at any one moment depends on patterns of sensory stimulation and on the momentary interests of the perceiver.

25 Aleatoricism is the incorporation of chance into the process of creation, especially the creation of art or media. The word derives from the Latin word *alea,* the rolling of dice.

type of chaos magic.[26] It creates the visualization bridge between form and intuition, as its uncertain images have more information in them than a clear certain image (or sound) where the information quickly becomes redundant. Thus *Odyssey Palimpsest* gives rise to new thought. It promotes the emergence of new forms of an old story: art.

As mentioned above, what is important in *Odyssey Palimpsest* is its intentional enigma. It needs to be obscure to the degree that its codes cannot be discerned. This phantasmagorical obscurity and mystery is increasingly desirable in a world that has become increasingly datamined, mapped, quantified, specialized, and identified in a straightforward matter-of-fact way. This will for enigma is the basis for discovering and entering into an immersion into the art of noise, even.[27]

Its goal is to disrupt instrumental logic and contradict, counteract, and cancel out false reason and hollow feeling. Suffering and joy, like figure and ground, are here tied together in frenzy, neither one without the other. Thus *Odyssey Palimpsest* suggests and produces stress in us; one might even say an urgent anxiety of disintegration. So dedication to its merits, if there are any, might well be described as vaguely heroic, because *Odyssey Palimpsest* suggests the revelation of a plentiful nihilistic life force. Thus *Odyssey Palimpsest* implies a cul-de-sac of ill communication (vacuole)[28] — the communication of enigma itself as experienced by the lyric poet.

26 Some common sources of inspiration for chaos magic include such diverse areas as science fiction, scientific theories, ceremonial magic, shamanism, Eastern philosophy, and individual experimentation.

27 As an example, see/hear Marina Rosenfeld's *Cephissus Landscape* (2002), an immersive noise work that undermines the central notion of "surround-sound" technology by locating viewers in an environment with no fixed center and numerous temporary sonic sweet spots, where short bursts of mingled electronic and acoustic sounds intersect and decay in expanding concentric circles that suggest oscillating landscapes.

28 This is a reference to Gilles Deleuze's notion of the *vacuole*. This concept of *noncommunication* comes from Deleuze's essay "Postscript on Control Societies." As I explain in *Immersion into Noise,* 14, Deleuze's notion of control is connected to information-communication technology — a concept

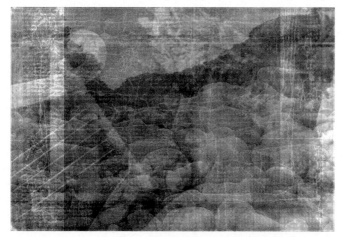

Fig. 4. Joseph Nechvatal, *Miasmic Confluence* (2014).

Thus *Odyssey Palimpsest* has something that words risk diminishing. Nevertheless, I obviously have felt that I must take that risk because if we are to continue to live among electronic vibrations that mine us, it may be helpful to talk back against them. But yes, *Odyssey Palimpsest* is the transmitter of unspeakable secrets. That is why art noise matters. It wants *more* from us. Moreover, it teaches us *to want more from art*. It teaches us to look *deeper,* to hear *more,* and to trust the inner noise.

There are now many artists who see the symbolic and metaphorical dimension of a work as of little importance. I am not one of them. For me, the real worth of vigorous contemporary art is in its ability to deliver to the commons excessive sensually embodied implications. As noise-art aesthetics are indistinguishable from that which it produces, as in *Odyssey Palimpsest,*

he pulled out of the work of the writer William S. Burroughs. A vacuole is like a sac in a cell's membrane, completely bound up inside the cell but also separate from it. Vacuoles play a significant role in autophagy, maintaining an *imbalance* between biogenesis (production) and *degradation* (or turnover) of many substances and cell-structures. They also aid in the destruction of invading bacteria or of misfolded proteins that have begun to build up within the cell. The vacuole is a major part of the plant and animal cell.

it might be considered as a panpsychic[29] sphere that contains systems of chance operations within it.

So, as you can see, for *Odyssey Palimpsest* I eagerly identified with Nietzsche's Dionysian attention to the frantic painful beauty of primal unity. For as he wrote, "The brightest clarity of the image did not suffice us, for this seemed just as much to reveal something as to conceal something."[30] My urge with *Odyssey Palimpsest* has been, in his words, to "tear the veil and to uncover the mysterious background" of life through the powerful analogy of art.[31]

Such a Dionysian approach to art includes the notions that *The Birth of Tragedy* emphasizes in its title — *eternal recurrence* — and the realization of "the eternal joy of becoming" that is the creative act.[32]

The Dionysian embraces the frenzied chaotic nature of experience as all-important, not just on its own, but also as it is intimately connected with the Apollonian. The Dionysian magnifies us, but only so far as we realize that it emphasizes the harmony that can be found within one's chaotic experience. Such a thinking of frenzy through the prism of Dionysian aesthetics was agitating my inner logic during the summer of 2012 when I did the lion's share of *Odyssey Palimpsest* in Corsica[33] and Provence.[34]

Nietzsche sees in eternal harmonious unification the genesis of the highest expression of art: tragedy that allows us to sense an underlying essence of primordial unity, which revives our Dionysian nature. This is an almost indescribably pleasurable

---

29 Panpsychism is the view that all matter has a mental aspect, or, alternatively, all objects have a unified center of experience or point of view.

30 Friedrich Nietzsche, *Nietzsche on Art and Life,* ed. Daniel Came (Oxford: Oxford University Press, 2014), 30.

31 Ibid.

32 Ibid., 193.

33 "[…] in a dense, desolate pocket in a beautiful mountain-valley in Corsica" (Josesph Nechvatal, "The Art of Nietzsche," *The Brooklyn Rail,* Oct. 4, 2012), http://www.brooklynrail.org/2012/10/books/The-Art-of-Nietzche. Thank you, Dominique and Isabelle Roussy.

34 Thank you, Jean-Charles and Jacqueline Blanc.

feeling to try to capture, but it was my goal for *Odyssey Palimp-sest*: art as means of self-transcendent turbulence.

Art is the great poetic stimulus to radical life, so from an aesthetic viewpoint we need not to look for purpose, for art is purpose in itself: the purpose of life. Indeed, for Nietzsche, art is the supreme delight of existence. With the eternal return at the heart of *Odyssey Palimpsest,* I hope to provoke many happy de-territorializations and turnings to ecstatic frenzy within the current construction of contemporary tragedy. And I hope to have taken you on an inner voyage, floating, like ancient Homer's lost hero, against the tide of our tragic postmodern carnival.

15

"Philosophizing With a Scalpel":
From Nietzsche to Nina Arsenault[1]

Shannon Bell

NWW.IV, April 13, 2013

Shan Bell: "Why shouldn't the Buddhist monk be an incredible, fabulously beautiful woman, the most beautiful woman in the world?"[2] And why shouldn't the most beautiful woman in the world become a shadow of beauty — a sovereign figure oscillating between the poles of the beautiful and the grotesque, the Apollonian and the Dionysian?

As Bill Hughes states in "Nietzsche: Philosophizing with the Body," "It takes a body to lift a hammer and smash it down. It takes a body to write philosophy. Therefore it takes a body to philosophize with a hammer."[3] If one brings together Hughes's enunciation with Nandita Biswas Mellamphy's claim in *The Three Stigmata of Friedrich Nietzsche* that the psycho-physiological theory of the body is the key link between Nietzsche's

---

1   I would like to thank Raan Matalon for the time he has given to reading, discussing, and theorizing Nietzsche with me. As always, I wish to thank Gad Horowitz for his theoretical and editorial assistance.

2   Shannon Bell, Interview with Nina Arsenault, Nov. 17, 2010.

3   Bill Hughes, "Nietzsche: Philosophizing with the Body," in *Body and Society,* Vol. 2, No. 1 (London, Thousand Oakes and New Delhi: SAGE, 1996), 31–44, at 31.

two most overworked concepts: eternal recurrence and will to power;[4] if we take the living enactment of Nietzsche's transvaluation of values as a manifestation of will to power and couple it with his urge to write with blood: "Of all that is written, I love only what a man has written with his blood. Write with blood, and you will experience that blood is spirit";[5] this will get us to the Nietzschean excess of Bataille combined with the shamanic interpretation of Nietzsche *à la* Bataille by Nick Land.[6] It doesn't, however, get us to Arthur Kroker's "Future that is Nietzsche."[7] Kroker questions: "Written today, would the *Genealogy* be compelled to conclude with an essay on artificial flesh, electric eyes and robotic intelligences — a transhuman legacy [...]?"[8]

I would answer *yea...* and who better as a techno-upgrade to the Nietzschean sage Zarathustra than a transhuman, transsexual, bio-techno medically created cyborg artist who makes her body the ground of her artwork and carves out a new body every few years, who attains ecstatic bliss "as the surgeon's scalpel carves pockets of fat out of her skin"?[9]

I am engaging the work of transdisciplinary artist Nina Arsenault, who has worked in theater, television, film, video, art,

---

4   Nandita Biswas Mellamphy, *The Three Stigmata of Friedrich Nietzsche* (London: Palgrave MacMillan, 2011), 14.

5   Friedrich Nietzsche, "On Reading and Writing," *Thus Spoke Zarathustra*, trans. Walter Kaufmann (New York: Penguin, 1954), §40.

6   Nick Land, "Shamanic Nietzsche," in *Fanged Noumena: Collected Writings 1987–2007*, ed. Ray Brassier and Robin Mackay (Falmouth: Urbanomic, 2011), 203–28.

7   Arthur Kroker, *The Will to Technology and The Culture of Nihilism: Heidegger, Nietzsche and Marx* (Toronto: University of Toronto Press, 2004), 85.

8   Ibid.

9   Nina Arsenault, "The Ecstasy of Nina Arsenault," *40 Days & 40 Nights: Working Towards a Spiritual Experience* (henceforth, *40–40*) (Toronto SummerWorks, August 2012). An excerpt of *40–40* is available at http://www.youtube.com/watch?v=baDGIou44UU. See Tobaron Waxman's excellent interview with Nina Arsenault discussing *40–40* at http://www.prettyqueer.com/2012/12/12/how-plastic-i-was-nina-arsenault-interviewed, and Richard Ouzounian's review of the performance at http://www.thestar.com/entertainment/stage/2012/08/15/nina_arsenault_presents_40_days_and_40_nights_working_towards_a_spiritual_experience.html.

photography, and print. In June 2012, *Trans{per}Forming Nina Arsenault: An Unreasonable Body of Work* was published; this is a book by international feminist and queer scholars engaging with Nina's work. In 2011 Arsenault's work was recognized by the Canadian Civil Liberties Association as having a profound impact on human rights in Canada, and Arsenault was the recipient of the 2012 York University Bryden Alumni Award: *Redefine the Possible*.[10] I will look into three of Nina's performance-works: *The Silicone Diaries, I w@s B*rbie,* and *40 Days & 40 Nights: Working Towards a Spiritual Experience.*

Paul Halferty in "Unreal Beauty: Identification and Embodiment in Nina Arsenault's *Self-Portraits*" positions Arsenault as

> a trans-gender heiress to Haraway's conception of a cyborg feminist: a self-conscious construction achieved through technological intervention and performative framing; a living representation of femininity, inspired by fantasy and Barbie Dolls, and achieved through surgical intervention and artistic practice.[11]

And I would add that she is also "a trans-gender heiress" to Zarathustra.

Nina is continuing the project of devaluation of existing meanings; she is doing what Nietzsche identifies as "philosophizing with a hammer"; however, she is doing it with her body and a scalpel. Arsenault's will-to-plasticity enacted by over sixty return trips to the surgeon and then back to the people in manifold art spaces to bring new values to the concepts of body, self, human, female, and feminist is a return with a difference to Zarathustra's way from the cave in the mountain to the people, again and again.

---

10 See Nina Arsenault accepting the 2012 York University Bryden Alumni Award for *Redefine the Possible* at http://www.youtube.com/watch?v=LNJxXuJX-wc.

11 Paul Halferty, "Unreal Beauty: Identification & Embodiment in Nina Arsenault's Self-Portraits," *Trans{per}Forming Nina Arsenault: An Unreasonable Body of Work,* ed. Judith Rudakoff (Chicago: Intellect, 2012), 32.

1. The Mannequin Cyborg

Nina Arsenault designed herself to embody what she at the age of five saw as the most beautiful woman in the world: a mannequin. In *The Silicone Diaries,* she recounts her first encounter with a mannequin. She was then the boy Rodney.

> Her face is perfect. The arch of her eyebrows has the same shape as the Cupid's bow in her lips. The upward swoop of the cheekbones is reflected in the upward swoop of her almond eyes; the tip of her pointed nose; the shape of the jutting chin; it's so harmonious. I don't think this at the time. I think: "She's more beautiful than Barbie." I stare at her. Into her eyes. They seem to shimmer. [...] "Is she real?"[12]

Yes, she is real; she is the *Lacanian* real: she is that which eludes, she is impossible, and she is designed and materialized as a live self-portraiture by Nina Arsenault. As Nina narrates the object of desire of the young Rodney, projected on the screen behind her are images of Nina posing with two mannequins[13] that look identical to her in size, proportion, facial structure and comportment. In two of the full-body images of three mannequins it is difficult to see which one is alive. What is most uncanny about these images is that Arsenault actualized — concretized — her version of Apollonian beauty, and lives it. On her currently-unavailable website Nina wrote this about the Mannequin photoshoot:

> Since I was a child I've been mesmerized by the visual harmony that has been sculpted into the designer faces of life-size mannequins. The tips of their noses reflect the shape in their jutting chins. The curves of their lips are echoed

12 Arsenault, "Sex/object (1979)," *The Silicone Diaries,* in *Trans{per}Forming Nina Arsenault,* 206.
13 The images were taken by Hamish Kippen for *Fresh* magazine's September 2007 issue.

in the elegant arches of their impossibly high eyebrows, as well as the swoops of their almond eyes and the gentle bulging of their cheek-bones. Moreover, their poreless plaster visages are perfectly symmetrical. Their false eyelashes are permanently attached, and their airbrushed make-up never smudges. These feminine works of art are supposed to represent women, but they are often too perfect to look like a real female.[14]

In a talk on "Self-portraiture, Transformation, Identity & Performance" Nina disclosed that "at some point, looking beautiful became more important than looking like a woman. It became more important than looking natural."[15]

When the mannequin comes to life through technological enhancement of the flesh-body producing a mannequin cyborg, one enters the territory of the Dionysian post-human encased in sculpted Apollonian elegance. For the first time in history, actually becoming the mannequin — looking out from the given-to-be-seen of a plasti-silicone body and having the gaze of the world reflect this very image back upon you — is a techno-physiological possibility.

But Nina doesn't merely do that (which is an identity-design feat in itself); Nina does something more — way more — which simultaneously marks her as the "most beautiful woman in the world" and a Feminist Nietzschean overhuman in the vein of a Fast Feminist.

What sets Arsenault apart from other "most beautiful women in the world" is that a part of her beauty consists in disclosing in vivid detail the design details that constitute it and the necessary rigorous daily maintenance regime. In "Venus/Machine (2007–2009)," the final segment of *The Silicone Diaries*, Nina

---

14 Arsenault, "Mannequin for *Fresh* Magazine," http://www.ninaarsenault. com/2009/10/605/#more-605; also quoted in Shannon Bell, "Nina Arsenault: Fast Feminist *objet_a*," in *Trans{per}Forming Nina Arsenault*, 100.

15 Arsenault, "Self-portraiture, Transformation, Identity & Performance," a talk at York University's Visual Arts Department's *The Body: From Liminal to Virtual* speaker's series of Canadian artists, Feb. 9, 2011.

indicates that she desired to overcome her anger "about the two hours a day I need to get ready." "I've built a perfection onto my face that needs make-up and hairstyles to complete it, or else I'm not aesthetically cohesive in my own vision."[16] In fact, Nina does transform the energy of anger through breath work and extensive exercise. And with the new endeavor, which she marks as "the next phase of my work with my body,"[17] Nina adds a new dimension to the mannequin cyborg: the Buddhist monk in preparation for her Dionysian post-beauty in *40 Days & 40 Nights*.

2. *The Buddhist Monk*

The monk comes into being on stage as Nina removes her wig to expose her shaved head and the beautiful scars of the surgical cuts. The gaze of the spectator is focused on that which the lure of accoutrement and enhancement has been obfuscating: the face denuded, the scars of creation. "The other who manifests herself in the face [...] breaks through her own plastic essence."[18] Nina's exposure of her scarred shaven head doesn't diminish the power of her beauty because what is driving the beauty is that which is more than accoutrement and enhancement — it is the glint, the gleam, the sparkle, the shimmer, the ecstasy of *overcoming*. Nina finds ecstasy in the process of beauty:

I live for beauty. I have suffered for it; the suffering is sadomasochistic. The pain of it is thrilling, the endurance, the feats to achieve it have been very much a part of it. It is the act of the forbidden, the joy of the forbidden. We have this horrible schizophrenic thing in our culture, which is, women must be inhumanly beautiful and inhumanly thin. These aes-

16 Arsenault, "Venus/Machine (2007–2009)," *The Silicone Diaries,* in *Trans{per} Forming Nina Arsenault,* 224.

17 Ibid., 225.

18 Emmanuel Levinas, "The Trace of the Other," trans. Alfonso Lingis, in *Deconstruction in Context,* ed. Mark Taylor (Chicago: University of Chicago Press, 1986), 351.

theticized beings. Yet, you're not allowed to want that or to try for it. I speak the forbidden, I speak the blasphemous: I say I have suffered for it, this suffering has been also ecstatic. Even to call it suffering is to reduce it to one thing. There's been ecstasy and joy. I enjoy going for surgeries, I like having people taking care of me, I like the anesthetic needle going in my veins, I like the feeling of the anesthesia, the ability to see myself one way, one day and then two weeks later having a "completely new face." It's an ecstatic experience.[19]

The anger at the daily rigor of beauty gets transmutated in a deep-breath practice: "One of the ways I get through the rigour is by breathing and going completely into the moment in the mirror."[20] This moment in the mirror is Nina the mannequin cyborg gazing at Nina the Buddhist monk gazing at Nina the mannequin cyborg, an anamorphic gaze in which each comes together as one in the image of the mannequin-cyborg-monk.

In her play *I w@s B*rbie*[21] Nina discloses her reaction when she received Mattel's request to be Barbie at Barbie's official fiftieth birthday in Toronto: "I want to say: *Do you really want to hire someone known for having massive amounts of plastic surgery to represent a doll that's accused of fucking-up the body-images of millions of little girls?*"[22] It is as if in their selection of Nina as the truest likeness to Barbie, Mattel simultaneously acknowledged the impossibility of Barbie's proportions and features and recognized that — with some sixty cosmetic surgeries and procedures, an exquisite eye for redesigning the flesh body, time in which to do so (eight years), monetary means ($200,000), aesthetic and ascetic discipline, geisha-like training and perhaps most importantly the will to "sacrifice being normal," to

19 Shannon Bell, Interview with Nina Arsenault, Nov. 17, 2010.
20 Ibid.
21 I saw Nina Arsenault performing "I was Barbie" at *PSi16: Performing Publics,* Buddies in Bad Times Theatre, Toronto, June 9–13, 2010. The quotations from the play are from her written text, *I w@s B*rbie* (2010).
22 Arsenault, "Barbie Pink PMS 219," *I w@s B*rbie* (2010), 3.

"be plastic," and to "be fabulous instead of reasonable"[23] — the impossible is attainable.

The projected images of the process of becoming the "most beautiful woman in the world" were images of surgically cut skin, a bandaged face, liquid silicone entering the body. This is the frenzied underside of beauty, the "cut" in beauty. What Nina is revealing in showing both her technologically designed cyborg-art object body and the deconstruction/reconstruction of human flesh body involved in this design is the *unseen*.

It isn't the vivid images of the operations, procedures and re-covering face and body that upsets people in the audience. Rath-er, it is the dissonance, disharmony, and discrepancy between what is seen and what is behind the look of Nina Arsenault. It is Arsenault's will-to-power as a will-to-beauty, a willingness to do anything it takes to be that beautiful, a willingness to undergo silicone injections in the States, surgeries in Mexico (because they were illegal in Canada), willingness to suck enormous amounts of cock to finance beauty, to be whatever the client's fantasy was, willingness to die for beauty, and then her willing-ness to disclose precisely what it takes to be just that beautiful. That's one of the reasons why a great many feminists love her.

After achieving the summit of beauty — real live Barbie — the peak and abyss begin to merge for Arsenault. *The Silicone Dia-ries* closes with the beginning of a new process:

> In my mind's eye, I see the next phase of my body. There will be the signs of aging on my body. There will be facelifts, re-surfacing, the ways I honour aging with make-up. There will be the spiritual pursuits, the meditations, the therapy, the art-making that allows me to deal with aging.[24]

---

23 Arsenault, "I Am My Own Self-Portrait (2004)," *The Silicone Diaries,* in *Trans{per}Forming Nina Arsenault,* 217.

24 Arsenault, "Venus/Machine (2007–2009)," *The Silicone Diaries,* in *Trans{per} Forming Nina Arsenault,* 227.

3. The Shadow of Beauty

Arsenault's "endurance performance" installation — *40 Days & 40 Nights: Working Towards a Spiritual Experience* (August 2012) — after her then most recent return to Mexico for face surgery — picks up from where *The Silicone Diaries* leave off. Nina performed nightly from 9pm to 5am for eleven nights in a row in what she described as "a cloister I have built for myself to live in, a sacred space […] also a decadent space."[25] In fact, it was a converted storefront with a red neon sign announcing "The Whore of Babalon."[26] Like those the aging Zarathustra encounters and invites into his cave in the fourth part of *Thus Spoke Zarathustra* — "Behold there goes the way to my cave; be its guest tonight"[27] — Nina invited artists, writers, filmmakers, and the public to join her. She prepared for the eleven-night public ritual by — among other actions[28] — spending four days in total darkness and isolation emulating "The Vow of Shadows" taken by medieval monks and nuns. In the shadows Nina accessed the active forces of the body: the energy force of the will-to-power.

> Behind your thoughts and your feelings there stands a mighty unknown sage — whose name is self. In your body he dwells; he is your body. The self seeks with the eyes of the senses; it listens with the ears of the spirit.[29] (Z §34, "On the Despisers of the Body")

About "The Vow of Shadows" Nina offers:

---

25 Arsenault, *40 Days & 40 Nights.*

26 Arsenault produced a 2013 calendar, *Whore of Babalon,* which documents her transmutation from most beautiful woman to monk to a shadow-of-beauty aging geisha. A number of the images are from *40 Days & 40 Nights.* See the interview of Arsenault regarding the calendar at http://www.youtube.com/watch?v=L5ycfkX6VVs.

27 Nietzsche, "The Voluntary Beggar," *Thus Spoke Zarathustra,* §271.

28 Other actions included fasting, celibacy, and sleep deprivation.

29 Nietzsche, "On the Despisers of the Body," *Thus Spoke Zarathustra,* §34.

I went through a lot of emotions — excitement, fear, much loneliness, peace, joy. I had the feeling that I was looking under the darkness and there was creative energy through it. It was an ecstatic feeling, but it also gave me serenity — a sense that I was living inside creative energy, and that I was also made of this energy.[30]

In the portion of the nightly event which Nina called "The Ecstasy of Nina Arsenault," her guests listened to the story of her surgeries. In a sense she has moved from the *outcome* of the sixty-plus surgical procedures (beauty) to the *process* of the surgery itself. Nina narrates:

For a very long time I wanted to be beautiful — I took a lot of very sexy pinup photos; I always felt that I had a wink in my eye and I was deconstructing iconic beauty, patriarchal beauty because I was so plastic. I never thought that I would find the surgical procedures erotic and they weren't until I finally stayed awake during the facelift and because of the mirror on the ceiling I could watch the knives going into my face, I could see myself being cut and feel no pain; the sensation registered because of the anesthetic as sparkly tingly feelings that were moving through me. I could see inside the Doctor's eyes, a beautiful man with his hands in my face; really stretching me; he wasn't just fucking my face, he had his whole hand in my face; [...] the post-surgical pain — recovering in this very beautiful hotel in Mexico, not having anything to do but just aching in pain, taking pain-killers and waiting for the doctor to come by — was like being taken care of like a doll.[31]

The nightly eight-hour event recurred eleven times according to the same format that included extreme stationary biking nude in front of a full-length mirror, while peddling at top speed Nina

30 Arsenault, "The Vow of the Shadows," *40 Days & 40 Nights*.
31 Arsenault, "The Ecstasy of Nina Arsenault," *40 Days & 40 Nights*.

repeatedly flogged her back; one-to-one sessions with audience members; collaborations between Arsenault and other artists; her sculpture — "Pure Form with Blood and Silicone" — of her discarded silicone implants; cleansing meditation. Each night closed with Nina stripping naked again, putting on a pig's head mask, the room filling with what one reviewer termed "a beat that sounds like crystal meth set to music";[32] Arsenault then enters an automatic state and writes aphorisms on the wall. "The question isn't *Is it working,* but *How far can it go?*"[33]

Nina lives Nietzsche's politically charged knowledge that "the knowing, thinking, objective subject is [...] an invention," that "the body acts, and thinking and contemplation will follow it."[34] Like Nietzsche, Nina hammers — or in her case, cuts — the so-called *Grand* in western thought, particularly the *Grand* in feminist thought, with what has been traditionally dismissed and despised as patriarchal body tyranny. Much like Nietzsche, whose own pain and suffering made his body "for him an everpresent thesaurus from which he culled a language to challenge [...] modernity,"[35] Nina deploys her body as a site from which to critique and challenge hegemonic (patriarchal and feminist) ideas of beauty and femininity. Her body acts as a visible will-to-power for transsexual women and men to be as they desire, in which "the doing, effecting, becoming — the deed is everything."[36]

Nina is Nietzsche's artist–philosopher par excellence, I would argue; one who brings forth the feminine from what was once male, one who redirects the new technologies of beauty — silicone injections, radical plastic surgery — to art, producing a new extreme body, and reveals with a scalpel just what it takes

32 Richard Ouzounian, "Nina Arsenault presents *40 Days & 40 Nights: Working Towards a Spiritual Experience,*" http://www.thestar.com/entertainment/stage/2012/08/15/nina_ arsenault_presents_40_days_and_40_nights_working_towards_a_spiritual_experience.html.

33 Ibid.

34 Hughes, "Nietzsche," 38.

35 Ibid., 41.

36 Nietzsche, *On the Genealogy of Morals,* trans. Walter Kaufmann and Richard Hollingdale (New York: Vintage Books, 1989), I §13, §45.

to achieve iconic beauty. The being that Arsenault brings forth is feminine in excess: a feminine that simultaneously *exposes* the feminine masquerade, *seduces* with it, and then willfully *abandons* it only to *repeat* it again, with a slight difference (another surgery, another performance, another body-directed inner experience). "We are to the degree that we risk ourselves."[37]

What sort of feminist, then, is Arsenault? Arsenault's redesign and reconstruction of "self" as body-in-action — never fixed, ever elusive and transformative — is one of the main principles of Fast Feminism: not to congeal the process of doing live theory into the identitarian logic of THIS IS.[38] "Fast Feminism is a feminism of affect — of intensity and movement."[39] Arsenault states in her talk on "Self-portraiture, Transformation, Identity & Performance" that "at each phase of my life I created a new self-portraiture and a new shape-shift, a 'new me': a new social role, a new fantasy I *wanted to be,* a new fantasy I *had become,* a new aesthetic *calling,* to make real. They are all me."[40]

4. Nina Arsenault: Fast Feminist Overhuman

The excess femme and the deconstructive radical techno-politics which Arsenault deploys and discloses in her construction of self make her a Fast Feminist according to the manifesto that I put forth in *Fast Feminism.*

> If Fast Feminism were to have a manifesto, the latter would have the following outline: 1) critique the world quickly; 2) interrupt intellectual scholarship; 3) position the body as the basis of intellectual work; 4) write theory as art; 5) do art as theory; 6) do theory from non-obvious points of departure; 7) do violence to the original context.[41]

37 Georges Bataille, *On Nietzsche,* trans. Bruce Boone (New York: Paragon House, 1994), 72.
38 Shannon Bell, *Fast Feminism* (New York: Autonomedia, 2010), 173.
39 Ibid., 174.
40 Arsenault, "Self-portraiture, Transformation, Identity & Performance."
41 Bell, *Fast Feminism,* 174.

Nina embodies and personifies the three principles of Fast Feminism: *theory* must be grounded in *action,* otherwise it is dead; we *are* to the degree that we *risk* ourselves; and never *write* about what you don't *do.*[42] And she performs all seven fast feminist manifesto points in all her work. Interestingly, so does Nietzsche. The overhuman has Fast Feminist credentials.

Nina Arsenault seems to be the answer to the riddle that Nick Land poses in "Meat": "What is an *animal* at dawn, a *human* at noon, and a *cyborg* at dusk, passing through [...] genetic *wetware* [...] [and] technocultural *software* [...] into the tertiary schizo[Venus]machine?"[43]

---

42 See the first chapter of my *Fast Feminism*: "The Fast Feminist & Fast Feminism," 10–29, which sets out the principles of Fast Feminism
43 Nick Land, "Meat," in *Fanged Noumena*, 428.

16

"Nietzsche in Drag": *Thinking Technology through the Theater of Judith Butler*

Arthur Kroker

NWW.III, October 1, 2011

> *Perhaps most importantly, we must recognize that eth-*
> *ics requires us to risk ourselves precisely at moments of un-*
> *knowingness, when what forms us diverges from what lies*
> *before us, when our willingness to become undone in rela-*
> *tion to others constitutes our chance of becoming human.*
> — Judith Butler, *Giving an Account of Oneself*[1]

Could there be any text more appropriate to both understanding and perhaps, if the winds of fate are favorable, *transforming* contemporary politics than Judith Butler's eloquent study of
moral philosophy, *Giving an Account of Oneself*? Resisting the
most powerful political currents of the times, breaking decisively with the regulatory regime of normativity, speaking eloquently, passionately, historically about another ethics, another
body, another space, Butler injects into contemporary public
debate something that was thought to have been lost forever:
what she herself once described as the "shameless impurity"
of Antigone — not Antigone as a haunting figure of the eternal

---

1   Judith Butler, *Giving an Account of Oneself* (New York: Fordham University
     Press, 2005), 136. — Ed.

struggle between state and kinship but that other Antigone, the forgotten Antigone of the burial chamber, who, in the end, preferred death to irresponsibility, the unrequited passion of love to self-preservation. It is this Antigone, this *ethical* remembrance of Antigone, who, against all reasonable expectation, returns from her incarceration in the burial chamber to finally break her silence in *Giving an Account of Oneself,* to say finally what needs to be articulated, namely, that now as then, an "ethics of responsibility" may be the only measure of real kinship in a culture patterned by an "ethics of violence" — and to say this not dogmatically, not with the certainty of an abstract universal but in a rhetorical analysis which in its hesitations, nuances, and sudden transfigurations does honor to the equally forgotten language of contingency.

Because that is what *Giving an Account of Oneself* specifically — and Judith Butler's thought in general — is really about: it is simultaneously a plea for the return of that which is most frail, vulnerable, unintelligible, unknowable, unrepresentable in political thought and a lament for that which has been lost in the coming to be of the most recent of the real-world iterations of Hegel's vision of the "universal homogenous state." In this ethical demand for the recovery of the contingent in human affairs, being *human* is itself, in the first instance, that impossibility of interpellation by the codes of abstract universalism — simultaneously constituted by and authorizing power — while, at the same moment, dwelling in the borderlands of other equally contingent *social* beings, each with their own hauntology of unknowability, unintelligibility, and unrepresentability. Which is why Butler can argue so persuasively in undermining Žižek that the real has never been understandable exclusively in the language of lack — fear of castration, fear of the law — but only in the more complex terms of silent foreclosures and fatal contestations. More than is customary, the thought of Judith Butler is a continuing, insistent reiteration of, and rebellion against, the abyssal silence of an ethics that would be vulnerable, finite, and unintelligible in this time after Antigone, not only in the sense that Butler's writings always trace the phantasmal, yet tangible, presence of life and death in all the great signifiers, whether of kinship, gender, sexuality, or power, but for a different reason. Butler is truly after Antigone because her writings represent most directly and powerfully the haunting question left by Antigone — namely, what are the lasting claims of kinship, love, and fealty, that is to say, the claims of compassion and social solidarity, in a world suddenly divested of its reasons by the presence of evil.

Now, of course, the mark designated by the appellation *After Antigone* is the evil demon of all models of power that originate in Nietzsche's caesura. Nietzsche could reflect with such devastating insight in *Thus Spoke Zarathustra* that the logic of the self-identical could never rest easy with the necessary contingency of "time's *it was*" precisely because the will to power would be based, then as it is now, on the death of death. Evacuating lived relationality from the moment of death — disavowing the fully contingent relation of our bodies to the cyclical wheel of time, the relation of bodies to the sacred, the profane, the mortal, and indeed to the "problem" of mortality itself — is the worm that turns in the post-Enlightenment mind and, before that, in the cosmologies of the Christian confessional, and most vividly in their full exposure to the light of anti-reason in all the genealogical texts of Nietzsche. But if the excommunication of knowledge of that which is most contingent, relational, intelligible, vulnerable from modern subjectivity is the mythological price exacted by the death of death, this also would suggest that the mark of death's singularity — our own — which has gone missing from the human story is fated to return as the specter that haunts human passions. Privilege the question of contingency and the narrative of all the master referents — power, gender, sexuality, knowledge, desire — immediately come unglued. Disavowal of the contingency of the human situation is the necessary gesture of a power, a body, a reason, a desire that would seek to substitute itself for the lost language of the gods who, in the face of this challenge, continue to maintain their long silence, hidden in shadows from human view.

But if we are not to passively mime the psychic strategy of disavowal nor lament the flight of the gods, we should, for all that, remain attentive to the sentiment of Antigone at work in *Giving an Account of Oneself.* Of Antigone herself, Judith Butler likes to repeat the beautiful refrain that she was always "between living and dying," a faithful — indeed, a *responsible* — sister and daughter whose loyalty to the honor of death in a land of evil made of her the first of all the post-humans, a post-moralist who recuperated the human by choosing the singularity of (her own) death. A "shameless impurity" certainly: remembering Antigone, recalling to mind the incommensurability of "between living and dying" is also to refuse the honor of the name of life of power, to add additional complexity to kinship based on blood. But more than that, the designation *After Antigone* calls to mind that those who would think the question of an "ethics of responsibility" in the imperial storm-center of an "ethics of violence" are also fated to represent a form of thought and practice which is itself beyond living and dying.

Antigone's Claim is, of course, the extended intellectual meditation that constitutes ,in all its philosophical intensity and social commitment, the life of Judith Butler. A philosopher, political theorist, deconstructionist of all things gendered and bodied and spoken and written and performed, her intellectual comportment does honor to the name of Antigone. By her voice, variously analytical, poetic, theoretical, and always a rhetoric machine, she returns the enigmatic fate of Antigone to public scrutiny — not only for a psychoanalytical practice that would finally turn from Oedipus to Antigone but for a political theory of the state, of the body, of desire in all its genders and sexes that would seek out the traces of intelligibility, of responsibility, of contingency in their living materiality. Someday, and why not this day perhaps, it may well be said of Butler what she once remarked about Antigone:

She acts, she speaks, she becomes one for whom the speech-act is a fatal crime, but this fatality exceeds her life and enters the discourse of intelligibility as its own promising fatality, the social forum of its aberrant, unprecedented future.[2]

All of Butler's speech acts are "fatal crimes" which only enter the discourse of intelligibility as their relentless overturning, the philosophical forum of its "aberrant, unprecedented future." A theorist of performance, performing *Gender Trouble,* performing *Bodies That Matter,* performing *Excitable Speech,* performing *Antigone's Claim,* performing *The Psychic Life of Power,* she is, for all of that, always seduced by her own undoing — not just *Undoing Gender,* the scandal of undoing power, undoing intelligibility, undoing violence, undoing representation, undoing Hegel, Freud, Foucault, Levinas, Žižek, and Agamben, and, of course, undoing Nietzsche most of all.

And why not? Judith Butler is Nietzsche in drag. Not the bitter Nietzsche with the bad conscience that he promptly circuited into the essays comprising *On the Genealogy of Morals* but that other spectral, imaginary Nietzsche — his double, who, until now, lurking in the shadows at the side of the stage of philosophy, finally makes his dancing entrance in the theater of Judith Butler in the drag outfit of the "transvaluation of values." As Butler shows with brilliant detail in *The Psychic Life of Power,* Nietzsche's thought always hovered around the stone that closed the burial chamber of "time's *it was,*" listening intently to the intimations of human deprivation, the first and best witness to the upsurge of the "last man," the earliest prophet of the dark future of ressentiment, the philosopher who would note that this, the most consciously post-Christian of all eras, would be the most marked by the sign of the crucified Christ. While Nietzsche literally threw speech ahead of his dying body, writing posthumously about the "turn" in the circuit of power that signaled the beginning of something radically original — something constituted by power yet, at the same time, its "fatal crime" — namely, the "transvaluation of values," he was by temperament unsuited

2   Butler, *Antigone's Claim: Kinship between Life and Death* (New York: Columbia University Press, 2000), 82.

to the task of illuminating the "dancing star" of this "unprecedented future." Bad conscience never escapes the mythological riddles of unhappy consciousness. In essence, bad conscience preserves while always disavowing its basis in unhappy consciousness.

But not Butler. She begins precisely where Nietzsche left off. That's the emotional capstone of *The Psychic Life of Power*. Certainly this text is an eloquent meditation on Hegel's unhappy consciousness, Nietzsche's bad conscience, Freud's melancholic ego, Foucault's normalizing power, and Althusser's concept of interpellation, but its deepest connecting thread is the stubborn, recalcitrant thought of Nietzsche — and not just any Nietzsche, but the "less than human" Nietzsche of *On the Genealogy of Morals*: the Nietzsche whose mind thinks its way into the galactic debris field left by the implosion of two thousand years of Christian metaphysics and the rising star, dim at first but then quickly burning luminescent, of the bourgeois ego. *This* Nietzsche is present everywhere in Butler's thought — certainly not always openly, but in the more subtle, and consequently pervasive, sense that Butler reading Nietzsche is, in effect, *Nietzsche undoing Butler*; that her thought is, in the best sense, undermined by the crucial insight that Nietzsche expressed in *On the Genealogy of Morals* concerning the appearance of a *purely perspectival will* — a "concept-fiction" — which, animated by bad conscience, turns back on itself, and on account of which modern subjectivity is doomed to be forever trapped in the logical circuitry — the "sorry bind" — of its own figuration and ground.

It has been remarked often enough that Butler is a Hegelian, her thought framed by the metaphysics of *The Phenomenology of Spirit*, by, that is, the challenge of articulating a form of thought that takes account of the dialectic of inclusion and exclusion while simultaneously effectively undermining this (epistemological) mirror of the self-identical. But Butler's purported subordination to Hegelian dialectics does not take into consideration that the passion of Nietzsche has itself effectively supplanted the world-spirit of reason. Like the classical tradition of Greek idealism before him, Hegel attempted to solve the historical riddle of the broken field of mind and body by appealing to the unifying capacities of the will to reason. That the Hegelian resolution of the problem of the divided will could not be resolved by a flight from human vicissitudes to the (self-identical) will to reason was signaled by those competing (political) futures in the *Phenomenology*: the fable of "Lordship and Bondage" as the foundational text of the critique of political economy and "Unhappy Consciousness" as the premonitory shadow cast sixty years in advance of Nietzsche's essays in the *Genealogy*. Perhaps herself a "less than human" Hegelian, a theorist who honors the name of Hegel by listening attentively to the clues to our shared historical destiny hidden in the textual interstices of the *Phenomenology,* Butler's instinct has always been to search for the Nietzsche in Hegel, tracing the "terror of the body" in all its violence from the pages of *On the Genealogy of Morals* to its original appearance in *The Phenomenology of Spirit*:

> Here, consciousness in its full abjection has become like shit, lost in a self-referential anality, a circle of its own making. In Hegel's words, "we have here a personality confined to its own self and its petty actions, a personality brooding over itself, as wretched as it is impoverished.[3]

This is Butler's excremental Hegel — not the unfolding of the world-spirit of reason nor the "self-referential" dialectic of reason but something more "abject," motivated by "negative narcissism," fully preoccupied with "what is most debased and defiled" about itself: in short, Hegel's "unhappy consciousness."

> Regarding itself as a nothing, as a doing of nothing, as an excremental function, and hence regarding itself as excrement, this consciousness effectively reduces itself to the changeable features of its bodily functions and features. Yet, since it is an experience of wretchedness, there is some consciousness

3   Butler, *The Psychic Life of Power: Theories in Subjection* (Stanford: Stanford University Press, 1997), 50.

which takes stock of these functions and which is not fully identified with them. Significantly, it is here, in the effort to differentiate itself from its excretory functions — indeed, from its excretory identity — that consciousness relies on a mediator that Hegel calls a "priest." This mediating agency relieves the abject consciousness of responsibility for its own actions.[4]

When self-negation becomes a body invader and "unhappy consciousness" invests itself fully in the future of its bodily functions, we are in the presence of a powerful current of thought migrating inexorably from the remains of *The Phenomenology* to the future that is the *Genealogy,* from Hegel's broken dreams to Nietzsche's bad conscience. That the Hegelian resolution of the world crisis of the divided will — the fatal splitting of mind and body, in short, "abject consciousness" — could not be achieved by an appeal to the unifying capacities of selfsame reason was rehearsed long before Hegel by the earlier futilities of Greek enlightenment. "Born posthumously," without (idealist) faith-based illusions in the "unchangeable" and the "immanent," Nietzsche knew better. The first and best of all contingent thinkers, he made of his thought a circuit through which all of the abjections, disavowals, and negations of two thousand years of Christian experiments aimed at resolving the crisis of divided consciousness would be projected onto that vulnerable, frail, resentment-driven, yet for all that dreamer of the vanished gods we call the contingent histories of the (human) body. While Butler provides in *The Psychic Life of Power* a dense knot of psychoanalytical reasons for her recovery of the Nietzsche in Hegel, there is always in the text a sense of something not yet named, still not recuperated, not said, something "perspectival," a "concept-fiction" put in play by Nietzsche. Because isn't that what the "psychic life of power" really is — a "concept-fiction," a purely *perspectival* reality that generates the concept of the body, gender, consciousness, identity, and, most of all, the abject self as

4   Ibid., 50–51.

ways of simultaneously drawing into presence and hiding from view the delirious nothingness, what Hannah Arendt described as the "negative will" of the modern project?

When Butler brushes the *Genealogy* against *The Phenomenology*, it is as if an astral gateway opens, out of which rushes all the Nietzsche in Butler. All the "concept-fictions" are there in all their primal violence: Nietzsche's "ascetic priests" return as the policing of "compulsory heterosexuality": the concept of ressentiment forms the psychogeography of Butler's critique of the culture of injury; Hegel's unhappy consciousness is revealed to be the ethical reflex of Nietzsche's bad conscience; everywhere "there is no formation of the subject without a passionate attachment to subjection";[5] the will "turns back" on itself; the (gendered) body "turns back" on itself; conscience "turns back" on itself; and everywhere Butler's overall political project — reoccupying the site of injury as the only way of working through possibilities for transformation, transfiguration, fabrication — has its origins as a compelling counter-challenge to Nietzsche's "ascetic priests," who only open the wound (of ressentiment) to stir up "chestnuts" of injured grievance.

And why not? More a theorist of the play of powers and dominations in cultural politics than a writer of intellectual history, Butler's teasing out of the Nietzsche in Hegel resonates with the contemporary public scene. The political culture that implicitly contextualizes all her work is that of the United States, the dynamic, planetary spearhead of the fully-realized "universal homogenous state." Technologically accelerating at the speed of light, social reality is itself now in the process of being consumed by the paradoxes of light time and light space, and *light power*. Social history is now perhaps best understood in the language of astrophysics, which implies that a culture moving at light speed is not exempt from the perturbations of space travel with its black holes, warp jumps, and unexpected ripples in the space–time fabric, like the violent rip in the cultural fabric that occurred post-9/11, in which the political universe, while

5   Butler, *The Psychic Life of Power*, 67.

continuing to accelerate technologically, began to curve back to its primal origins in anxiety, distrust, panic, and "bad conscience." This explains why we can live simultaneously in the much hyped world of global cybernetic development while being embroiled in the most recidivist of fundamentalist religious passions. Today the body of flesh and blood has been literally split in two — part flesh, part machine — with no easy reconciliation on the horizon. Cognitively, we may be the first generation to exist in that peculiar situation bequeathed to those who are truly after Antigone, not only "between living and dying" but already aware that even the language of the prohibited — the excluded — is a constitutive condition for the affirmation of power.

Consequently, when Butler senses the presence everywhere of Nietzsche's contingent power — in gender, sexuality, consciousness, public policy, psychoanalysis — she makes of the *Genealogy* a guide to understanding not only the violent history of the will but also its possible future. For Nietzsche, the debate on the natural and discursive body is a purely "perspectival" event, hiding from view the incorporation of the body by "the passionate attachment to subjection." Call it what you will — the languages of reification, alienation, simulation, and the virtual, or in the more searing terms of Judith Butler, "excretory identities" in an "excretory culture" — today the hint of death is everywhere, animated and seductive but still a resurrection-effect of a culture that only now begins to live. Oscillating wildly between hyperaesthetics and excremental culture, the body desperately clings to any floating sign: the signs of death, panic, fear; the signs of insecurity and instability; but perhaps also the signs of a new multiplicity that is struggling to be born, exist, and thrive.

It is this story of power, this story of *contingent* power, that is recovered by Butler's theoretical imagination. It is, of course, customary to limit understanding power to the logic of inclusions and exclusions. Here the language of exclusions does not operate independently of normative regimes of inclusion but the opposite. Precisely because they are the prohibited — the outcast, the forbidden term — the logic of exclusions designates the essential condition for the affirmation of power. Marking the limits of the psychic life of power, power would no longer operate as a force from the outside — a pressure from the exterior — but as the basic condition of possibility for that which has itself been forbidden. Consequently, *The Psychic Life of Power* can be so politically consequential because it focuses on the doubled nature of power — certainly power from the outside, but more important, the *preontological* constitution of subjectivity by a regime of power that would make of its prohibitions the essential locus of "the passionate attachment to subjection."

Politically, this would culminate in the *paradox* of cynical power — power framed by the apparent oppositions of inclusion and exclusion — that the insurrection of the prohibited (Foucault's famous "insurrection of subjectivity") can never really be confident that the terms of contestation have not been, in fact, staged in advance to amplify the psychic life of power itself. For example, this is the informing logic of Luce Irigaray's evocative theorization of the self-identical logic of masculinist sexuality. It is as well the foundation for Paul Gilroy's insight that the critique of racism is itself constituted, and effectively undermined, by its production as a perspectival effect of the language of racialism itself.

But what if, as in the meditation on power that is the psychic life of Butler, the closed logic of inclusions and exclusions is itself exceeded by a new psychic figuration — a prohibition functioning as its own *singularity moment* — simultaneously enmeshed in the matrix of power yet all the while expressing something incommensurable? And what if this is not simply creative mimesis but a fatal challenge to power by the emergence of psychic complexity itself? Here the language of the outcast, represented finally only in terms of psycho-analysis, would have something about it of the contingency of life itself, expressing that which cannot be fully absorbed by power yet all the same comprising the most perfect inflection of power. Ironically, what if the lasting importance of *The Psychic Life of Power* is, in the end, not rhetorical but astronomical? Like a massive object in deep outer space intervening between the human gaze and an otherwise invisible planet to reveal by its very darkness the presence of something otherwise undetectable by human vision, *The Psychic Life of Power* slides between ourselves and that which is otherwise hidden in the astral object of power, lighting up for the first time that which is figurative, fabricated, and creative.

A keen student of contingency, of the vulnerable, the frail, the fragile, Butler's thought begins and ends with the failure of power. Specifically, this is why she can reflect so eloquently about Althusser's concept of interpellation, noting its unique challenge to "being elsewhere or otherwise, without denying our complicity in the law we oppose."[6] Absorbing fully Nietzsche's insight that power always turns back on itself, Butler writes that

> Such possibility would require a different kind of turn, one that, enabled by law, turns away from the law, resisting its lure of identity, an agency that outruns and counters the conditions of its emergence. Such a turn demands a willingness not to be — a *critical desubjectivation* — in order to expose the law as less powerful than it seems [...]. How are we to understand the power to be as a constitutive desire? Resituating conscience and interpellation within such an account, we might then add to this question another: However is such a desire exploited not only by law in the singular, but by law of various kinds such that we yield to the temptation in order to maintain some sense of social "being"? [...] Such a failure of interpellation may well undermine the capacity of the subject to "be" in a self-identical sense, but it may also mark the path toward a more open, even more ethical, kind of being, one of or for the future.[7]

Of this "failure of interpellation" we might question in turn its origins and how the passion for subjection is to be countered by a "critical desubjectivation." Alluding to Jacqueline Rose's utopian gesture toward "unconsciousness as resistance,"[8] to Freud's

6 Butler, *The Psychic Life of Power*, 130.
7 Ibid., 130–31.
8 Ibid., 97.

"postmoral gesture,"[9] which calls into question the values of morality, Butler has brushed against Nietzsche too deeply not to recognize that the moment of "critical desubjectivation" will have to pass through the psychological storm-center of the bad conscience. For example, speaking of Foucault, she dwells on the paradoxical qualities of the "injurious term":

> He understood that even the most noxious terms could be owned, that the most injurious interpellations could also be the site of radical reoccupation and resignification. But what lets us occupy the site of discursive injury? How are we animated and mobilized by that discursive site and its injury, such that our very attachment to it becomes the condition for our resignification of it? [...] As a further paradox, then, only by occupying — being occupied by — that injurious term can I resist and oppose it, recasting the power that constitutes me as the power I oppose. In this way, a certain place for psychoanalysis is secured in that any mobilization against subjection will take subjection as its resource, and that attachment to an injurious interpellation will, by way of a necessarily alienated narcissism, become the condition under which resignifying that interpellation becomes possible. This will not be an unconscious outside of power, but rather something like the unconscious of power itself, in its traumatic and productive iterability.[10]

If identity were to be permanently attached to the site of its injury, this would only make of it a site of Nietzsche's bad conscience. But what if there is an "unconscious of power" hidden within the language of power itself as its "traumatic and productive iterability'? And what if the "alienated narcissism" that would emerge from the "failure of interpellation" would take as its challenge not to exceed power from its exterior but to "rework and unsettle the passionate attachment to subjec-

9   Ibid., 82.
10 Ibid., 104.

tion without which subject formation and reformation cannot succeed"?[11] For Butler, *being contingent* is the real world of the bad conscience, which is why she can remark of the "chiastic" moment in Nietzsche when the conscience turns back on itself that this is not only "the condition of the possibility of the subject, but the condition of possibility of fiction, fabrication, and transfiguration."[12] Neither a liberal humanist committed to abstract universalism nor a post-structural deconstructionist, Butler occupies a third space in the theorization of power. Silently streaming her thought with other nomadic thinkers before her, she sets out to *undo* interpellation, to *undermine* signification, to *work through* bad conscience, and to do this in a way that is neither universal nor particular but deeply reflexive. Because that is what she truly is — a theorist of psychic complexity — the unconscious of power — seeking to make of the "failure of interpellation" a possible opening to the fictional, the fabricated, the transfigurative. If this makes her a hopeless utopian, it is for all that a utopia of impossibility, which is and, for that matter, has always been the irreducible singular moment of the human condition.

Of course, in these dark times, utopias, particularly utopias of impossibility, are not permitted. Nietzsche correctly anticipated this when he envisioned a future of suicidal nihilism with its orgies of cynical power led by ascetic priests as "blond beasts of prey," and all this driven onward by the passion for subjection so powerfully captured by the concept of the bad conscience. It is our specific historical fate to actually live today within the body politic thought "posthumously" by Nietzsche, that point where the philosophically universal has been made historically particular. The savagery of the weak will of the "last man" has been realized in political history by what the Pentagon likes to describe as the "long war" of viral terrorism. Metastasizing through the body politic — sometimes assuming the administrative form of hypersurveillance, at other points legitimating it-

11 Ibid., 105.
12 Ibid., 67.

self by apparent threats from the exterior of power — the specter of terrorism has quickly become the "constitutive outside" necessary for the operation of power. Functioning under the sign of cynicism, power flips randomly today from the "homeland" of normative inclusion to an increasingly virulent sense of persecutory anxiety aimed at those nominated for exclusion. Politically unilateral, suspicious of expressions of internal dissent, filled with a crusading sense of missionary consciousness, close-circuiting itself in the domestic bunker, the ambivalent relation of truth and power has now resolved into an epoch of "speaking power to truth." No exceptions are permitted to the logic of the selfsame; no subjectivity is authorized that exceeds normative regimes of inclusion and exclusion; no ethics are allowed that do not privilege the violence of condemnation; no moral perspective is enjoined that does not close ranks with the logic of imperial exceptionalism; and no bodies are to be constituted that are not perfectly mimetic of the ruling standards of representation and intelligibility.

Cautious in her rhetorical claims, pragmatic in her critical aspirations, Butler's utopia of impossibility steers between performativity and lament to discover the third space of a power that would be its own undoing. Her thought draws into presence that which is always most vehemently disavowed by power, namely, the necessary interpellation of figure and ground. Making of her own writing a concept-fiction, an apparent reality, a perspectival simulacrum, she proceeds to undo the disavowal necessary to all power by a strategy of *reflexivity* — Butler's version of Nietzsche's transvaluation of values:

> More precisely, what does it mean to say that a subject emerges only through the action of turning back on itself? If this turning back on oneself is a trope, a movement which is always only *figured* as a bodily movement, but which no body literally performs, in what will the necessity of such a figuration consist? The trope appears to be the shadow of a body, a shadowing of that body's violence against itself, a body in

spectral and linguistic form that is the signifying mark of the psyche's emergence.[13]

Noting that there is "no subject except as a consequence of this reflexivity,"[14] Butler begins with a subject trapped in a "logical circularity" — a subject that "appears at once to be presupposed and yet not formed, on the one hand, or formed and hence not presupposed on the other." It is a fully contingent subject born out of a "strange way of speaking" — strange, because like the language of the will turning back on itself before it, "it figures a process which cannot be detached from or understood apart from the figuration."[15] With this fateful conclusion,

> what emerges is not the unshackled will or a "beyond" to power, but another direction for what is most formative in passion, a formative power which is at once the condition of its violence against itself, its status as a necessary fiction, and the site of its enabling possibilities. This recasting of the "will" is not, properly speaking, the will of a subject, nor is it an effect fully cultivated by and through social norms; it is, I would suggest, the site at which the social implicates the psychic in its very formation — or, to be more precise, as its very formation and formativity.[16]

If the term "queer" is to be a site of collective contestation, the point of departure for a set of historical reflections and futural imaginings, it will have to remain that which is, in the present, never fully owned, but always and only redeployed, twisted, queered from a prior usage and in the direction of urgent and expanding political purposes.[17]

---

13 Butler, *The Psychic Life of Power,* 68.
14 Ibid.
15 Ibid., 69.
16 Ibid., 66.
17 Butler, *Bodies That Matter* (New York: Routledge, 1993), 228.

So, then, queer bodies are the "site at which the social implicates the psychic in its very formation" — definitely not queer bodies only at the level of the sexual register (although that, too) but queer bodies as a tangible hint of that which is most irrepressible, most present in the moment, most utopian in this doubled language of power as subjection and subjectivation. Here beginning in the psychic economy of gay and lesbian sexuality, mindful of the foreclosures necessary to institute and maintain the hegemony of heterosexual normativity, queer bodies can so easily break the skin barrier because the utopian gesture of "queering" is itself a premonitory sign of the return of the contingent, the ambivalent, the ambiguous. "Never fully owned, and only redeployed, twisted, queered from a prior usage," the term *queer* has a more general philosophical, and then political, significance beyond the languages of pleasure and desire. Reversing as a matter of survival the productivist logic of political economy, queer bodies do the impossible by representing a form of power that would be its own undoing. From the foreclosed space of queer sexual economy, from the libidinal energies of gays and lesbians and transsexuals, emerges a counter-logic to the times in which we live, simultaneously its "necessary fiction" and "enabling possibility." Understood retroactively, the future alluded to by the act of queering sex, queering gender, queering politics, has always been with us as that fatal symbolic gesture, the palpable traces of which spread out everywhere today. *Queering history*: that's Walter Benjamin's *Theses on the Philosophy of History,* with its rebellion on behalf of a form of political resistance that would instantly link present and future, making of the forgotten language of the Parisian communard, the Spanish anarcho-syndicalist, the always liquidated poet, the foreclosed space of the artist, the avatars of a political history that would stir again, like Klee's *Angelus Novus,* to the storm of the future breaking in on the gathering debris of the past. *Queering ideology*: that's Slavoj Žižek's brilliant, but highly instructive, failure to achieve a radically socialist, radically democratic critique of the elementary *forms* of ideology, because he forgot that the sublime object of trauma, this irreducible trace of emptiness, this singular remainder in the human condition is always shadowed by the remainder's double — the actual contents, the ambivalent, deeply contested citations — of ideological struggle. *Queering love*: that's Luce Irigaray's *To Be Two,* which introduces a violent, but no less seductive, sudden swerve into the philosophical canons surrounding the question of identity and difference, by recuperating in all its challenge and fragility the ethical demand "to take care of the difference between us, not merely because of its role in generation, because it represents the means of humanity's production and reproduction, but in order to achieve happiness and make it blossom."[18]

In her important essay "Critically Queer," Judith Butler has this to say about drag and the heterosexual imaginary:

If drag thus allegorizes *heterosexual melancholy,* the melancholy by which a masculine gender is formed from the refusal to grieve the masculine as a possibility of love; a feminine gender is formed (taken on, assumed) through the incorporative fantasy by which the feminine is excluded as a possible object of love, an exclusion never grieved, but "preserved" through the heightening of feminine identification itself. In this sense, the "truest" lesbian melancholic is the strictly straight woman, and the "truest" gay male is the strictly straight male [...]. What drag exposes is the "normal" constitution of gender presentation in which the gender performed is in many ways constituted by a set of disavowed attachments or identifications that constitute a different domain of the "unperformable." [In a culture of heterosexual melancholy], "the straight man *becomes* (mimes, cites, appropriates, assumes the status of) the man he "never" loved and "never" grieved"; the straight woman becomes the woman she "never" loved and "never" grieved. It is in this sense, then, that what is most apparently performed as gender is the sign and symptom of a pervasive disavowal.[19]

---

18 Luce Irigaray, *To Be Two* (New York: Routledge, 2001), 57.
19 Butler, *Bodies That Matter,* 235–36.

It is not just Butler queering gender — adding, that is, to the question of gender a very real element of Lacan's sense of the perverse (making of gender a play of disavowal, melancholy, and foreclosure on one hand, and undecidability and uncertainty on the other) — but Butler queering, as well, the question of ideology. Not content with creating real gender trouble by rubbing the panic speech acts of gender as performativity against Luce Irigaray's unspoken, wordless world of sexual desire, this world of "two lips that would be one"; definitely not ready to settle for a compromised world of bodies that matter, with what is an exclusively *theoretical* explanation that posits embodiment as the polar opposite of gender (lesbian and gay sexuality as that which is necessarily foreclosed, never grieved, never loved by the straight man and the straight woman, the straight world, that is, of compulsive heterosexual normativity as drag on speed); and not content to reinscribe the boundaries between gender, bodies, and sex that all her writing has struggled to deconstruct, Judith Butler is that rarity of a thinker, a theorist of whom it might be said what Heidegger once remarked about Nietzsche, that in his thought first he would argue, and Butler's next I would argue, there is to be found a theoretical imaginary that represents the self-overcoming of the respective cultures in which they lived. In Heidegger's perspective, Nietzsche's thought, represented in all its passion and denials in *The Gay Science, The Twilight of the Idols, On the Genealogy of Morals, Thus Spake Zarathustra,* and *The Will to Power,* represents the self-overcoming of nihilism; Judith Butler's self-overcoming is more complex. Certainly her theorisations represent the self-overcoming of heterosexual normativity in favor of a form of thought that is radically, playfully, passionately — critically — queer, but something else, too, something else in her thought that is just at the other edge of queer politics; something that is not exclusively about the compulsive, mimed, cited, appropriated mechanisms of compulsive heterosexuality; something that goes beyond even the still unexplored sexualities of gays, lesbians, and trans people; something that in Nietzsche's words is human, all-too-human; a haunting aporia that has to do with a fatal pause in Butler's theoretical project. Who knows why? Maybe it's the inexplicability in straight/queer discourse of comprehending the full dimensions of the gathering darkness of the human condition — sites of bodily and cultural injury used now as political opportunities for projecting all the madness of *ressentiment* onto an always crusading, always missionary, never grieving, never loving, re-animated world historical project of American imperialism. Or perhaps Butler's thought was fatally undermined by all those disappeared bodies that really did matter to her — the bodies of the ethnically scapegoated, those bodies trapped in "indefinite detention," the bodies of the disappeared, the oppressed, bodies that are ethically rendered in the grisly terms of Heidegger as objects of "*abuse value*," bodies that exemplify the exact opposite of Levinas's resurrection of the face as the basis of an ethics of responsibility — namely, bodies reduced to the cruel ethical tutelary of the "*injurious neglect of the thing*."[20]

Now given the certain uncertainty of the human heart and the undecidability of any individual human's response to a time of real political emergency, I don't know, or perhaps have no real need to know, the genealogy of Butler's self-overcoming, that point where her thought came to represent the self-overcoming of being critically queer in the direction of something that touches deeply not simply our sexual condition but our human condition — *being critically human.*

I do know this. Under the impress of the gathering darkness, her thought has changed, has mutated from the mirror of gender and the rhetoric of excitable speech to something more intangible, more uncertain, and more ethically responsive. Perhaps this transformation was prefigured in the title of one of her books — *Precarious Life: The Powers of Mourning and Violence.* Or perhaps Butler moving from *queering gender* with memories of bodies that matter to Butler *queering ideology* with memories of *Precarious Life* is prefigured by something else, by a political register in her thought which, until now, was always foreclosed,

---

20 Martin Heidegger, *The Question Concerning Technology and Other Essays,* trans. William Lovitt (New York: Harper & Row, 1977), 48; emphasis added.

excluded, never really noticed. Perhaps the entire theoretical project of Judith Butler specifically and of the queer community generally has always been in the way of a complex prefiguring, a premonitory rehearsal in the codes of panic gender and prohibited sexualities, of a more ominous turn in contemporary ideology — not just drag now in its exclusive gender citations as an index of that which is foreclosed by the straight man and the straight woman of all the club scenes, but an entire political culture that is in *imperial drag,* that generalizes the psychoanalytics of compulsive heterosexuality from the theater of sexual representation to the theater of world politics. All the signs of compulsive heterosexuality are there — panic responses to the contamination of bodily fluids that was the immediate response to HIV have now become surveillance strategies of the new biometric state; the hysterical male who thrives in faith-based politics with its panic about same-sex marriage and fear of, and seduction by, gay desire; and all the unmourned, ungrieved violence that is the everyday life experience of women suffering domestic violence and of disappeared sex workers and gays and lesbians and trannies when they walk the streets of *Stone Butch Blues.* What is all this but a vast, inflected rehearsal in the language of sexual denial and compulsory gender performativity of a political culture that functions now by displacing its previously isolated sexual politics onto its imperial missionary ambitions — and in a straight way, too. Power now is always in drag, always performing that which it refuses to love, to grieve, to mourn. Power now is heterosexual melancholy in its most dangerous phase: that ambivalent stage of triumphant self-recognition of its own fierce strength and panicked self-denial about those bodies, those sexualities, those "faces" of Levinas, those memories it must de-cite, dis-appropriate, de-index if it is to flourish.

Now, in the first stage of this story of nihilism, Nietzsche came on stage to play the part of the madman in the marketplace who announces the death of God. In the final stage of nihilism — completed nihilism, the projection of heterosexual melancholy as the spearhead of contemporary political history—it's not Nietzsche of *The Gay Science* and *The Twilight of the Idols* who appears on stage but Nietzsche in drag, Nietzsche channeled through Judith Butler to perform the "unperformable," Nietzsche's prophecy of nihilism mimed and cited and appropriated by Judith Butler as a way, perhaps the only way, of bringing into presence that which is excluded and foreclosed by an imperial politics of compulsive heterosexual performativity.

And why not? Butler's rhetoric always plays the game of the doubled sign. Not Lordship and Bondage but something more complicated, something that makes of gender, sex, ideology, and power the incommensurable politics of the performative. In her writing, not only gender but the whole compulsive language of phantasmatic identification is burning. Butler can write so eloquently about the lesbian phallus because in her thought the meaning of being queer has escaped its exclusively sexual register to become the burning sign of the unconscious of a power that is never about the real as lack but rather real bodies, real injuries, real sexualities as sites of foreclosure and contestation.

Most unusual and certainly noteworthy about the thought of Judith Butler is that her intellectual project is fully suspended between critical proximity to the larger issues of contemporary political ethics and a gathering intimation, present in all her reflections, that we are witness today to a larger cultural crisis, one that may find brutal expression in the disappeared subjects and abused bodies of the imperial reign of power but that has its basis in the origin story of the Christian self. In her writing, it is as if the fabric of spacetime itself splits open, bringing into presence the more profound dimensions of a cultural crisis that, while expressed most brutally in "excitable speech" as political ethics, is deeply inflected with the more infelicitous language of metaphysics.

Everywhere Butler's thought touches on the urgent questions of contemporary political ethics: issues related to indefinite detention, media censorship, suicide bombers, Islamic religious martyrs, ubiquitous surveillance cameras in an infinitely receding war on terror, the resurgence of Christian fundamentalism in the politically potent form of crusading, missionary con-

sciousness, and the bitterness of the heart that may well represent an early sign of a coming global reaction on the part of the
dispossessed against the excesses of capitalism under the sovereign sign of imperialism.

Reflecting on the political context that gave rise to the political ethics of *Precarious Life: The Powers of Mourning and
Violence,* we can acknowledge with confidence that some historical tendencies are now effectively completed. For example,
the twentieth-century experiment in the politics of late modernity — the illusion of a bipolar world frozen in the hegemonic
codes of communism versus capitalism, American versus Soviet
empires — ended decisively with the fall of the Berlin Wall in
1989. Indeed, the city of Berlin can rise once again as a major
cultural capital of the West because on that night in 1989, the political history of the twenty-first century effectively began. Ours
would be a future not bipolar but multipolar, not capitalism versus communism, but one driven by the specter of capitalism triumphant — which, finally liberated of its constraining binary of
socialism, would finally be open to seduction by the siren call of
its always repressed, always present dark underside — fascism.
Already wing strokes can be heard in the nighttime air of Hegel's
owl of Minerva returning to the political history from which it
first took flight.

And something else has been completed as well. In the
short interval between the fall of the Berlin Wall and the violent events of 9/11 in New York and Washington, DC, another
world-historical project — the much-hyped new world order of
globalization — quickly rose and just as suddenly disappeared.
Perhaps it was the global protests of student activists, workers,
feminists, and environmentalists who revolted in the late 1990s
against the policing regime of the World Trade Organization
and the International Monetary Fund; or maybe it was the revolt from the south — the electoral rebellion of popular forces
in Bolivia, Peru, and Venezuela — that rose against the manifest
destiny of US hegemony; or perhaps it was the counter-gift of a
bodily death that cannot be refused by Islamic religious martyrs — what Bataille once described as the gift of the "accursed

share" — that finally broke the solipsistic power of empire. As the Chicago political theorist Michael A. Weinstein has argued, globalization was always just the bait dangled to hook the world on a diet of consumer-capitalism. When that did not work, the politics of American political unilateralism was immediately called on to jam the hook of compulsory capitalism down the throat of an often unwilling global population. For all the discussion today concerning the digital wonders of information technology and the information economy, what increasingly now prevails is the logic of primitive capitalism and predatory power.

Consequently, political paradoxes proliferate. For example, at the same instant futurist genetic laboratories are conjuring android successors to the human species, the remainder of the all-too-human species lives in a growing archipelago of radical destitution and despair — Mike Davis's *Planet of Slums* with its one billion occupants denied the most minimal forms of recognition and reciprocity. Or consider the rhetoric of *panic terror* that dominates the administrative apparatus of homeland security in most of the countries of the Western world. Panic terror? That's the contemporary counterreaction of hegemonic binaries with a strict normative logic of inclusion and exclusion. In an age of intense securitization, the system of power itself is increasingly haunted by paranoiac fears of revenge by those who have been excluded from the spectacle of consumption. A hauntology of the dispossessed, the excluded, and those violently excommunicated from the Western ethical order of the "human" remains the most pervasive psychological feature of imperial power. This could also explain why there now takes place the active criminal prosecution in the United States of over two hundred postmodern artists. Their apparent crime? In a time of heightened security, control of the symbolic framework is everything. Understood in these terms, postmodern artists are always necessarily sign-criminals. By its very aesthetic nature, postmodern art works to disturb dominant frameworks of understanding — transgressing boundaries, privileging the complex, the hybrid, the incommensurable. When the specter of an art of complexity haunts power, then we finally know that we are living in the final days of a fully nihilistic power.

In these dark times, a sense of apocalypse surrounding the triumph of Nietzsche's "last man" is everywhere. After five hundred years of technological abuse — making of nature what Nietzsche said would be a future of cruel experiments and vivisectioning — nature itself has finally rebelled. In the twenty-first century, this great rebellion of nature will likely be played out in the increasingly catastrophic scenarios of global climate change. For all the predictions concerning the fast disappearance of the body at the behest of cybernetic technology, images of the very material body are everywhere — hostage bodies, bodies that are genocided, tagged, biochipped, surveilled, and electronically scanned. But for all that, bodies always incarnate a wayward heart, an irrepressible spark of individuality that is capable always and anywhere of suddenly rising to seek a greater truth. Precarious life can only arise again in union with an equally precarious nature.

It is precisely the global political crisis that makes the lessons of Butler's *Precarious Life* so astute, producing a lucid meditation on the psychic reality that is simultaneously the precondition and object of contemporary politics. An American confessional, this book does that which is as improbable as it is difficult. In a solitary, courageous act of speaking truth to power, *Precarious Life* interrogates, first and foremost, the origins of the malice of strife in the wounded American heart. Here the psychological formations present in contemporary displays of a near-universal state of injury, unfathomable rage, a "narcissistic preoccupation with melancholia,"[21] hostility toward the Other, the alien, the immigrant, is dissected with a logic that is as psychoanalytically clinical as it is emotionally remorseless. Nothing is spared — not the executive branch of government, which is held to exploit public grieving for its own predetermined political ends; not the judiciary, who are found to be receptive to politically prescribed

---

21 Butler, *Precarious Life: The Powers of Mourning and Violence* (London & New York: Verso, 2004), 30. — Ed.

limits on free speech at the behest of the new security state; not the larger majority of the voting public, which has made its private compromises with the carceral politics of indefinite detention, surveillance cameras, and the suppression of inconvenient truths; and certainly not the mass media, which is exposed not for excessive indulgence in the lesser games of image manipulation but for the more problematic ethical issue of "evacuating the human through the image." Always a faithful political student of the incommensurability of power, it is Butler's thesis that the will to violence today is supported, not so much by the effacement of the Other, but by a media strategy of continuously calling up the face of the Other — the Afghan woman, the political dissident, the always fugitive immigrant — only to instantly dehumanize her. Like power itself, the visual norm of the human contains the usual double logic of simultaneous representation and disappearance, *nomination* as the specter of the unrepresentable and *designation* as the visual symbol of primitive victimization, terror, porous borders, incomprehensible resistance:

> Indeed, all of these images seem to suspend the precariousness of life; they either represent American triumph, or provide an incitement for American military triumph in the future. *They are the spoils of war or they are the targets of war.* And in this sense, we might say that the face is, in every instance, defaced, and that this is one of the representational and philosophical consequences of war itself.[22]

Butler can undertake such a searing confessional of American psychic reality, faithfully transcribing the deepest interiority of the American mind — its psychic oscillations between fear and the technological sublime — because her thought has always been inflected with what Foucault once described as a "language of dissent," a form of thought that, while brushing against the immediacy of political life, follows a deeper trajectory to the metaphysical origins of the crisis of precarious life. Conse-

22 Ibid., 143.

quently, if in books such as *Excitable Speech* and *Precarious Life,* Butler diagnoses so accurately the self-confirming logic of inclusion and exclusion that circuits power today, it is because her project has never been posterior to the question of political ethics but philosophically anticipatory of the contemporary crisis of nihilism. It is no coincidence that she so brilliantly recovers the haunting voice of Antigone, not only as a way of critiquing political authority but as a means of rupturing the language of power supportive of the psychic reality of oedipalization. For example, Butler concludes *Precarious Life* with a prophecy and a warning phrased in the classical language of lament:

> If the humanities has a future as cultural criticism, and cultural criticism has a task at the present moment, it is no doubt to return us to the human where we do not expect to find it, in its frailty and at the limits of its capacity to make sense. We would have to interrogate the emergence and vanishing of the human at the limits of what we can know, what we can hear, what we can see, what we can sense. This might prompt us, affectively, to reinvigorate the intellectual projects of critique, of questioning, of coming to understand the difficulties and demands of cultural translation and dissent, and to create a sense of the public in which oppositional voices are not feared, degraded, or dismissed, but valued for the instigation to a sensate democracy they occasionally perform.[23]

In these words can be heard once again the dissenting voice of Antigone, speaking kinship to authority, responsibility to cynicism, affirming against the hard winds of political power the possibility of those indispensable virtues of the human, those *human* frailties that have long been practiced as the limit experiences of reciprocity, love, and compassion. While these frailties may function "at the limits of [their] capacity to make sense," perhaps this is because the human begins, now as always, with that which is beyond sense, with those fragments of life

23 Ibid., 151.

that have somehow succeeded in revolting against the spirit-flesh of power that circuits our bodies, cultures, and politics.

∗

This reflection on contingency in the philosophy of Judith Butler would be incomplete if it didn't seek to make of its own interpretative strategies a fully contingent inquiry, concluding with a question to which — while there may be no satisfactory response — there remains an indubitable and entirely satisfying element of doubt: is it possible that all of Butler's work to date has been in the order of a great preparation for another philosophical task, one not consciously adopted nor theoretically designated but one to which the question to which all of Butler's thought is a continuing response — namely, how to make *unfinished* the closed rhetoric of sex, bodies, power, gender, and knowledge — inevitably recurs, and on behalf of which Butler's thought is of necessity simultaneously classically ancient and post-human in equivalent degrees? Is it possible that Butler's thought has effectively never been after Nietzsche, *but always before Nietzsche*? Does Butler's continuing meditation on the crisis of split subjectivity represent in all its intensity the main problematic to which all of Nietzsche's thought struggled to respond? Indeed, if Butler can write so passionately about the complex translations and dissents of being human today, about the frailty of the human condition, does the reason for this have less to do with the urgency of her political analysis than the fact that her thought is the privileged site at which a deeper crisis in the modern project has broken out once again?

Definitely not nostalgic, Butler can enjoin the question of the human as an effective riposte to a form of power that would make the human disappear because her writing effectively seeks to complete in advance Nietzsche's *On the Genealogy of Morals.* And how could it not? Butler's impassioned recurrence to the voice of Antigone, her brushing *Bodies That Matter* against *Gender Trouble,* her exploration of *The Psychic Life of Power,* and her ethics written out in the pages of *Precarious Life* and *Excitable*

Speech represent the horizon of a critical philosophy of completed nihilism written at the height of its times. Here we find
ourselves engaged in a language of descent that draws thought
downward to the gravity well of *On the Genealogy of Morals*. But
not concluding with Nietzsche — or should we say not impeded
by the received interpretation of Nietzsche as an early student
of normalized power — Butler's is a form of thought that actually follows the fatal glance of Nietzsche as he follows his own
language of descent to the Christian origins of the genealogy of
morals. Indeed, given the uncertain direction of time's arrow in
the passage of thought from one writer to another in the great
chain of philosophical being, Butler may not so much follow
Nietzsche as actually precede Nietzsche by illuminating the genealogy of the crisis of split subjectivity.

In Butler's Nietzsche, it is the figure of Antigone who haunts
Genealogy, and it is precisely by uncovering the Antigone in
Nietzsche that Butler traces Nietzsche's own descent into the
psychic reality of the human-all-too-human. Here the genealogy of the human is finally brought into presence: not only the
distinctive human instinct for revenge-taking — *being reversed
against itself in self-loathing* — that forms the basis of so much
of contemporary politics, but something more ominous...
namely, constituting the modern subject on the anvil of the
death of instinctual behavior and the politics of reactive being.
In Butler's thought, there is a very real *political problematic,* specifically, that the same metaphysical crisis to which all of Nietzsche's thought represented a sustained response has broken out
again in the form of contemporary American empire politics;
and there is an equally real *political ethic* — the reworking of the
politics of reactive being and the death of instinctual behavior
with the rhetoric of that which is for all its frailties indispensably
human: *Antigone's Nietzsche.*

Nietzsche may have written *On the Genealogy of Morals* in
1887, but the cultural context out of which the book appears itself has a longer descent, a genealogical trace bringing together
texts from the fourth and the twentieth centuries, namely, Augustine's *Confessions* as the book that *Genealogy* interpellates.

More than anything, *Genealogy* immediately revolts against the traditional canons of philosophy, beyond critiques of Plato and Kant, to directly engage the conditions under which morality itself is staged — namely, the conditions under which Christian confessionality first created the modern subject as we know it, and once having been set in place, this subject has at once become both condition and end of all valuing.

With the *Genealogy,* we descend deeply into the repressed dreams of modernity, where that which is most ancient (debates between Athanasius and Ambrose, Augustine's predecessors in fourth century North Africa as Bishops of Carthage, battling the heresy of Arianism, with its implicit denial that Christ is the Son of God and thus the living Incarnation of the Holy Spirit) and this which is most futuristic (our abiding faith in scientific rationality played out now most hysterically in the search by contemporary physicists for the "God Particle" as the most elementary force of nature) are brought together in a genealogy of morals, past, present, and future. There are always three bodies circulating in the *Genealogy* — *spirit-flesh* ("the soul stretched as a membrane across the confessional self"), *mnemotechnic flesh* (how subjects are rendered "regular, calculable" by the power of the modern state through the propadeutic practice of burning remembrance into conscience by making it hurt to forget), and bodies constituted by the *will to truth* (inscribing consciousness with the mythic aims of a science that would deny its own foundations in mythology). Nietzsche is a genealogist whose thought descends into the gray matter of these three sedimented strata of the modern subject.

How could it be otherwise? More than a strictly religious impulse that would eventually war with the language of scientific rationality, Christian confessionality represented a successful metaphysical resolution to a paralyzing cultural crisis that neither philosophy nor secular culture could resolve. This crisis — the crisis of radically divided experience with power, represented by Roman pragmatism on the one side and reason figured by Athenian tragedy on the other — evaded all pragmatic resolutions that were only *externally* posited. Power itself could never provide a satisfactory response to the compelling existential question, namely, now that we have won an empire, now that we have conquered the world with spear and axe, what are to be the ultimate ends of the will to power itself? And reason also, which even in the noblest moments of Epicurean sensibility could never discover an adequate rejoinder to the question concerning the ultimate ends of reason: why is it that a life of reason is not to culminate in a universe of the absurd?

It was precisely at the moment of greatest crisis — power without substantive purpose and reason tinged by the absurd — that the Christian formulation first appeared, provoking in its wake the great debate among Rome, Athens, and Jerusalem. Represented in all its religious passion, yet philosophical subtlety, by the Trinitarian formula — God the Father, God the Son, and God the Holy Ghost, in other words, by the signifying logic of will, intelligence, and affect — Christianity moved the metaphysical center of Western experience from power and reason on the outside, externally posited, to the most intimate moment of interiority, the *directly experienced* confessionality of the Christian subject. Henceforth the internal principle of unity of Western experience would not be the instrumentalism of power without ultimate ends or reason without limits but that momentous fusion of conversionary belief, apostolic action, and determined willpower that became first the Christian subject and later, when the entire horizon had been wiped clean of the language of the sacred, the modern subject. With the invention of the Christian self, *personality* was made the creative principle of will, intelligence, and affect — simultaneously a redemptive sign of salvation and a psychic foreclosure against sinfulness. Here being human would come to mean *being spirit-flesh,* being possessed fully by the power of Incarnation. Henceforth the will to power would be animated by the *death of wild, instinctual behavior* and the *triumph of reactive being.* In the form of the will to power, the reduction of being human to spirit-flesh would be repeated daily as the overriding psychic reality of modernity.

Just as Nietzsche's *Zarathustra* was a parodic rewriting of the New Testament, the *Genealogy,* with its three enigmatic essays — "Good and Evil," "Good and Bad," "Guilt," "Bad Conscience" and the like; and "What is the Meaning of Ascetic Ideals?" — is itself a parody of the Christian Trinity, with "god the father as the source of all evil" as the subject of the first essay; God the Son, this fateful sign of sacrificial violence and the origin of all *ressentiment,* as the subject matter of the second essay; and the Holy Ghost, the ascetic ideal, as the meaning of the third essay. Stated in a more liturgical way, to read the *Genealogy* is to participate in Nietzsche's parodic reenactment of the great Christian rituals of Good Friday, Holy Saturday, and Easter Sunday, with this patient, gray genealogy of the complex subject who appears under the sign of the "cross, the nut, and the light," this subject who is constituted by *ressentiment,* by what Heidegger will later call a "malice of strife," who first carried out a relentless vivisectioning of his every motive ("cruelty turned inward," "itching for revenge," "feeling bad about himself," always eager for "orgies of feeling" associated with the great spectacles of sacrificial violence), and who only awaits for its *ressentiment* to be given a direction by Nietzsche's "ascetic priests," the keepers of ascetic ideals).

With the appearance of the self-identical subject formed out of the crucible of Christian confessionality, we find ourselves suddenly in the presence of a deeply paradoxical self. Undoubtedly influenced by Foucault's interpretation of Nietzsche, but definitely exceeding Foucault's understanding of the radical implications of *Genealogy,* Butler demonstrates in all her writing that the real issues today are not limited to issues of body and discipline nor to the migration of power as death to power as life. Anterior to these concerns, although obscured by the religious discourse of confessionality, there remains that enigmatic quality that Nietzsche identified in the *Genealogy* under the sign of the "transvaluation of values," which is to say that the subject, whether the subject of the fourth-century Christian confessional or the modern subject of *Precarious Life,* only emerges — indeed *can* only emerge — through the action of *turning back on itself.* For the modern subject no less than the Christian confessional self, the triumph of purely reactive being and the death of instinctual behavior is its psychic essence.

I want to suggest that everything in Butler's thought has been in the order of an intense preparation for understanding the full dimensions of the cultural crisis of the split subject. Consequently, if I have dwelt on the genealogy of the *Genealogy,* it is with the dual purpose of privileging the missing mass of Christianity as Nietzsche's hauntology and also to note that after Nietzsche, Butler is the one contemporary theorist fully alert to the psychic genealogy of the Christian self and its radical implications for the constitution of the modern subject. When she speaks about the appearance of a self that turns back on itself, about the creation of a fully fictitious self as the constitutive vocabulary of modernism, about the immersion of the psyche in the social, her thought is fully present with Nietzsche's at the moment of the Augustinian resolution of the crisis of split subjectivity. After all, the original formulation of the "logical circularity" of the modern subject is to be discovered in the confessional self, whereby the goal of the confessional self is also its abiding justification.

Butler studies in the twenty-first century key precisely what happens when the circularity of the self-identical subject breaks down — the violence of *Precarious Life,* the struggles of *Bodies That Matter,* the dissents of *Gender Trouble,* the voices of *Excitable Speech,* and the human reciprocity of *Antigone's Claim.* True to her own claims on behalf of that which is undecidable, uncertain, doubtful, hesitating in the bodily conditions of an always frail human community, Butler's lasting achievement is to make of the quality of *being unfinished* a double moment of danger and enablement. When the modern subject turns back on itself only to find, in its past as much as in its future, a psyche that has been inhabited by spirit-flesh, a body invested by the pain of mnemotechnics, and a will to truth edging toward cynicism and abuse value, then Butler's injunctions on behalf of *Precarious Life* are also appeals on behalf of the small, fragile mercies of precarious thought.

Printed in Great Britain
by Amazon